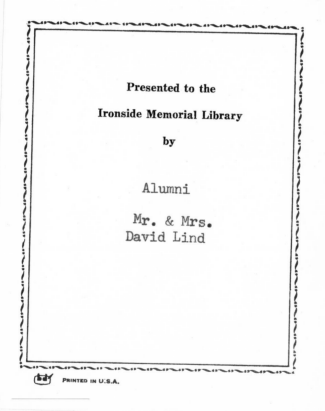

THE FREE MAN'S LIBRARY

A Descriptive and Critical Bibliography

by

HENRY HAZLITT

D. VAN NOSTRAND COMPANY, INC.
PRINCETON, NEW JERSEY
TORONTO   LONDON
NEW YORK

D. VAN NOSTRAND COMPANY, INC.

120 Alexander St., Princeton, New Jersey
257 Fourth Avenue, New York 10, New York
25 Hollinger Rd., Toronto 16, Canada
Macmillan & Co., Ltd., St. Martin's St., London, W.C. 2, England

*All correspondence should be addressed to the
principal office of the company at Princeton, N. J.*

2 5 9 6 9

CONTENTS

Freedom of men under government is to have a standing rule to live by, common to every one of that society, and made by the legislative power vested in it; a liberty to follow my own will in all things, when the rule prescribes not, and not to be subject to the inconstant, uncertain, unknown, arbitrary will of another man.

—JOHN LOCKE

It is seldom that liberty of any kind is lost all at once.

—DAVID HUME

The common people of England . . . so jealous of their liberty, but like the common people of most other countries never rightly understanding wherein it consists. . . .

—ADAM SMITH

The people never give up their liberties but under some delusion.

—EDMUND BURKE

The worth of a State, in the long run, is the worth of the individuals composing it. . . . A State which dwarfs its men, in order that they may be more docile instruments in its hands even for beneficial purposes, will find that with small men no great thing can really be accomplished; and that the perfection of machinery to which it has sacrificed everything will in the end avail it nothing, for want of the vital power which, in order that the machine might work more smoothly, it has preferred to banish.

—JOHN STUART MILL

INTRODUCTION

This book is a descriptive and critical bibliography of works
on the philosophy of individualism. I have applied the term
"individualism" in a broad sense. The bibliography includes
books which explain the processes and advantages of free
trade, free enterprise and free markets; which recognize the
evils of excessive state power; and which champion the cause
of individual freedom of worship, speech and thought.

Such a compilation seemed to me to be increasingly urgent
because so few writers and speakers on public questions today
reveal any idea of the wealth, depth and breadth of the litera
ture of freedom. What threatens us today is not merely the
outright totalitarian philosophies of fascism and communism,
but the increasing drift of thought in the totalitarian direction. Many people today who complacently think of themselves as "middle-of-the-roaders" have no conception of the
extent to which they have already taken over statist, socialist,
and collectivist assumptions—assumptions which, if logically
followed out, must inevitably carry us further and further
down the totalitarian road.

One of the crowning ironies of the present era, in fact, is
that it is precisely, especially in America, the people who flatteringly refer to themselves as "liberals" who have forgotten or
repudiated the essence of the true liberal tradition. The typical butts of their ridicule are such writers as Adam Smith,
Bastiat, Cobden ("the Manchester School"), and Herbert
Spencer. Whatever errors any of these writers may have been
guilty of individually, they were among the chief archi-
tects of true liberalism. Yet our modern "progressives" now
refer to this whole philosophy contemptuously as *"laissez
faire."* They present a grotesque caricature of it in order to

1

refute it to their own satisfaction, and then go on to advocate more and more governmental power, more centralization of government in Washington, fewer and fewer powers for the States or localities, more and more power for the President, more and more discretionary power for an appointed bureaucracy, and less and less power for Congress, which is usually ridiculed by our self-styled "liberals" and given to understand that its sole function is to "support the President"—in other words, to act as a rubber stamp. And none of this group seem to recognize that they differ from the totalitarians only in that the totalitarians want *unlimited* government power, *complete* centralization, unlimited power in the President or "Leader," and no legislature at all except as window-dressing, or as sycophants to proclaim the greatness of the Leader.

This present-day reversal of the traditional vocabulary in itself sets up great obstacles to the compilation of a bibliography of freedom. But these difficulties and obstacles go much further, of course, than those created by a reversal in the popular meaning of the word "liberalism." "Oh, Liberty!" Madame Roland is said to have exclaimed as she passed a statue to that goddess on her way to the guillotine, "what crimes are committed in thy name!" Looking at the world today, we are tempted to stress the intellectual crimes committed in the name of liberty as much as the moral crimes. Never were men more ardent in defense of "liberty" than they are today; but never were there more diverse concepts of what constitutes true liberty. Many of today's writers who are most eloquent in their arguments for liberty in fact preach philosophies that would destroy it. It seems to be typical of the books of our intelligentsia to praise one kind of liberty incessantly while disparaging or ridiculing another kind. The liberty that they so rightly praise is the liberty of thought and expression. But the liberty that they so foolishly denounce is economic liberty. They dismiss this contemptuously as *"laissez faire"*—a phrase, as I have already pointed out, which they almost always use in a merely invidious rather than in any seriously descriptive sense. In fact, no literature is more soaked in semantics than that concerning freedom. "Freedom" and "liberty" are the honorific terms for the liberties that the particular writer is defending; *"laissez faire"* or "license" are the disparaging terms for the liberties he is decrying.

Unfortunately the authors who have fallen into this practice include some of the finest minds of our generation. (I think particularly of Bertrand Russell and the late Morris Cohen.) Such writers seem to me to be at least in part reflecting an occupational bias. Being writers and thinkers, they are acutely aware of the importance of liberty of writing and thinking. But they seem to attach scant value to economic liberty because they think of it not as applying to themselves but to businessmen. Such a judgment may be uncharitable; but it is certainly fair to say that they misprize economic liberty because, in spite of their brilliance in some directions, they lack the knowledge or understanding to recognize that when economic liberties are abridged or destroyed all other liberties are abridged or destroyed with them. "Power over a man's subsistence," as Alexander Hamilton reminded us, "is power over his will." And if we wish a more modern authority, we can quote no less a one than Leon Trotsky, the colleague of Lenin, who in 1937, in a moment of candor, pointed out clearly that: "In a country where the sole employer is the State, opposition means death by slow starvation: The old principle: who does not work shall not eat, has been replaced by a new one: who does not obey shall not eat."

Liberty is a whole, and to deny economic liberty is finally to destroy all liberty. Socialism is irreconcilable with freedom. This is the lesson that most of our modern philosophers and littérateurs have yet to learn.

I write all this to explain why certain books which some readers might expect to find in this compilation will not be found here. They may say some eloquent and even true things about liberty; but their net influence is not on the side of liberty. The test I have tried to apply here is whether any book, regardless of the reservations I may personally have on the position it takes on this issue or that, is still *on net balance* on the side of true liberty.

I have long contemplated a compilation like the present one. But I kept postponing the task because it seemed too formidable. My hesitation was broken at last when a friend informed me of the existence of a 95-page pamphlet published by the Individualist Book Shop of London in 1927, which might be the kind of bibliography I had in mind. I immediately sent to London for this book, and quite as promptly received a copy from Miss Marjorie Franklin, General Secretary of The Society for Individual Freedom. Miss Franklin warned me, however, that not only had the pamphlet been long out of print, but that I was getting a "precious file copy."

I read this pamphlet with satisfaction and delight. If it could not be republished simply as it stood, it was at least the ideal nucleus to build around. It was both scholarly and penetrating; its standards of selection were at once discriminating and catholic; its judgments were sound, and it was written with charm.

The pamphlet was anonymous; but I learned by inquiry that it had been prepared by Professor W. H. Hutt, the British economist, now Dean of the Faculty of Commerce at the University of Cape Town, South Africa. Professor Hutt informed me in correspondence, however, that while he was responsible for the greater part of the pamphlet he "did everything in collaboration with" the late Francis W. Hirst, the well-known British Liberal and former editor of *The London Economist,* "and if there is any acknowledgment in the preface, his name should be mentioned as well as mine."

This compilation and discussion for the Individualist Bookshop had only one major defect: it was more than a quarter of a century old. But this defect, it seemed to me at first, could very easily be remedied. It would simply be necessary to drop one or two score of its 166 entries (because they were books now obsolete or superseded), to shorten the comments on some of the rest, and to add a score or two of entries to cover the important libertarian books that had been published in the nearly thirty years since 1927.

The work of elimination proved no more difficult than I had supposed. But the work of addition took on a far different aspect. I was surprised to find, for example, that even some of the classics of freedom and individualism—the relevant works, say, of Milton, Montesquieu, Burke, de Tocqueville and Lord Acton—had been omitted. These gaps were of course easily filled. Much more formidable was the task of selecting from the mass of books published since 1927.

This raised many problems. I will expand on only one by way of illustration. This was the problem of whether to include or exclude the more important works that have appeared in the last quarter-century denouncing the immorality or warning against the internal or external perils of communism. The Hutt pamphlet had been mainly devoted to books expounding the positive philosophy of freedom and individualism. Yet it had freely listed the books primarily critical of socialism. On the same principle there was every reason for including the books critical of communism. The two terms were used by Karl Marx, in fact, interchangeably. The Russian Communists still call their domain the Union of Soviet *Socialist* Republics. Communism is not merely the logical and inevitable end-product of socialism; it is also another name for a socialism that is really complete. We must subscribe, in short, to the definition of Bernard Shaw that "A communist is nothing but a socialist with the courage of his convictions."

Yet the decision to add the leading anti-communist books not only swelled the dimensions of this bibliography, but presented a problem of another kind. The authors who attack socialism have generally based their criticism on the explicit premises of a free, competitive, private enterprise. But probably a good half of the books of the last quarter-century which attack communism do so on the basis of socialist assumptions. They attack Russian communism as a "betrayal" of true socialism. (The works of Arthur Koestler are an outstanding example.) They attack even Stalinism as a betrayal of "true Leninism." In fact, most of the best known anti-communist books, including some that are admirable in other respects, attack the end-product without seeming to realize that it is socialist ideals that inevitably create this end-product. The authors of these books attack the despotism in Russia, for example, without recognizing that you cannot carry out the centralized economic planning of socialism without despotism. They attack the communist suppression of freedom of speech and thought without recognizing that once you give government complete power over jobs and employment—the power to promote or demote, to hire or fire, to say, in short, whether a man is to live or starve—you at the same time give government complete power to control or suppress speech and thought. They fail to recognize that in prescribing the means they are prescribing the end. They fail to recognize that the immorality and the intellectual and spiritual suppression that they denounce flow inevitably out of the centralized economic planning and governmental omnipotence that they applaud.

Yet some anti-communist books of disillusioned communists who are still socialists or planners are among the most eloquent and powerful denunciations that have yet been written on the end-products of communism. I have therefore decided to include them, often accompanied by a warning against acceptance of their premises.

This decision to include anti-communist volumes, as I have indicated, created as many problems as it solved. It substantially increased the length of this book. I soon found that by adding one book after another to my list I had raised the number of entries from 166 in the original Hutt bibliography, notwithstanding my numerous omissions from it, to a new total of more than 550.

As a result of these inclusions other decisions were forced upon me. My original purpose had been to offer my own judgments of all the works included, except when I was satisfied with those given in the Hutt pamphlet. But as my ideas expanded concerning the volumes that ought to be included I was forced by sheer growth of number to fall back in many cases, as the reader will see, on the judgments of others. This decision was forced for a double reason. It was as impracticable as it would have been supererogatory to read through from cover to cover each of the 400 or so additional volumes listed in order to write a half-dozen lines about it. I found, in addition, that even where I had read a substantial part of a book, or even where I had read it through—but years ago— my present memory did not leave me with sufficient confidence in my own judgment of it. In these cases I have fallen back upon critics whose judgments seem to me to deserve confidence, or writers who have spoken with special authority or justness on the book in question. In some cases I have also added such judgments in the hope of reinforcing my own.

By following this eclectic procedure I have of course lost whatever advantages might have accrued in the following compilation from a completely uniform style and uniform standard of judgment. But such a disadvantage, it seems to me, is more than compensated by greater comprehensiveness than I could otherwise have achieved. And I early decided that the application of a uniform standard was in any case next to impossible. The reader will find in the following compilation books of very different "weights." He will find the works of Locke and Adam Smith and Mill cheek by jowl with modern books just out last year. He will find the works of the great pioneers and trail blazers next to popularizations written mainly for beginners. I do not know how this kind of heterogeneous mixture can be avoided if this book is to fulfill the functions for which it is designed. For it is designed to guide the reader not merely to the great classics on liberty and individualism, but to introductory works.

A further word should be said here regarding the standards I have applied in deciding whether or not a given work should be included in this compilation. I already see myself being buttonholed occasionally by some angry reader who asks: "Why on earth did you include Pumpernickel's book in your bibliography? Don't you know that on page 155 he writes this outrageous sentence—?" And then my questioner will probably quote or misquote some pronouncement that I do not at all feel like defending. In an effort to answer as many as possible of such objections in advance, I should like to say here that the inclusion of a book in this bibliography certainly does not imply that I myself subscribe to every doctrine or sentence in that book or that I think every opinion it enunciates is an essential part of the libertarian or individualist tradition. What inclusion does imply is that in my judgment the book, to repeat what I have said earlier, makes *on net balance* a factual or theoretical contribution to the philosophy of individualism, and that at least some readers may derive from it a fuller understanding of that philosophy.

The inclusion of any book in this list, in brief, implies recommendation. Therefore, with few exceptions, I have confined myself to making or quoting comments which emphasize the merits of a book rather than its defects. A primer, for example, may ably serve its modest purpose without necessarily constituting a major contribution to the subject with which it deals. A book may contain, in parts, collectivist or confused thinking and still be one from which a student of liberty could greatly profit. In my comments, therefore, I have tried to keep reservations, misgivings and objections to a minimum.

Nor is the reader to take the amount of space devoted to the discussion of any book as a necessary measure of my own judgment regarding its relative merit or importance. A classic may be so well known, and there may be so many sources from which a reader can learn about it, that a few lines of comment may be sufficient for the purpose of this bibliography. Another work, less meritorious and less important, may yet rightly, for some special reason, call for longer comment. But I cannot do better here than to quote with approval a footnote in the Hutt bibliography on the lengthy entries under the name of Auberon Herbert: "It may seem incongruous to give far more space to Auberon Herbert than to Locke or Bentham. But the object of making this list is to put information before the student, and, if important matter is neglected or inaccessible, it needs more space than is required by works known, by name at least, to 'every schoolboy.' "

With some reluctance, however, I have made it a general rule to exclude pamphlets from my list, notwithstanding the many admirable ones that have appeared in recent years. I have done this not only because their inclusion would have swollen this bibliography far beyond useful dimensions, but because it is usually so difficult for readers to obtain pamphlets, particularly after they have been allowed to fall out of print, that their inclusion might too often merely arouse a curiosity could not be satisfied. I must add, in fact, that in spite of my *general* rule against including pamphlets, I have felt simply compelled to make a few exceptions because of their outstanding importance.

This points to one of the insoluble problems of the bibliographer in dealing with practically any great subject. He finds it next to impossible to draw sharp boundaries, to be completely consistent, to defend confidently his every inclusion or omission. If he tries to make his list "complete," his task becomes a labor of Sisyphus; and even if he were to succeed, his list would be unmanageable and useless to most readers. If he makes his bibliography "selective," he is inevitably accused of being arbitrary or capricious in his selections.

I became increasingly conscious of this dilemma as my work proceeded. I am aware that for a great number of readers the more than 550 entries here may seem more bewildering than helpful. The device of marking with an asterisk those books "specially recommended" would, I fear, have created more problems than it solved. Therefore, for the sake of those who would appreciate the guidance of a shorter list, I have resorted to a practice that has become a traditional annual event with many American book reviewers, and drama and motion picture critics. I have compiled a list of "the best ten." This, of course, adds the limitations of an arbitrary number to the other arbitrary factors in selection. To make my task just a little less provocative of indignation, I have in fact compiled *two* lists of ten—first, the "ten best" historic classics on liberty and individualism; and secondly, the "ten best" contemporary works.

Here is the list of "classics" in chronological order:

JOHN MILTON, *Areopagetica*
JOHN LOCKE, *Second Treatise on Government*
DAVID HUME, *Essays Moral, Political and Literary*

ADAM SMITH, *The Wealth of Nations*
EDMUND BURKE, *Works*
FRÉDÉRIC BASTIAT, *Economic Sophisms*
ALEXIS DE TOCQUEVILLE, *Democracy in America*
JOHN STUART MILL, *On Liberty*
HERBERT SPENCER, *The Man vs. the State*
LORD ACTON, *Essays on Freedom and Power*

Here are the "ten best" contemporary works, in alphabetical order:

B. M. ANDERSON, *Economics and the Public Welfare*
F. A. HAYEK, *The Road to Serfdom*
F. A. HAYEK, *Individualism and Economic Order*
F. A. HAYEK et al., *Capitalism and the Historians*
JOHN JEWKES, *Ordeal by Planning*
LUDWIG VON MISES, *Socialism: an Analysis*
LUDWIG VON MISES, *Human Action*
GEORGE ORWELL, *Nineteen Eighty-Four*
LIONEL ROBBINS, *The Great Depression*
WILHELM RÖPKE, *The Social Crisis of Our Time*

If the reader is tempted to smile at the presumption and crudity of selecting a list of the "ten best" works in this field, either classic or contemporary, he may at least be assured that I smile with him. If he is unhappy about the particular selection even within the arbitrary number of ten, I may add that I am a little unhappy about it myself—though perhaps not for his reasons.

In restricting the list of classics to ten, I have been forced to leave out Montesquieu's *Spirit of the Laws,* the writings of Jefferson, the speeches of Cobden, Calhoun's *A Disquisition on Government,* the writings of Jacob Burckhardt, and the essays of William Graham Sumner—all of which would have been included had my list been slightly larger, and one or two of which, no doubt, some readers will think should have been included in my list of ten at the expense of one or two already there.

I am sorry that in the case of Burke I have felt compelled to list his collected works rather than any particular book or

speech. This is because his finest aphorisms and most luminous passages on liberty are scattered throughout his work
and have not been satisfactorily extracted and collected, to my
knowledge, in any single volume. Many of us have been
brought up to believe that, although Burke may have begun
as a liberal (as exemplified in his speech on *Conciliation with
America*), he ended as a vehement reactionary (as in his *Reflections on the Revolution in France*). Yet any open-minded
reader, even though he is opposed to Burke's main conclusions on the French Revolution, as William Hazlitt so strongly
was, will agree with the latter that "in arriving at one error
[Burke] discovered a hundred truths." Therefore, Hazlitt considered himself "a hundred times more indebted to [Burke]
than if, stumbling on that which I consider as the right side
of the question, he had committed a hundred absurdities in
striving to establish his point." We, too, I think, must agree,
as Hazlitt did, with the judgment that in political philosophy
Burke "was the most eloquent man of his time; and his wisdom was greater than his eloquence."

Burke in his later years was certainly a conservative; and
the prominent inclusion of his works in a bibliography of
freedom may seem to some readers, accustomed to associate
the case for freedom with the case for "liberalism," to call for
explanation. But there is no necessary conflict between intelligent conservatism and real liberalism. On the contrary, at
least in the peculiar climate and conditions of the present age,
they have come to mean nearly the same thing.

Historically, the liberals fought against government tyranny; against governmental abridgment of freedom of speech
and action; against governmental restrictions on agriculture,
manufacture, and trade; against constant detailed governmental regulation, interference and harassment at a hundred
points; against (to use the phrases of the Declaration of Independence) "a multitude of new offices" and "swarms of officers"; against concentration of governmental power, particularly in the person of one man; against government by whim
and favoritism. Historic liberalism called, on the other hand,
for the Rule of Law, and for equality before the law. The

older conservatives opposed many or most of these liberal demands because they believed in existing governmental interferences and sweeping governmental powers; or because they wished to retain their own special privileges and prerogatives; or simply because they were temperamentally fearful of altering the status quo, whatever it happened to be.

Those who flatteringly call themselves "liberals" today, and to whom confused opponents allow or even assign the name, are for nearly everything that the old liberals opposed. Most self-styled present-day "liberals," particularly in America, are urging the constant extension of government "planning." They constantly press for a greater concentration of governmental power, whether in the central government at the expense of the States and localities, or in the hands of a one-man executive at the expense of any check, limitation, or even investigation by a legislature. And they look with favor on an ever-growing bureaucracy, and on the spread of bureaucratic discretion at the expense of a Rule of Law. Those who oppose this trend toward a new despotism, on the other hand, and plead for the preservation of the ancient freedoms of the individual, are today's conservatives. The intelligent conservative, in brief, is today the true defender of liberty.

This conclusion should not seem too paradoxical. It was always possible to reconcile intelligent conservatism with real liberalism. There is no conflict between wishing to conserve and hold the precious gains that have been achieved in the past, which is the aim of the true conservative, and wishing to carry those achievements even further, which is the aim of the true liberal. Burke not only recognized that these two aims were compatible; he summed up that compatibility in one of his memorable aphorisms: "A disposition to preserve and an ability to improve, taken together, would be my standard of the statesman."

Let us go on, after this long digression, to consider the list I have put forward of the "ten best" contemporary books on the philosophy of individualism.

My contemporary list is even more unsatisfactory to me than my historic one, especially in what I am forced to exclude. My reasons for including each of the twenty books in the two lists will be found under the entry for that book in the bibliography that follows. However, I should perhaps say a word in explanation of the fact that there are three entries under the name of Professor Hayek. Hayek's *The Road to Serfdom* is the most acute and impressive analysis of the modern drift to totalitarianism that has been written in our time. It deserves a place in any contemporary list no matter how short. His essays collected under the title of *Individualism and Economic Order* have been included in the list chiefly because of the leading essay, *Individualism: True and False,* which no open-minded individualist can read without having his ideas enlarged and clarified; for true individualism certainly does *not* consist in mere eccentricity, intransigence, or contempt for voluntary social cooperation. It is the mistaken association of these qualities with "individualism" that has given that philosophy a dubious reputation with many who would otherwise be won to it. Professor Hayek is not the author of the third volume, *Economics and the Historians;* he is simply the editor and one of the contributors. The selection of this short book from among some excellent economic histories is perhaps arbitrary; but it performs, better than any other work I know of, the negative function of informing the reader how grossly some of the most celebrated economic historians of the last half century or more have misrepresented the meaning of the Industrial Revolution and the growth of capitalism.

Those who think my contemporary list unbalanced can substitute for Hayek's *Individualism and Economic Order,* say, Max Eastman's *Reflections on the Failure of Socialism,* or Walter Lippmann's *The Good Society* (at least the first half of that book).

To offer an abbreviated list of "best" books is one thing; to suggest a "reading course" is quite another. It is not always advisable for the novice to begin with the masterpieces; he must be educated to the point where he can understand and appreciate them. But this is a subjective problem in which no two readers are likely to be in precisely the same position; and the ideal reading program should be individually tailored to fit a particular reader's requirements. A major purpose of the present extensive bibliography, in fact, is to act as a guide to the reader in making his own individual choices. The tyro will learn more or faster from one set of books, the proficient from another.

Bearing in mind these reservations, however, some readers may still find it helpful if I suggest at least one "introductory course." Fortunately this task is not too difficult, because the finest books of the past and present are usually as distinguished for lucidity as for wisdom. So even an introductory course could easily be built exclusively from our two lists of the "ten best." An introductory course of five books, for example, might be this: The reader might begin with (1) a contemporary book, F. A. Hayek's *The Road to Serfdom.* He might then read in this order: (2) John Stuart Mill's classic essay *On Liberty;* (3) Ludwig von Mises' *Socialism;* (4) Hayek's essay, *Individualism: True and False,* or Max Eastman's *Reflections on the Failure of Socialism;* and (5) Ludwig von Mises' *Human Action.*

The most formidable books on the foregoing list, in length and difficulty, are the two volumes by von Mises. For readers to whom this program may seem too arduous or ambitious, therefore, I suggest this introductory list of only three books, each short and relatively simple: (1) Hayek's *The Road to Serfdom;* (2) Mill's *Liberty;* (3) von Mises' short collection of essays, *Planning for Freedom.*

The reader should be able to steer his own course from there on, a process in which I hope this bibliography will still prove helpful.

The main purpose of this bibliography, to repeat what has already been said in substance, is to bring to the attention of the modern reader the most important, useful or available books in the true liberal tradition—the tradition of free trade, free enterprise, free markets; of limited and decentralized government; of freedom of speech, of religion, of the press, and of assembly; of security of person and private property—

the tradition, in brief, of the freedom and dignity of the individual.

Now this tradition, rich and deep and noble as it is, is being treated by most present-day intellectuals almost as if it had never existed. When they speak of it, they usually speak merely of some grotesque caricature in their own minds, which they contemptuously dismiss as *"laissez faire"* or "the Manchester School." Yet as Friedrich Hayek has pointed out in *The Road to Serfdom* (p. 13), what the modern trend to socialism means "becomes clear if we consider it not merely against the background of the nineteenth-century, but in a longer historical perspective. We are rapidly abandoning not the views merely of Cobden and Bright, of Adam Smith and Hume, or even of Locke and Milton, but one of the salient characteristics of Western civilization as it has grown from the foundations laid by Christianity and the Greeks and Romans. Not merely nineteenth- and eighteenth-century liberalism, but the basic individualism inherited by us from Erasmus and Montaigne, from Cicero and Tacitus, Pericles and Thucydides, is progressively relinquished."

This bibliography, I hope, will help to clarify as well as to mobilize the case for individualism and true liberalism. It is designed to strengthen individualists in their knowledge and convictions, to place in their hands the intellectual weapons that will help them to combat the totalitarian trend. It is designed, also, to call attention to the richness of the truly liberal tradition, to the excellent books and the many noble minds that have helped to shape it.

But this compilation would fail of part of its purpose if it gave readers the impression that the literature of freedom and individualism is already so rich that it does not need to be supplemented and expanded. On the contrary, there are deplorable gaps in this literature, particularly in recent writing. It would take me too far out of my way to try to call attention in detail to these gaps. The task, moreover, would be odious. Frankly, I have occasionally included a book in the following list because, in spite of serious shortcomings, it happens to be the only book which covers some special subject from the libertarian point of view. But it is my hope that this bibliography will indirectly call attention to some existing gaps, and thereby stimulate the writing of better books to fill them.

It is partly, in fact, in the hope that it may encourage translations that I have listed a number of books in French and German that have not yet been made available in English.

A similar hope may be expressed about pamphlets. There are many of the first rank, some by the same author, some on different phases of the same subject, that urgently need to be brought together and made permanently available in book form.

As a final word, I must emphasize again my sad discovery that a bibliographer's lot is not a happy one. If he is "selective," his selections are likely to be called arbitrary, subjective and capricious. If he seeks to be "comprehensive," his troubles multiply beyond counting. In the present case, I have been constantly troubled by the problem of exactly where to draw my boundary lines. This is essentially a bibliography on the philosophy of individual freedom. A few economic classics and a few contemporary economic analyses and textbooks are included because they either explicitly or by logical implication support this philosophy. But other economic volumes, which considered purely as technical economic analysis are as good as or perhaps in some respects even better than some of those included, have been omitted either because most of their discussion is only remotely relevant to a libertarian philosophy or may even veer off to support a socialist or statist philosophy. Yet between the easily classifiable cases there are any number of borderline cases in which the decision to include or exclude is very difficult and cannot fail to be in some respects arbitrary.

An essential part of the philosophy of individualism, again, is the doctrine of the Rule of Law. This calls for the inclusion of some works on jurisprudence. But at exactly what point does one stop? And so for a score of other fields. The philosophy of individualism can be reflected in works on jurisprudence, on administrative law, on politics, on ethics, on general economics, on agriculture, on labor relations, on interest rates, on money and banking policy, and so on. How much weight should one attach to the technical excellence or importance of works of this type in their special fields as compared with that of an individualistic philosophy which may merely be implied in such works?

I have found no satisfactory answer to questions of this sort, no clear-cut pigeonholes that satisfy my bibliographic conscience. In any case, the process of compiling a critical bibliography is at best an art and can never be reduced to an exact science. It is at the mercy of accident and subject to the limitations of the compiler. I shall not be completely astonished to find, for example, after this book has been printed and bound beyond alteration, that I have omitted an entry or two from sheer oversight. In still other cases, when some kind lady corners me at a social gathering and asks with a puzzled expression, "Why did you leave Professor X's book out of your list?", I may have to reply, as the great Samuel Johnson had the courage to do to a woman who asked him to account for an error in his dictionary: "Ignorance, madame. Pure ignorance."

Fortunately for readers and writers alike, a book not free from shortcomings may still perform a useful and necessary function; and it is in the belief that this volume will prove helpful not merely to individual readers, but to the great cause of human liberty itself, that it is put forward.

A word should perhaps be added about the title of this bibliography. In calling it *The Free Man's Library* I do not, of course, mean to imply that books on the philosophy of individualism, or in defense of personal liberty, are the only books that a "free man" should carry on his shelves. The free man is free to take all human knowledge for his province. His full library, let us hope, will contain the Bible and Shakespeare, Homer and Plato, and other well-chosen selections from the world's treasuries of drama, fiction, poetry, history, art, philosophy and science. By *The Free Man's Library* I mean to indicate merely the books that a man may wish to know about, to read or have in his home specifically in his role *as* a free man—as a man who wants to understand how he may best restore, preserve, or increase his own freedom and the freedom of others. In the same way we should expect a bibliography called "The Physician's Library" to be confined to the books that a physician should know about or read in his special capacity *as* a physician, and a bibliography called "The Engineer's Library" to be confined to the books that a man should know in his capacity *as* an engineer. But neither the physician nor the engineer, let us hope, will be *solely* a physician or an engineer, but will have the range of intellectual interests that we associate with a liberal education and a broad, humane culture. And the "free man," we may hope also, whatever his special calling, will have the same wide range of intellectual interests, the same broad, humane culture, for these are among the finest fruits of freedom; and it is partly because it has these fruits that freedom is so precious.

Acknowledgments

I have received so much help from writers and friends in suggesting the consideration of this or that book for inclusion in my list that I regret to be unable to give individual credit. I have also used research help in verifying literally thousands of details—dates of publication, page numbers, spelling of names, etc. I am especially in debt to my wife for help in so many directions that it would take too much space to list them. My most obvious indebtedness is, of course, to the bibliography, already mentioned, compiled for the Individualist Book Shop of London. The anonymous introduction to that list (which I have since found was written by W. H. Hutt) is so excellent and informative that I have inserted it in full after this introduction of my own.

Next to the Hutt bibliography, I owe most to the back files of the *Book Review Digest,* sometimes making use of its summary of the theme or contents of a book, as well as of its quotations from reviews. I should have made more use of the multigraphed list of 100 titles compiled by F. A. Harper, of the Foundation for Economic Education, if my own list had not been virtually completed when I saw this compilation.

ARRANGEMENT AND ABBREVIATIONS

No effort has been made in the following list to give the price of any book or to indicate whether or not it is still in print. Prices are often changed; and books going out of print, or new editions of old books, would soon make the latter information inaccurate. In nearly all cases, however, I have given the number of pages in a book. Where more than one edition exists, the number of pages should of course be understood to refer merely to that of one of these editions. The purpose of giving the number of pages is simply that the reader may have a rough idea of the length of the book. Nothing is more unhelpful or irritating, I have found, than a bibliography which does not enable a reader to know whether a listed title refers to a pamphlet of a dozen pages or a work in four volumes.

A short form of their name is used for all well-known publishers, British as well as American. The city of publication is not given for any American book unless the publishing house is small, or relatively new, or not familiar to the book trade in general. The names of foreign publishers (except prominent English publishers) are given in full—accompanied, of course, by the city of publication.

The year of the original publication of a book is given in nearly all cases, and sometimes the year of the latest or most accessible edition. When a date appears immediately after the title, or *preceding* the name of any specific publisher, it means the date of original publication. When a date is given *after* the name of a particular publisher, it refers to the volume printed by that publisher. When two editions are known to exist, both dates are usually given. Where more than two editions exist, the word *etc.* is often inserted after the original date in lieu of any attempt to list all editions. Wherever the name of a publisher and a date of publication are enclosed in a common parenthesis, it means that that particular edition is either the most available or is recommended among numerous editions. Wherever a book is available in both British and American editions, usually only the American publisher is named, even if the book originally appeared in England.

Wherever, as frequently happens, more than one title is listed by the same author, the titles are not necessarily listed in the chronological order of their appearance. Rather the effort has been made to list and discuss first the work or works by that author which are most important for the present bibliography, or which lend themselves most conveniently to comment on the qualities and contribution of that author. Occasional inconsistencies will be found in citing the same author's name. This usually happens when the author's name is not printed in a consistent form on the title pages of his various works.

PI at the end of a quoted descriptive comment on a book indicates that the comment is quoted from *The Philosophy of Individualism: A Bibliography*, the out-of-print pamphlet published in London in 1927 which is referred to earlier in this introduction. In all other cases where comment is quoted, the name of the author, periodical, or other source is spelled out.

All other abbreviations (such as *pp*. for *pages*) are those in common use.

INDIVIDUALISM IN POLITICS
AND ECONOMICS[1]

The term Individualism was cited by Henry Reeve (of *Edinburgh Review* fame) in William IV's reign as "a novel expression." John Stuart Mill is (wrongly) credited with having given it currency and popularity. Although he discusses the subject at great length in his *Political Economy,* he seldom if ever uses the exact term— his judicious and well-balanced mind was adverse to the manufacture of labels. He preferred to employ such expressions as "individual freedom," "individual property," "those who have been called the *laissez-faire* school," etc. Even in *Liberty,* published much later, which is rightly regarded as a classic of Individualism, he avoids the term, although he uses (perhaps not more than once) the word "Individuality" in that sense.

However, the term is an extremely convenient one to express the views of those who would confine the functions of the State and various public authorities to a relatively small province, i.e., maintaining law and order, the army, the navy and other means of national defence, the enforcement of contracts, the maintenance of public services which cannot conveniently be entrusted to private enterprise, and in general the provision of a fair field for the play of individual energy. It is opposed to Collectivism, Socialism, Communism, and the various other means of restricting liberty, whether these be adopted by public authorities, quasi-private corporations, private firms, hereditary autocrats, military dictators, or the like. It should be remembered that in Mill and many writers of the older generation the terms Socialism and

[1] This was the introduction to *The Philosophy of Individualism: A Bibliography* published in 1927 by The Individualist Bookshop of London. Because it gives so compact, informative and balanced a survey of the intellectual history of individualism I am reprinting it in full. Although it was originally anonymous, I have since learned (see my own introduction) that the author was W. H. Hutt. The footnotes are also his, except one or two which are signed with my own initials.

Communism are used as equivalents; and it is hardly necessary to remind any serious student that words, especially general terms,[2] are very slippery articles, and that many discussions are barren and lead to complete misunderstanding, because the parties engaged in them have no clear definition of the terms in their minds, or, at any rate, are using the terms in a sense different from that employed by their opponents.

Modern as the term Individualism may be, the thing itself is older. Undoubtedly traces of the theory may be found in Latin and Greek writers; but it is needless to go back further than the seventeenth century, for three very good reasons:

1. In the Greek world the City State was supreme—the individual citizen lived and moved as a member of the State.[3] So Pericles is made by Thucydides to say: "If a man prospers individually when his country is destroyed, he is none the less joined in the general ruin, while he comes through in complete safety if the State prospers, even though he himself suffers calamities." In the Roman Empire citizens had only legal rights. The State was autocratic.

2. The medieval theory of politics and economics was feudal and paternal. To Macaulay's schoolboy, and even to people less well informed, this fact is so familiar that the mere statement will suffice. It is clear that up to 1500 A.D. there was little scope for a theory of Individualism.

3. The Classical Revival, though it revolutionized a large part of modern thought, at first did nothing to change the general attitude toward the State. This was only to be expected, seeing that the State was supreme in Classical theory.

At last, in the seventeenth century, came the rise of Individualism, and this was due to several causes:

1. The Protestant Reformation brought private judgment into theology, and the new habit of thought soon extended to other questions, and, above all, to the problems of individual rights and the functions of the State.

2. The wars of Religion which devastated Europe, made men distrust the principle of authority, which had seemingly led to those horrors. The wars, having been conducted by Governments,

---

[2] *Latet dolus in generalibus*—"Fallacy lurks in general terms"—is an old and true maxim of the Schoolmen.

[3] "The Hellenic State, like the ancient State in general, because it was considered all powerful, actually possessed too much power."—Blumschli, *The Theory of the State* (Book I., c. iii).

helped to undermine confidence in official wisdom, i.e., in governments. A careful reader of Pope's poetry will notice that almost every line is permeated with scorn, not only for the general human capacity but for "the great" in particular; and nearly all the leading eighteenth century writers hold similar opinions. Thus Gray, in contemplative mood, exclaims:

> "How low, how little are the proud,
> How indigent the great!"

But long before Pope, the Swedish Oxenstiern (1654) had summed up the whole matter in his renowned saying: "Behold, my son, with how little wisdom the world is governed."

3. The action of despots, benevolent or otherwise, who introduced innumerable and vexatious regulations to control the business and daily life of their subjects, caused thoughtful men to distrust government action. The restrictive policy carried out by Colbert, under Louis XIV, with a multitude of protective regulations, provoked a reaction to the *laissez faire* school of France; and the French merchants' cry *"let us alone"* [4] became the motto of economic and political reformers. But before this, in the reign of Charles II., there had come forward the English founder of Individualism, the master builder in that school of empiric philosophy which is one of the most characteristic products of England. This man was John Locke.[5] His name and writings are not today very familiar to the general reader, because nearly all his principles were translated into practice by other men, famous in their day and tolerably well known to posterity, while Locke is little more than a name, venerated but nowadays seldom read. And yet he is, directly and indirectly, perhaps the most influential writer[6] who has appeared in the last two hundred years.

We are here only concerned with his political philosophy. Its direct influence in England was immense. The "Glorious Revolution" of 1688 sprang naturally from his theory of government. Adam Smith's doctrine of Natural Liberty and Bentham's general theory of Individualism owe much to him. John Stuart Mill acknowledged him as one of his masters in philosophy. But great

---

[4] *Laissez faire* might be translated "Leave us to act as we please." Its literal meaning is, of course, "Let do."

[5] Much of Locke's most important work was *written* in that reign, though not published till later.

[6] "On the whole, the most important figure in English philosophy."—Sorley. *Camb. Hist. Eng. Lit.* Vol. VIII., c. 14.

as was his direct influence in England, it produced even more striking effects in France and America. The Declaration of Independence may be traced largely to the philosophy of Locke, who (though his constitution for South Carolina was a practical failure) may also claim to have had a share in the Constitution of the United States. Adam Smith drew from the physiocrats who drew from Locke. Tom Paine and the other "Friends of the People" found in Rousseau a like intermediary.

The precursors of Revolution in eighteenth century France owed much to Locke. Voltaire and the Encyclopaedists were all more or less his disciples. Though Rousseau is also in one sense a founder of Socialism, his famous and unhistorical Social Contract was taken from Locke, who borrowed it from Hobbes, converting it from an argument for an all powerful despot to an argument for a limited constitutional monarchy, free and tolerant. Everyone knows the far-famed declarations of Rousseau's *Social Contract* and the Constitution of the United States—that all men are born free and have a natural right to freedom and security.[7] But few have read them in Locke's *Of Civil Government,* where they appeared much earlier.

For Locke and his disciples, including Adam Smith, Thomas Jefferson, and a long line of British and American statesmen, the main object of Representative Government is the freedom and happiness of the individual citizens who control it by their votes and support it by their taxes. Thus Locke's political philosophy crossed the Channel, and became the groundwork of Quesnay, Turgot, Bastiat, and other advocates of *laissez faire,* which was a French synonym for Individualism. Crossing the Atlantic it became the groundwork of American policy in internal affairs. Locke was the first considerable publicist to lay down the momentous doctrine that the State is secular—that it has a well-defined province in which alone it may act, i.e., that its business is to secure to men their civil rights, leaving all other matters to individual volition or voluntary co-operation. Thus he says in *A Letter Concerning Toleration:* "The commonwealth seems to me to be a society of men constituted only for the procuring, preserving, and advancing their own civil interests. Civil interests I call life, liberty, health and indolency [freedom from pain] of body; and the possession of outward things, such as money, lands,

[7] These assertions, of course, are found in the Declaration of Independence, but not specifically in the Constitution.—H. H.

houses, furniture, and the like. It is the duty of the civil magistrate, by the impartial execution of equal laws, to secure unto all the people in general, and to every one of his subjects in particular the just possession of these things belonging to this life."

In refusing to extend toleration to Roman Catholics, Locke followed Milton in his *Areopagitica*. In those times it was believed that Rome, if it regained power, would overthrow constitutional liberty. The Inquisition was still active. No one advocated universal toleration except members of persecuted minorities. In the reign of James II, most English Dissenters, when offered toleration on condition that the Roman Catholics should also be tolerated, declined the boon.

Locke, it may be said, laid down the theory so frequently set forth by Macaulay—that the duty of Government is to preserve the lives and property of its subjects, and that their other activities must be left in the main to moral influences and to free competitive enterprise. Locke did his business so thoroughly that the English theory remained unchanged for more than a century and a half. Indeed, if tendencies admitted of exact dates, we might say that Locke's theory was almost unchallenged until the publication of the Fabian Essays in 1889.

In *Civil Government* Locke expounds the Individualistic view of private property, and again lays down the quintessence of Individualism: "The great and chief end, therefore, of men's uniting into commonwealths, and putting themselves under government, is the preservation of their property." He qualifies his theory of a Social Contract, Compact, or Covenant, by pointing out that "men when they enter into society give up . . . liberty" of a kind; "yet it being only with an intention in every one the better to preserve himself, his liberty and property," the power conferred "can never be supposed to extend farther than the common good, but is obliged to secure everyone's property," etc., etc. This artful qualification of the *common good*, serves as a complete defence of the "Glorious Revolution," which gave us effective parliamentary government.

As Locke is of capital importance in our subject, those who wish to study it thoroughly should at least read his monumental essay. Some critics may object that we have over-valued Locke, seeing that he was anticipated in many respects by Hobbes as well as by Milton and other Republican writers. It is true that Hobbes, like Locke, was in a sense Individualist. But his influence, for various reasons, was much smaller. Besides, though Hobbes and Locke adopted many of the same premises, they drew from them quite different conclusions. Locke argued in favor of a free commonwealth, while Hobbes pointed to an absolute monarchy.

Locke's victory over all opposing schools of thought was so complete that Emancipation and Liberty became for more than a century after his death the keynotes of English political philosophy. Under the early Georges individual liberty was not only the admiration of all intelligent foreigners, but it had gone quite as far as public opinion approved. With the American revolution democratic reformers came to the front. But all progress was stopped by the French Revolution.

One of the few able men who wrote in nominal opposition to Locke's point of view was Bolingbroke, whose brilliant *Patriot King* (published in 1749) is probably more admired today than it was at the time of his death. But Bolingbroke, though he had a more extended view of the functions of Government than Locke, did not write in strong opposition to his principles. His ideal, "a patriot king at the head of a united people," was capable of a more or less "democratic" interpretation.

The policy of Walpole, and indeed his successors, was *Quieta non movere,* "Let sleeping dogs lie." A politician might have said, "We are all individualists now." Tory Dr. Johnson and non-party Goldsmith joined in composing the couplet:

> "How small, of all that human hearts endure,
> That part which kings or laws can cause or cure!"

In the same year that the *Patriot King* was published appeared the far more important *L'Esprit des Lois* of Montesquieu, a revolutionary book because it introduced the historical method. It helped to confirm the prevalent mode of thought, because it held up the British Constitution to the admiration of mankind.

We may then take it for granted that among thinkers and writers there was little effective opposition to Individualism in the eighteenth century.

In the economic sphere Hume, Tucker and Burke were all advocates of free trade and industrial emancipation from red tape regulations. But Adam Smith was the great architect. Individualism, already firmly rooted in England, was made impregnable in economics for generations by his *Wealth of Nations,* which appeared in 1776. At second hand or otherwise this work is so well known that it would be waste of time to dilate upon it. Until Adam Smith came into the field the Individualistic practice in politics had not, as a rule, extended to trade in spite of Walpole's experiments in that direction. But within seventy years the triumph of *laissez faire* in economics was complete. Pitt, the first great modern Tory statesman, absorbed Adam Smith's teaching and educated his party. This was a decisive factor; till then the one check upon Individualism had been Tory hostility to the Whigs—the political heirs of Locke. Henceforward the Tories, though as a body inclined to Protection and State control of trade, could be persuaded by leaders like Huskisson or Peel (however unwillingly) to remove restrictions from commerce and industry; indeed, in late Victorian days their leader, Lord Salisbury, and the bulk of his Parliamentary followers remained Free Traders. Free Trade means the absence of a Protective Tariff. Freedom of Trade means freedom not only from tariffs but from restrictions and regulations of all kinds, including those imposed by Trade Unions or combinations of employers, as well as those imposed by Government. This robust growth of economic Individualism was largely due to the seed sown by the *Wealth of Nations* and to the popular arguments of Cobden and the Manchester School.

It is impossible here to do more than glance at the important developments of *laissez faire* in France and the United States. In France the movement for economic emancipation was led by the Physiocrats, who by their contemporaries were called "Economistes." Many of their members, as Quesnay and Turgot, were great and beneficent figures in the history of France. The zeal they displayed for industrial and commercial liberty was natural in reflective men contemplating the feudal servitude of the French people, who were, like Rousseau's Man, everywhere in chains. They rightly attributed the poverty and misery of France to the obsolete regulations which everywhere sterilized effort and enterprise. Writing in the *Encyclopédie,* Turgot condemns "le malheureux principe qui a si longtemps infecté l'administration du commerce, je veux dire la manie de tout régler, et de ne jamais s'en rapporter aux hommes sur leur propre intérêt." The Physiocrats detected the fallacies of the Mercantile Theory and the Balance of Trade. Adam Smith owed much to them; but his judicious mind rejected their "crank" doctrine—that land is the sole source of wealth. Unhappily for France, Turgot fell, and instead of his wise reforms came revolutionary violence and the wars that made

Napoleon the military despot of France. Napoleon created a new bureaucratic state, more efficient than the old monarchy but hardly less subversive of freedom. Nevertheless Individualism revived in France after Waterloo and found a brilliant protagonist in Frédéric Bastiat, whose writings are a most lively exposure of the fallacies of Socialism, Protectionism and Militarism.

When we turn to the United States, we find there in Thomas Jefferson the master Individualist—for ability and consistency he has few if any rivals in the practice of that political creed. Having received the pure doctrine of Locke, he found during his residence in France a kind of laboratory in which he watched the French experiments in government. In the end he was able to establish in the United States a form of political thought which dominated it from the first decade of the nineteenth century and still prevails.[8] This may be called a triumph in observation and experiment, extremely rare in practical politics. The American tariff, indeed, is contrary to Jefferson's philosophy. But it must be remembered that the United States constitutes the largest and richest free trade area in the world with forty-eight states enjoying complete liberty of exchange for all their products and a maximum of freedom from economic restrictions.

We must now turn to England and the Industrial Revolution which will engage our attention more closely than its twin French sister. This vast change, which lasted roughly from 1760-1846, is now described in all text-books. England passed from home industries to factory industries. The Individualist régime, which then prevailed, enabled her to effect the change with comparative ease, and a period of wonderful expansion followed. For the second half of the nineteenth century Great Britain led the world in manufactures, commerce and shipping. Capital accumulated. Wages rose steadily. All classes prospered. The eighteenth century had been the age of optimists, and Adam Smith was one of them. He believed that Heaven would help those who helped themselves, and his anticipation of the prosperity which would follow commercial freedom was realized in Victorian England. One of his doctrines was that, if the individual trader were left to himself, the study of his own advantage would lead him to a course of action which would also be advantageous to society. Let him pursue his own interest, and he would be "led by an invisible hand to promote an end which was no part of his intention."

[8] This statement was written, it must be remembered, in 1927.—H. H.

In the literature of Individualism after Locke, Bentham is perhaps the leading figure; he was to the nineteenth century what Locke was to the eighteenth, and he showed how an Individualistic conception of society might be made the basis of wonderful improvements in public administration. He was a strong advocate of public economy, and was careful to insist that the functions of central and local authorities should be limited to police, public health and other services which do not lend themselves to voluntary effort. His small *Manual of Political Economy*, published in 1798, puts the economic case in a nutshell: "With the view of causing an increase to take place in the mass of national wealth, or with a view to increase the means either of subsistence or enjoyment, without some special reason, the general rule is, that nothing ought to be done or attempted by government. The motto, or watchword of government on these occasions, ought to be—*Be quiet;* . . . The request which agriculture, manufacturers, and commerce present to governments, is modest and reasonable as that which Diogenes made to Alexander: *'Stand out of my sunshine.'* We have no need of favour—we require only a secure and open path."

That Utilitarianism, Individualism, and Political Economy enjoyed so long a reign, and even held sway at the Universities, was largely due to the philosophy of John Stuart Mill, a very great man, who to all his other gifts added a candour, rare in controversy, which secures the confidence of the reader and makes him feel that he is not reading propaganda but accompanying the author on a journey in search of truth. Mill's lucidity of thought and style helped to extend his influence, and he soon took the place of Bentham as the leading exponent of utilitarian Individualism. His virtues and unselfish public spirit won him the title of "the Saint of Rationalism." Among Mill's books *Political Economy, Representative Government,* and above all, *On Liberty,* are the most important for our subject. They influenced, and still influence, the views of intellectuals on the critical problem of what should be the relationship under democratic institutions between the people and their government. Mill's analysis of the whole subject provides a most valuable contribution to political and economic science. There is a fine moral elevation of tone which lifts his arguments and conclusions far above the level of mere party controversy or the narrow and selfish interests of classes. The argument for free speech and complete toleration, and for individual liberty in general, has never been developed with such persuasive force as in Mill's brief but masterly treatise *On Liberty*. Among Mill's contemporaries the most brilliant of the writers who took part in this controversy was Macaulay. There is no more crushing exposure in our literature of the fallacies of State Socialism and of the theory that a government ought to be extravagant and meddlesome than Macaulay's essay on Southey's *Colloquies of Society*. It is worthy to be printed alongside Bastiat's unmasking of the French experiments in Communism.

The most powerful political force on the side of Individualism in the middle years of the nineteenth century was, of course, the Manchester School under the leadership of Cobden and Bright, supported by economists like Henry Fawcett and Thorold Rogers. It was equally opposed to Protectionism, Militarism and Socialism. With its support Gladstone introduced a severe economy into all departments of State and instituted the financial control of an efficent Treasury Department on the principles already laid down by Sir Robert Peel.

Among the apostles of Individualism after the death of Cobden and Mill were Herbert Spencer and his disciple Auberon Herbert. Herbert Spencer's *The Man versus the State* is an effective pamphlet against the Socialistic tendencies which began to permeate both the Liberal and Conservative Parties in the 'Eighties and the 'Nineties of last century. Among the politicians who aided this movement the most conspicuous was Joseph Chamberlain. His Radical Programme was issued in 1885, and when he passed over to the Conservative Party he took with him some of its items, including free education, which was carried by Lord Salisbury's Government.

Meanwhile, a Socialist Party was being gradually formed under such leaders as Hyndman, Morris and Keir Hardie. In 1889 there appeared the *Fabian Essays,* which won many converts to a moderate and progressive type of Socialism. Its most brilliant exponent was Mr. Bernard Shaw; but it owed even more to the researchful industry and incessant activity of Mr. and Mrs. Sidney Webb. A little later appeared Blatchford's *Merrie England,* which caught the popular fancy and helped to turn many working class Radicals into Socialists. But it was not until the Great War, with all the terrible suffering and economic loss which accompanied and followed it, that British industry and capital were at last confronted with a strong Labour Party and threatened by an active group of

Communists who aimed at the expropriation of property and at the Marxian ideal known as the "Dictatorship of the Proletariat." Since then Socialist propaganda has been very active among the working classes, and a considerable section of the British Press has been inclined to compromise with its proposals rather than to meet them and counter them by the principles and arguments of Individualism, opposing free competition and enterprise to monopolistic combinations and bureaucratic red tape.

THE FREE MAN'S LIBRARY

ACTON, LORD. *Essays on Freedom and Power.* Beacon Press. 1948.
452 pp.

Lord Acton (1834-1902) is chiefly remembered today through a single quotation: "All power tends to corrupt, and absolute power corrupts absolutely." But he was one of the most deeply learned men of his time, and recognized as few have ever done the true nature and value of liberty. It is, he declared, "not a means to a higher political end. It is itself the highest political end."

His lifelong object was to write a great "History of Liberty," but he immersed himself so deeply in reading and research that he never lived to complete it. Only two essays resulted from all this laborious preparation: "The History of Freedom in Antiquity" and "The History of Freedom in Christianity." Both are included in this collection selected by Gertrude Himmelfarb, who contributes an excellent introduction. In the opinion of F. A. Hayek, the tradition of true individualism is most perfectly represented in the nineteenth century in the work of Alexis de Tocqueville in France and Lord Acton in England.

ACTON, LORD. *The History of Freedom and Other Essays.* Macmillan.
1907. 638 pp.

An earlier collection of Acton's essays.

ADAMS, JOHN. *The Political Writings of John Adams.* Edited by
George A. Peek, Jr. Liberal Arts Press. 1955. 223 pp.

John Adams' enduring title to fame was his grasp of the principles of republican conservatism. He "vindicated with vigor and consistency such basic ideas of the American Constitution as the balanced and limited powers of the government, the right of the minority to protection against the tyranny of the majority and the inseparable connection between liberty and property. . . . The heart of the second President's political philosophy is summed up in one brief sentence in his *Defense of the American Constitution.* 'Power is always abused when unlimited and unbalanced.' "—William Henry Chamberlin, in *The Freeman.*

ALLEN, C. K. *Law and Orders*. London: Stevens. 1946. 385 pp.

An inquiry into the nature and scope of delegated legislation and executive powers in England. "In this scholarly study Dr. Allen, who holds to the liberal view of the state, wrestles with the problem of how a proper balance between the legislative and executive powers in Britain's government can be restored and maintained."—*Foreign Affairs*. The book is valuable for Americans because this problem of balance has become even more serious for us than for Britain.

ALLEN, C. K. *Bureaucracy Triumphant*. Oxford University Press. 1931. 156 pp.

"This little collection of essays is highly instructive to both the lawyer and legislator and while its references are solely to the situation as it exists in England, its lesson is one that might well be heard in the United States."—S. H. Hofstadter, in *Columbia Law Review*.

ANDERSON, BENJAMIN M. *Economics and the Public Welfare*. Van Nostrand. 1949. 602 pp.

An economic and financial history of the United States from 1913 to a little beyond the end of World War II. I take the liberty of quoting from my own foreword to the book: "[Anderson's] *The Value of Money* [1917] is one of the classics of American economic writing. . . . The present work is destined to take a similar rank among American economic and financial histories. It is already the outstanding economic and financial history for the period it covers. . . . Few economic histories have ever interlaced theory and interpretation so completely and successfully with the record of the facts. . . . Its sense of drama, its unfailing lucidity, its emphasis on basic economic principles, its recognition of the crucial roles played by outstanding individuals, its realistic detailed description of the disastrous consequences of flouting moral principles or of trying to prevent the forces of the market from operating, combine to give this book a sustained readability seldom found in serious economic writing."

ANDREWS, MATTHEW PAGE. *Social Planning by Frontier Thinkers*. Richard R. Smith. 1944. 94 pp.

A satire on social planning and planners by an historical scholar. It consists in large part of quotations from recent writings by so-called "advanced thinkers."

ANGELL, NORMAN. *The Great Illusion*. Putnam. 1911.

Several years before the outbreak of World War I, Norman Angell challenged the then almost universally accepted theory that military and political power give a nation commercial and social advantages.

He contended that the wealth of our modern world is founded upon credit and commercial contract which vanishes before an invading host and leaves nothing to reward the conqueror, but involves him in its collapse. His theme, in brief, was that nobody wins a modern war. "It may be doubted whether, within it entire range, the peace literature of the Anglo-Saxon world has ever produced a more fascinating or significant study."—A. S. Hershey, in *American Political Science Review,* 1911.

ANGELL, SIR NORMAN. *After All: The Autobiography of Norman Angell.* Farrar, Straus and Young. 1952. 370 pp.

"Although Sir Norman is wholly unconscious of this, the picture is of a rarely elevated and noble life. Besides the record of that life, this book is enriched by Sir Norman's reflections—veritable little essays in some cases—on a wide variety of topics . . . [including] The Incredible Gullibility of Believers in Freedom under Socialism."—Max Eastman, in *The Freeman.*

ANGELL, NORMAN. *The Public Mind.* Dutton. 1927. 232 pp.

"A stimulating book. . . . Its importance to Individualists lies in the emphasis it indirectly gives to the desirability of restricting State action to spheres in which popular passion and prejudice, and the ability of politicians to exploit them can have least effect."—PI.

ANSHEN, RUTH NANDA (ed.). *Freedom: Its Meaning.* Harcourt. 1940. 686 pp.

A symposium in which forty-one contributors have expressed their views on what freedom means to them. The volume runs to over a quarter of a million words. The contributions reflect little consistency with each other in viewpoint or philosophy.

ARENDT, HANNAH. *Origins of Totalitarianism.* Harcourt. 1951. 477 pp.

A search by a German-born author and scholar for the deeper roots of anti-semitism, imperialism, and totalitarianism. Virginia Kirkus called it "a highly serious and commanding study." One reviewer objected to it on the ground that "too much of her interpretation is taken from the particular experience of Germany"; and another reviewer on the ground that: "She attempts to give scholarly support to the increasingly widely held dictum that Soviet Communism is nothing but Red fascism."

ARISTOTLE. *Politics.* 330 B.C. Many editions. 337 pp.

In his introduction to the 1920 Oxford edition (translated by Benjamin Jowett), H. W. C. Davis reminds us that this classic embodies "theories of perennial value, and refutations of fallacies which are always re-emerging." There is a brilliant answer to Plato's proposals to abolish private property and to communize wives and children.

ASHTON, E. B. *The Fascist: His State and Mind*. Putnam. 1937. 320 pp.

"Helps one to understand the system of ideas ruling our enemies and the differences which separate their minds from ours."—F. A. Hayek.

ASHTON, T. S. *The Industrial Revolution*. Oxford University Press. 1948. 167 pp.

For at least a century (in part under the influence of Karl Marx) most of the economic historians have portrayed the Industrial Revolution as a catastrophe which caused the working class untold misery and brought about a sort of economic and spiritual Age of Darkness. In this remarkable little book Dr. Ashton, professor of economic history at the University of London, with more careful scholarship presents the Industrial Revolution as what it was—an achievement which, through the application of science to industry and the increased use of capital, led not only to a rapid growth of population but to a rise in the real incomes of a considerable section of the working class. Dr. Ashton stresses the intellectual and economic as well as the technical aspects of the movement. (See also his contribution to *Capitalism and the Historians*, listed under F. A. Hayek.)

AUSTIN, BERTRAM H., AND LLOYD, W. F. *The Secret of High Wages*. Dodd. 1926. 124 pp.

In 1925, at a time of great industrial depression in Britain, the authors, two English engineers, came to the United States in an effort to discover the secret of our unprecedented prosperity. Their inquiry was mainly concerned with the causes of high wages in industry combined with low cost of production. The book was originally a confidential report, but was published following a suggestion from the City Editor of the London *Times*.

BACKMAN, JULES. *Wages and Prices*. Irvington, N. Y.: Foundation for Economic Education. 1947. 88 pp.

An excellent statistical reference work on the levels and relationships of wages, prices, costs and profits in recent years. The author points out how these facts are ignored or misread by those who are trying to fix or change wages and prices by force. The evils of price-control, labor monopolies and currency inflation are dealt with incidentally.

BAGEHOT, WALTER. *Physics and Politics.* 1869. Several editions. (Knopf. 1948.) 230 pp.

An original and penetrating study of the impact of science and invention on politics, and of political institutions on knowledge. Bagehot shows how in the early history of mankind blind obedience to usage and custom seemed necessary to social cohesion and survival, but after the transition from the principle of status to that of contract was finally achieved, it was liberty that ensured the greatest social strength and progress. "As soon as governments by discussion have become strong enough to secure a stable existence, and as soon as they have broken the fixed rule of old custom, and have awakened the dormant inventiveness of men, then, for the first time, almost every part of human nature begins to spring forward. . . . And this is the true reason of all those panegyrics on liberty which are often so measured in expression but are in essence so true to life and nature. Liberty is the strengthening and developing power."

BAGEHOT, WALTER. *The English Constitution.* 1867. Oxford University Press. 1933. 312 pp.

This classic work was the first to make clear the real nature of the British constitution in its modern development. That constitution is not based, as Montesquieu thought, on the "separation of powers," but, on the contrary, on "the close union, the nearly complete fusion, of the executive and legislative powers." In this respect Bagehot contrasted the British and American constitutions to the disadvantage of the latter. As the preservation of ordered liberty depends upon the existence of a sound political system, Bagehot's book deserves the close study of Americans as well as Englishmen. He was a brilliant stylist as well as a brilliant thinker.

BAGEHOT, WALTER. *Economic Studies.* 1880. Stanford, Calif.: Academic Reports. 1953. 236 pp.

The essays in this book mainly elaborate classical English *laissez-faire* economics. They deal with Adam Smith, Malthus, Ricardo, "the late Mr. Mill," and such subjects as "The Postulates of English Political Economy" and "The Growth of Capital." "Bagehot, Editor of *The Economist,* was one of the finest thinkers and writers of his time. He was always an advocate of individual and commercial freedom. His best known books are on the *English Constitution* and *Lombard Street.*"—PI.

BAILWARD, W. A. *The Slippery Slope and Other Papers.* London: Murray. 1920. 236 pp.

"A collection of essays and articles written over a period of twenty years during which the author was engaged in Poor Law and charitable administration. By 'the slippery slope' is meant the path of least resistance in dealing with social problems, that is, the path of pauperism and Socialism."—PI.

BAILWARD, W. A., AND LOCH, C. S. *Old Age Pensions.* 1903.

"A well-argued case against old age pensions. Its interest is chiefly historical, but it might well be read by students interested in the history of ideas."—PI.

BAKER, JOHN R. *Science and the Planned State.* Macmillan. 1945. 120 pp.

Dr. Baker, a lecturer in zoology at Oxford University, contends that central planning and direction of scientific research do more to inhibit than to promote the growth of true scientific knowledge and discovery.

BARBER, THOMAS H. *Where We Are At.* Scribner's. 1950. 255 pp.

The author, who has been a lawyer, city official, and cowpuncher, describes his book as "a guide for enlightened conservatives." He urges removal of all price-fixing, subsidies and special group privileges and return to a free market economy.

BASTABLE, C. F. *The Theory of International Trade.* 1897, etc. Macmillan. 197 pp.

This short book, which first appeared in 1897, long held the field as the standard exposition of the "classical" theory of foreign trade and policy. It is balanced, vigorous and lucid, and uncompromisingly defends freedom of trade. Bastable's "principal conclusion as to conduct" is that "Governments in their dealings with foreign trade should be guided by the much-vilified maxim of *laissez faire*. To avoid misinterpretation, let it be remembered that the precept rests on no theory of abstract right, or vague sentiment of cosmopolitanism, but on the well-founded belief that national interests are thereby advanced, and that even if we benefit others by an enlightened policy, we are ourselves richly rewarded."

BASTER, A. S. J. *The Little Less.* London: Methuen. 1947. 161 pp.

A witty and well-informed little book on "the political economy of restrictionism." It consists mainly of a satiric history of the "lunatic years" in Great Britain between 1919 and 1939, when various ingenious devices were introduced by which everybody expected to get a little more for producing a little less. The story is told under the separate chapter headings of Producing Less, Growing Less, Working Less, Transporting Less, and Trading Less. There are also chapters on The Politics of Restrictionism and The Political Economy of Freedom.

BASTIAT, FRÉDÉRIC. *Economic Sophisms.* 1843-1850. Many editions. 2 vols. 548 pp. 564 pp.

"Bastiat, a friend of Cobden, was opposed to all descriptions of public waste and government interference. Both by his writings and by his action as a politician, he waged unceasing war against Bureaucracy, Protection and Socialism. The book cited above gained a great reputation; it is very witty and written in an attractive style. The Petition of the Candlemakers against the sun, which interfered with their industry, is well known. Each short study attacks some economic error, or pleads for the removal of some restrictions. The truth to be brought out is often enforced by dialogue or some other lively method. Bastiat was an optimist. His view was that the various human impulses and activities would, under free competition and an honest and peaceful government, result in steady progress and increasing prosperity and happiness. This was the theme of his *Harmonies Économiques,* of which only the first volume appeared owing to his untimely death.

"His complete works with introductory biography were published in France in 1855 shortly after his death. They include many brilliant pamphlets and articles against the fallacies of State Socialism and Communism, which were rampart in Paris in the last years of Bastiat's life."—PI.

"In *Sophismes Économiques* we have the completest and most effective, the wisest and wittiest exposure of protectionism and its principles, reasonings, consequences which exists in any language. Bastiat was the opponent of socialism. In this respect also he had no equal among the economists of France."—*Encyclopedia Americana.*

BASTIAT, FRÉDÉRIC. *The Law.* 1850. Irvington, N. Y.: Foundation for Economic Education. 1950. 75 pp.

A separate publication of a new translation (by Dean Russell) of one of Bastiat's most famous pamphlets. "Law," Bastiat maintains, "is solely the organization of the individual right of self-defense which existed before law was formalized. Law is justice." But the law has been perverted, and applied to annihilating the justice it was supposed to maintain. Protectionism, socialism and communism are all forms of legal plunder.

BAUDIN, LOUIS. *L'Aube d'un Nouveau Libéralisme.* Paris: Librairie de Médicis. 1953. 220 pp.

An acute, scholarly, documented, but extremely readable account of "the dawn of a new liberalism"—a liberalism resting economically on faith in the free market and politically on individual freedom within a proper framework of law and morals. On pages 144 to 150 the author presents a useful survey of the literature of "neo-liberalism" and mentions several French-language works not included in the present bibliography.

BAUDIN, LOUIS. *Les Incas du Pérou*. Paris: Librairie de Médicis. 1947. 188 pp.

A shorter study of the same subject that Professor Baudin covered so thoroughly in his *L'Empire Socialist des Incas,* in 1928. When the Spaniards overcame the Incas of Peru they found that a socialist society had existed there in the fourteenth and fifteenth centuries more totalitarian than perhaps any other known to history. Baudin analyzes this society and shows the consequences of that total socialization, many of which have remained with the native Indian population to the present day—the complete suppression of family sentiment, the immobilization of the individual, the disappearance of initiative and foresight, the complete petrifaction of life, the creation of a slave mentality. The book is written with great lucidity and vigor. Professor Baudin has a final chapter discussing the lessons of the empire of the Incas for our own time.

BEAULIEU, P. LEROY. *Collectivism*. London: Murray. 1908. 343 pp.

"An important analysis and criticism of Collectivism. That progress has always followed the substitution of individual ownership for collective ownership is clearly brought out. The relatively simple example of collective ownership in land is first dealt with and industrial collectivism is then examined. Schäffle's *Quintessence of Socialism* is taken as the only available source of information on the *practical application* of Collectivism, and yet Leroy Beaulieu succeeds in proving its inherent incapability of performing its duties mainly by quotations from the book itself."—PI.

BECK, JAMES MONTGOMERY. *Our Wonderland of Bureaucracy*. Macmillan. 1933. 290 pp.

A study, by a former Solicitor General of the United States, of the growth of bureaucracy in the federal government, and its destructive effect upon the Constitution.

BENDA, JULIEN. *The Treason of the Intellectuals*. Morrow. 1928. 244 pp.

This celebrated book first appeared in France under the title *La Trahison des clercs*. "That the intellectuals of the world have sold out to utilitarianism, leaving their proper devotion to truth and humanity, is the theme of Julien Benda's scorching analysis of the current leaders of thought. By taking on political passions, the intellectuals have played the game of the state, espoused war and conflict and lost that universalism which is their true reason for existence."—*World Tomorrow*.

Greatly needed today is a study with a title and theme similar to Benda's, which would not only cover developments in the twenty-five years since his book appeared, and describe the intellectual and sometimes quite literal treachery of some present-day physical scientists, but would cover the whole drift of our litterateurs and other intellectual leaders over the last three-quarters of a century into a sentimental socialism—including Bernard Shaw, H. G. Wells, and the Webbs in England, Anatole France in France, and the corresponding figures in Germany and America. It would be important to analyze not merely individual figures but the mob psychology of our modern intellectuals and the ease with which they were blown about by the fashionable winds of doctrine.

BENHAM, FREDERIC, AND BODDY, F. M. *Principles of Economics*. Pitman. 1947.

A textbook intended for an introductory course, to provide "the simple tools of modern economic analysis." Considerable attention is also given to the effects of government intervention upon a capitalistic system.

BENN, SIR ERNEST. *Confessions of a Capitalist*. London: Hutchinson. 1925. 287 pp.

"A telling defense of individual initiative."—*London Financial News*. "A book which is unique in economic literature. Sir Ernest's pen is as vivid as his mind is fearless and independent. . . . He tells us the most intimate details of his business. . . . The whole is accompanied by a running line of argument on the fundamental problems of economics, which is set out so skillfully as to be as entertaining and arresting as the autobiographical details."—Lionel Robbins.

BENN, SIR ERNEST. *The Return to Laisser Faire*. London: Ernest Benn. 1928. 221 pp.

An argument against the extension of governmental activity and interference in England and a plea for a return to individualism. Public aid to housing and the growing burden of bureaucracy are special targets. Even reviewers hostile to the author's thesis paid tribute to "the entertaining style, the caustic wit, the arresting illustration."

BENN, SIR ERNEST. *The State the Enemy*. London: Ernest Benn. 1953. 175 pp.

The author reviews the British experiment in state intervention and socialism all the way from Lloyd George, who inherited a budget of £100 million, to Attlee, who left it at £4,000 million, and sums up the record of failure: "Nationalization has not brought the expected smile to the face of the worker, full employment has not encouraged production, the management of money has not improved its quality; in fact, all the anticipations of the original Fabian Essays, the bases of modern Socialism, have proved disappointing, if not entirely fallacious." The style is lively, witty and aphoristic.

BENTHAM, JEREMY. *Works*. Edited by John Bowring. 1838-1843. Edinburgh: Tait. 11 vols.

"A considerable amount of Bentham is still worthy of study. He may be considered as the philosophic founder of modern British democracy. He held that the State exists to promote the individual happiness of the citizens who compose it and that ministers are the servants of the electors. For our purposes, the more important works are: (1) *A Fragment on Government* (1776), (2) *Defense of Usury* (1787), (3) *An Introduction to the Principles of Morals and Legislation* (1789). As a Utilitarian, an Individualist, and a reformer of laws and institutions, he deserves more attention than he now receives. Bentham is, like Locke, influential, but known chiefly through the work of his pupils and disciples."—PI.

BENTHAM, JEREMY. *Defense of Usury*. 1787. Many editions. 232 pp.

Jeremy Bentham, whose reputation has hitherto been that of a moralist, a founder of Utilitarianism, a logician, a great political and legal philosopher and reformer, was also, it is now being discovered, an outstanding economist. Until very recent years, by far the greater part of Bentham's economic work was completely unknown—locked up in chaotic and illegible manuscripts. The Royal Economic Society commissioned Dr. W. Stark to make a closer scrutiny of this material, which in 1952 was published in three volumes under the title *Jeremy Bentham's Economic Writings* (London: Allen and Unwin).

The *Defense of Usury,* however, which is included in these volumes, was published in 1787 and acquired immediate celebrity. Bentham was a great admirer of Adam Smith, whom he called "the father of political economy" and "a writer of consummate genius." But he was not an uncritical admirer, and in the *Defense of Usury,* which he published eleven years after the appearance of *The Wealth of Nations,* he ventured to take the master to task for his inconsistency in approving so-called anti-usury laws while opposing government price-fixing in practically every other field.

"The liberty of bargaining in money matters," wrote Bentham, is "a species of liberty which has never yet found an advocate." Yet "fixing the rate of interest, being a coercive measure, and an exception to the general rule in favor of the enforcement of contracts, it lies upon the advocates of the measure to produce reasons for it." Examining the reasons that had been offered, Bentham rejected them as invalid, and proceeded to explain the positive "mischiefs" done by the anti-usury laws. He concluded that there is "no more reason for fixing the price of the use of money than the price of goods."

BENTLEY, ELIZABETH. *Out of Bondage*. Devin-Adair. 1951. 311 pp.

In this autobiographical account Miss Bentley, an American college girl, describes how she entered the Communist party, took part in its secret underground for ten years, and later collaborated with the Federal Bureau of Investigation after she left the party. Although her story on its appearance was ridiculed by some reviewers as "school-girlish" and "phoney," many of her most startling charges have been confirmed by later investigation.

BERGER-PERRIN, RENÉ. *Vitalité Libérale*. Paris: Éditions SÉDIF. 1953. 93 pp.

M. Berger-Perrin is Secretary General of *L'Association de l'Enterprise à Capital Personnel*. "After a quarter of a century of the pre-dominance of authoritarian and collectivist ideas," he writes, "liberal thought today is reappearing with increased force and profundity." To prove this he has put together a little anthology of excerpts from more than fifty writers—French, English, American, German, Norwegian, Swiss, Dutch, Mexican, etc. These include not only economists, but sociologists, historians, journalists, and businessmen.

BERLIN, ISAIAH. *Historical Inevitability*. Oxford University Press. 1954. 79 pp.

The main purpose of this lecture is to consider a tendency which has, in the West, been growing since the eighteenth century, to regard human history as the product of impersonal "forces" obeying "inexorable" laws; with the implied consequence that individual human beings are seldom responsible for bringing about situations for which they are commonly praised or blamed, since the real culprit is "the historical process" itself—which individuals can do little to influence. "A magnificent assertion of the reality of human freedom, of the role of free choice in history."—London *Economist*.

BLUM, WALTER, AND KALVEN, HARRY, JR. *The Uneasy Case for Progressive Taxation*. University of Chicago Press. 1953. 107 pp.

"Progressive-tax theory has been due for an overhauling, and the authors do a highly competent job. . . . The work is distinguished by penetrating analysis, comprehensive coverage of sources, and excellent documentation . . . Rates high honors in the field."—*Annals of the American Academy of Political and Social Science*.

BÖHM-BAWERK, EUGEN VON. *Karl Marx and the Close of His System.* 1896, etc. London: Unwin. 221 pp.

Until the appearance of *Socialism* by Ludwig von Mises (q.v.), this was by far the best criticism of the economics of Karl Marx. For the points that it covers—chiefly the fallacies of the Marxian labor theory of value—it is still superb, unanswerable, and irreplaceable.

BÖHM-BAWERK, EUGEN VON. *The Positive Theory of Capital.* 1888. (Macmillan. 1891.) 428 pp.

One of the most brilliant and original contributions—if not *the* most brilliant and original—ever made to the theory of capital and interest. Böhm-Bawerk, declares the *Encyclopedia of the Social Sciences,* "was at a very early age one of the first to accept the teaching of Karl Menger, giving all his powers to the development and the defense of the subjective theory of value: it is to him that both the success and the formulation of the theory are largely due." According to Frank W. Taussig, *The Positive Theory of Capital* "is a landmark in the development of thought. As an intellectual performance, there are few books on economics in any language that can be ranked with it. One may not agree with all that is said, but the book bears the unmistakable impression of a great mind."

BOWLEY, A. L. *The Division of the Product of Industry. The Change in the Distribution of the National Income, 1880-1913.* Oxford: Clarendon Press. 1919. 1920. 60 pp. 27 pp.

"The Socialist case obtains support primarily through the existence of a widespread idea that wealth is so unfairly distributed that a large and permanent improvement in the material condition of the working classes could be obtained merely by means of a redistribution. . . . These two works attempt to determine, by a careful examination of all the existing relevant data, what the true position is. The following quotations, although not fairly indicating the nature of Professor Bowley's conclusions, show the immense importance of these essays to those who believe that social amelioration is to be sought along the lines of redistribution.

"Discussing the problem of an advance in the scale of wages, he says: 'In the majority [of industries] no such increase as would make possible the standards of living now urgently desired, and promised in the election addresses of all the political parties, could have been obtained without wrecking the industry.'

"As regards the change in distribution over the thirty-three year period analyzed, he says: 'The constancy of so many of the proportions and rates of movement found in the investigation seems to point to a fixed system of causation and has an appearance of inevitableness.'—

The Change in the Distribution of the National Income, 1880-1913."
—PI.

BOWLEY, A. L., AND STAMP, SIR JOSIAH. *The National Income.* Oxford: Clarendon Press. 1924. 1927. 59 pp.

"The general conclusion of this book is that comparing the years 1911 and 1924, the real Social Income of [Britain] was very nearly the same at the two dates, and that although real income per head had fallen a little, distribution had altered slightly in favor of the manual worker. After allowing for taxation, there was definitely less real income available in the hands of the rich for saving or expenditure, and whilst luxurious expenditure by the rich had diminished, a good deal of income was available for cheaper amusements. The standard of living of the employed working classes had clearly risen."—PI.

BOWLEY, A. L. *Wages and Income in the United Kingdom Since 1860.* Macmillan. 1938. 151 pp.

"Professor Bowley is to be congratulated on publishing this short résumé of a lifetime's research into wages and incomes. . . . A comprehensive and systematic guide."—London *Economist.* "The best reference on wage and employment indices is to the outstanding work of A. L. Bowley."—Joseph A. Schumpeter.

BRADFORD, GOV. WILLIAM. *Of Plymouth Plantation.* 1622. (Knopf. 1952.) 448 pp.

When the Pilgrim Fathers landed on the shores of Massachusetts they established a communist system of land holding and cultivation, and were soon brought to a state of famine. The governor of the colony, in his contemporary account, describes how they finally decided that they "should set corne every man for his owne perticuler . . . and so assigned to every family a parcell of land." The result was an immediate transformation in their habits of industry; and at the next harvest, "instead of famine, now God gave them plentie . . . so as any generall wante or famine hath not been amongest them since to this day."

BRANDT, KARL. *Reconstruction of World Agriculture.* Norton. 1945. 416 pp.

An exiled German scholar, now professor of agricultural economics at the Food Research Institute of Stanford University, surveys the history of world agriculture and food supply from the beginning of the first European war to the present, and offers suggestions and programs for libertarian agricultural policies in the postwar world. "This book, by one of the world's foremost agricultural economists, should be required reading for all post-war planners."—E. deS. Brunner, in the *Political Science Quarterly*.

BRANT, IRVING. *Life of James Madison*. Bobbs-Merrill. 1941. 1950. 4 vols.

"A very comprehensive biography; thoroughly reliable as well as readable."—Felix Morley. "The third volume of Brant's *Madison* is a magnificent study of one of our greatest statesmen at the climax of his career . . . and a startlingly original account of that much-discussed document, the Constitution of the United States."—Douglass Adair, in the *New York Herald Tribune*.

BRESCIANI-TURRONI, CONSTANTINO. *The Economics of Inflation*. 1931. London: Unwin. 1937. 464 pp.

Inflation not only wipes out the purchasing power of savings but always constitutes a threat to economic liberty. This is the most comprehensive and authoritative account of the great German inflation from 1914 to 1923. As Lionel Robbins writes in his foreword: "It was the most colossal thing of its kind in history: and, next probably to the Great War itself, it must bear responsibility for many of the political and economic difficulties of our generation. It destroyed the wealth of the more solid elements in German society: and it left behind a moral and economic disequilibrium, apt breeding ground for the disasters which have followed. Hitler is the foster-child of the inflation."

BRIGHT, JOHN. *Speeches on Questions of Public Policy*. Macmillan. 1878.

"Eloquent expositions of public policy on many subjects. The principles are Individualistic, favoring peace, free trade and public economy on the lines of his friend Richard Cobden."—PI.

BROMFIELD, LOUIS. *The Farm*. Harper. 1933. 346 pp.

A novel, probably in part autobiographical, dealing with the fortunes of four generations of a family living on a farm in northern Ohio. It begins in 1815 and ends a century later. "Surpasses many sociological treatises in insight."—Wilhelm Röpke.

BROMFIELD, LOUIS. *Pleasant Valley*. Harper. 1945. 302 pp.

Partly autobiographical reminiscence, and partly an exposition of the author's theories of farming and farm life. He relates how, after many years spent abroad, he returned to his native Ohio and there built up a new home and a new way of life founded on the old ways of the pioneer American farmer. Mr. Bromfield puts great stress on the virtue of self-reliance in a climate of economic liberty.

BROMFIELD, LOUIS. *A New Pattern for a Tired World.* Harper. 1953. 314 pp.

"Vigorously written by an obviously sincere and devoted American, who is neither isolationist nor suspected on any other score, but who profoundly believes that the key to our future existence and our future happiness lies in improving our economic status and the economic status of our neighbors by achieving the ultimate in free trade."
—C. W. Weinberger, in *San Francisco Chronicle.*

BROOKINGS, R. S. *Industrial Ownership.* Macmillan. 1925. 107 pp.

"The Economic Emancipation of Labor" is suggested by the author as an alternative title for this book. It deals principally with the remarkable tendency toward diffusion in the ownership of property taking place in the United States, a movement that Professor Carver regarded as "an economic revolution."

BROOKINGS INSTITUTION. *Economics and Public Policy.* Washington, D. C. 1955. 157 pp.

These are the Brookings Lectures for 1954 as delivered by four American economists, Arthur Smithies, Joseph J. Spengler, Frank H. Knight and Jacob Viner, and by two British economists, John Jewkes and Lionel Robbins. Two of the lectures bear especially on the subject of the present bibliography. Professor Knight's lecture on "Economic Objectives in a Changing World" is instructive, but rather for the questions it raises than for those it answers. Professor Robbins' lecture on "Freedom and Order" is lucid and illuminating.

BRUTZKUS, BORIS. *Economic Planning in Soviet Russia.* London: Routledge. 1935. 234 pp.

An acute discussion, by an exiled Russian economist, of the difficulties and problems of central economic planning. It is especially valuable because the author combines theoretical insight with a wide factual knowledge of Russian conditions. He explains, for example, why the great Dnieprostroy dam and hydroelectric plant, the prewar pride of Soviet Russia, was not justified economically.

BRYCE, JAMES. *The American Commonwealth.* Macmillan. 1888, etc. 2 vols. 743 pp. 963 pp.

A classic work on the American political and social system, written half a century after de Tocqueville's *Democracy in America* and surpassed only by that work insofar as their fields overlap. Viscount Bryce declared that his purpose, unlike de Tocqueville's, was less to discuss the merits of "democracy" than "to paint the institutions and people of America as they are." In this he succeeded far beyond any native observer of the time. His interpretations are made from the standpoint of the liberal tradition.

BRYNES, ASHER. *Government Against the People*. Dodd, Mead. 1946. 265 pp.

"A scholarly and well written study of the growth and development of the police systems in Russia, Great Britain and the United States as illustrative of a basic factor making for war or peace in the modern world."—F. R. Dulles. The author contends that where people are free, the police force is decentralized, limited in scope, and nonpolitical.

BUBER, MARGARETE. *Under Two Dictators*. Dodd, Mead. 1951. 331 pp.

In 1925 the author and her husband, Heinz Neumann, deposed leader of the German Communist party, went to Moscow to translate for the Comintern. In 1937 her husband was arrested and she never saw him again. She herself was arrested the next year. Her book is the account of her sufferings in the Soviet slave camp of Karaganda, and in the Nazi concentration camp at Ravensbruck, where she spent five years. In 1945 she was liberated by the American Army. "This book can destroy the last outposts of the Soviet apologists in the West. It should be read by all the fellow-travelers, the Stalinoids, the double-standard 'liberals' and the phoney 'progressives' who have acted as Stalin's stooges when humanity needed every decent man and woman to defend itself against the onslaughts of those who thirst for concentrated power."—Peter Blake, in *The New York Times*.

BUCKLEY, WILLIAM F., JR. *God and Man at Yale*. Regnery. 1951. 240 pp.

A recent Yale graduate examines and criticizes the teaching of religion and economics at his university. As John Chamberlain sums up in his Introduction, Mr. Buckley concludes that the values inculcated at Yale "are agnostic as to religion, 'interventionist' and Keynesian as to economics, and collectivist as applied to the relation of the individual to society and government." Of the five chapters in the book, the most important for the purposes of this bibliography is the second, "Individualism at Yale," in which the author takes telling quotations from the leading textbooks used in Yale undergraduate economics courses to prove his case that the teaching is dominantly collectivist. What broadens the significance of this chapter is the probability that a like case could be made out against the economics teaching in many other leading American universities today.

BUDENZ, LOUIS F. *The Techniques of Communism*. Regnery. 1954. 342 pp.

"The present book," declares the author in his Introduction, "is an analytical and critical study of Communism. It deals with Communist ideology, strategy, and 'movement' as presented by the Marxist-Leninist classics themselves and by current Communist documents and directives. . . . It analyzes Communist activities as the Communist is instructed to carry them out."

Various chapters deal with the communist philosophy and apparatus; communist phraseology ("Aesopian language," involved "scientific" argumentation, double-talk, definitions turned on their heads, and the Big Lie technique); the strategy and tactics of communism; the training of communists; the role of the communist press; and various other methods of affecting public opinion and infiltrating unions, the schools, minority groups, and government agencies. There is a final chapter on "How to Fight Communism." The book is vigorous, clear and carefully documented. Every Congressman, high government official, and newspaper editor ought to master the lessons it contains.

BUDENZ, LOUIS F. *This Is My Story*. Whittlesey. 1947. 379 pp.

The former managing editor of *The Daily Worker,* the American organ of the Communist party, describes how he joined the party in 1935, served in various editorial capacities, became for six of his ten years with the party a member of the Communist National Committee, broke and was converted to Catholicism in 1945.

BUDENZ, LOUIS F. *Men Without Faces*. Harper. 1950. 305 pp.

Here the former high-ranking communist, who returned to the Roman Catholic Church in 1945, discusses the operations of the Communist party in the United States, describes in detail the methods it employed, and accuses it of forming a fifth column directly under the control of Soviet Russia. In a chapter on "The Capture of the Innocents" he explains how "some of our best minds are moved around by the Communists like pawns." "The master key to the Soviet conquest of the United States," he concludes, "might well be our own complacency."

BUDENZ, LOUIS F. *The Cry Is Peace*. Regnery. 1952. 242 pp.

An exposure of the Soviet "crusade for peace" and a criticism of American "appeasement" policies. "This is by all odds one of the best available books on the important subject of the Communist conspiracy against the United States."—W. H. Chamberlin.

BUER, MABEL C. *Health, Wealth and Population: 1760-1815.* London: Routledge. 1926. 290 pp.

"A critical contribution to the study of economic history. Its importance is wider than the . . . title would suggest, and it is a book with which all students of social history should be acquainted. Miss Buer holds that the Industrial Revolution has become the 'villain of the drama of economic history' through the habit of 'writing history backwards'; she shows that the positive assertion at the end of the period by Francis Place that the habits and conditions of the working classes showed a great improvement on their condition half a century previously, was amply justified. . . . The period was one of enterprise and experiment in social betterment in many spheres, and one in which philanthropy and benevolence 'were never more assiduously preached' and practiced. This attitude is contrasted with the extreme callousness on the part of the governing classes in the previous century."—PI.

BURCKHARDT, JAKOB. *Force and Freedom: Reflections on History.* Pantheon Books. 1943.

Jakob Burckhardt (1818-1897), a Swiss historian and humanist, was one of the great individualist philosophers of the nineteenth century. His profound and searching mind foresaw the coming of collectivism. "People today," he wrote in 1875, "feel lost and they shudder if they are not together in their thousands." He predicted the coming of the Mussolinis, Hitlers and Stalins: "My mental picture," he wrote in a letter in 1889, "of those terrible *simplificateurs* who will one day descend upon our old Europe is not an agreeable one. In my imagination I can visualize these ruffians in the flesh." The present book is the first English translation of a collection of short pieces. It contains a valuable introduction by James Hastings Nichols. "It is a book which ranks among the classics of historico-political writing, comparable to Edmund Burke, de Tocqueville and Fustel de Coulanges."—Karl Lowith, in the *Journal of Philosophy.*

BURGESS, JOHN W. *The Reconciliation of Government with Liberty.* Scribner's. 1915. 394 pp.

A scholarly study of modern constitutional government in Europe and America. The author, who was dean of the faculty of political science at Columbia University, saw in the tendency to increase the authority and functions of those holding public office a very real menace to liberty. "We are further away today from the solution of the great problem of the reconciliation of government and liberty," he wrote in 1915, "than we were twenty years ago."

BURGESS, JOHN W. *Recent Changes in American Constitutional Theory.* Columbia University Press. 1923.

Dr. Burgess takes the position that any movement contrary to limiting the powers of government and defining and guaranteeing individual liberty is in the wrong direction. The book traces the development of constitutional law between 1898 and 1918.

BURKE, EDMUND. *Works.* Oxford University Press. 6 vols.

"The man who to me seems to be one of the greatest representatives of true individualism."—F. A. Hayek. "To do Burke justice, it would be necessary to quote all his works; the only specimen of Burke is, *all that he wrote.*"—William Hazlitt. For individualists, however, the most important and most representative of his works are: *Thoughts on the Present Discontents* (1770); address *To the Electors of Bristol* (1774); the speech on *Conciliation with America* (1775); and *Reflections on the French Revolution* (1790). Even William Hazlitt, who was vehemently opposed to Burke's stand on the French Revolution, said: "In arriving at one error, Burke discovered a hundred truths."

BURNHAM, JAMES. *The Coming Defeat of Communism.* John Day. 1950. 278 pp.

The author believes that communism can and will be defeated, and without large-scale war—if the western nations, and particularly the United States, follow some such plan of action as he presents. Even reviewers who refused to accept this plan acknowledged the skill and brilliance of Burnham's writing.

BURNHAM, JAMES. *The Web of Subversion.* John Day. 1954. 248 pp.

A study based on examination of the records of Congressional investigations since 1948 of communist underground networks in the U. S. Government. "It would be less than just to call Mr. Burnham's new book a good digest of an enormous amount of material, deftly arranged, and neatly presented. It is indeed that, to begin with—but it is also a penetrating analysis which reveals the pattern of the fatal web spread for us by traitors and their associates."—Joseph McSorley, in the *Catholic World.*

BYE, RAYMOND T. *Principles of Economics.* Crofts. 1941. 632 pp.

A well-known college textbook that presents the free enterprise point of view.

CAIRNES, J. E. *The Character and Logical Method of Political Economy.* Macmillan. 1857. 229 pp.

John Elliott Cairnes (1823-1875) in his day held an authority in economics second only to that of John Stuart Mill, and is usually regardad as the last of the English classicists. The book here listed represents the part of his work that is still most alive; it deserves far more study than it gets. Another leading work was *The Slave Power* (1862), in which Cairnes expounded the inherent disadvantages of slave labor and helped to turn British opinion in favor of the North in the American Civil War. He accepted *laisser faire* in government economic policy "not as based on a scientific doctrine . . . but as the surest and most practical rule of conduct."

CALHOUN, JOHN C. *A Disquisition on Government*. 1851. (Included in *Calhoun: Basic Documents*. State College, Pa.: Bald Eagle Press. 1952. 329 pp.)

Calhoun (1782-1850) openly defended slavery as a positive good, and frankly repudiated the doctrine of human equality as expressed in the Declaration of Independence. This fact has thrown into undeserved neglect his brilliant defense of States' rights and the rights of minorities. "Calhoun was concerned with one of the permanent problems of government; and whatever one may think of the practical results of his logic, it should be recognized that the theoretical analysis which he presented in his *Disquisition on Government* was a contribution to political theory of permanent importance. The protection of minority rights had been one of the main objectives of the American Constitution. . . . The powers of the Federal government must be limited, and a minority section must be allowed to block action detrimental to its interests."—Henry Bamford Parkes, in *The United States of America: A History*.

CANNAN, EDWIN. *Wealth*. 1914, etc. Staples Press. 292 pp.

"One of the best expositions of the elements of economics ever published. It is much more than a textbook; it is the result of deliberate and original thought by a master economist able to see his subject in perspective and distinguish the most essential and relevant considerations. . . . It might well be made a sort of Individualist's bible, more especially because it does *not* advocate Individualism or any other system of social organization. . . . It is nevertheless true that nearly all Collectivist proposals obtain support through the existence of misconceptions which an understanding of this book would dispel." —PI.

CANNAN, EDWIN. *History of the Theories of Production and Distribution*. London: King. 1924. 422 pp.

"A critical account of the writings of the classical economists. The study of an acute history of economic theory such as this will prove useful to those who wish to acquire the ability to detect the many fallacies that lurk in discussions of economic problems by politicians and popular writers. Apart from this, the book is useful as a work of reference and the summing up in the last chapter should be read by all. The last sentence of the book is worth quoting as representing Prof. Cannan's views in 1903, when the second edition was published. '[The economist] is certain to disagree frequently with both Socialist and Individualist fanatics, who support and oppose changes, not on their merits, but according to the opinion they have formed, often on wholly insufficient grounds, as to their being movements towards or away from their ideal.' "—PI.

CANNAN, EDWIN. *Money*. 1918, etc. Staples Press. 136 pp.

This little work was projected as a supplementary chapter to the same author's *Wealth*. It is a model of lucidity and economic reasoning, and particularly good in explaining the connection between monetary policy and rising and falling prices. Although I would dissent from one or two of its conclusions, it seems to me to be still the best book on money of its length. It has gone through more than eight editions.

CANNAN, EDWIN. *An Economist's Protest*. London: King. 1927. 438 pp.

A collection of papers written over fourteen years. "Nothing that has been published in recent years will do so much to clarify doctrine and promote a grasp of essentials in Economics; while amateurs of literature, who are commonly repelled by an economic title, will find in the collection much that will hold its own among the classics of controversial literature."—London *Times Literary Supplement*.

CANNAN, EDWIN. *A Review of Economic Theory*. London: King. 1929. 448 pp.

A lively but authoritative history of economic theory. It begins with the ideas of ancient and medieval philosophers and discusses the doctrines of the classical economists and others up to the time of the book's publication.

CANNAN, EDWIN. *The Economic Outlook*. London: Unwin. 1912. 312 pp.

F. A. Hayek writes of the essays in this book, as well as those in *An Economist's Protest* (1927), that they "deserve, even now, renewed and wider attention, and translation into other languages. Their simplicity, clarity and sound common sense make them models for the treatment of economic problems, and even some that were written before 1914 are still astonishingly topical." Among the pupils of Edwin Cannan who have since exerted considerable influence are Sir Theodore Gregory, Lionel Robbins, F. C. Benham, W. H. Hutt and F. W. Paish.

CANNAN, EDWIN. *Coal Nationalisation*. London: King. 1919. 36 pp.

"This is a précis of evidence given before the Sankey Commission. Only parts were read aloud by the Chairman, who obviously failed to grasp its importance and relevance. Professor Cannan concluded that nationalization would not benefit the taxpayer, the consumers of coal or the miners themselves. As he indicated, the Commission and the Government had 'apparently decided "that something must be done" before finding out whether they knew of any remedy better than the disease.' "—PI.

CARLSON, OLIVER. *Handbook on Propaganda*. Los Angeles: Foundation for Social Research. 1953. 110 pp.

The purpose of this handbook is "To make available to alert citizens in all walks of life . . . some basic facts about propaganda—what it is—how it functions—and how to combat it." There is a discussion of the vehicles of propaganda, and separate chapters on nationalist and internationalist, racist, government, collectivist and communist propaganda.

CARR-SAUNDERS, SIR ALEXANDER M. *The Population Problem*. Oxford: Clarendon Press. 1922. 516 pp.

"This is thought by some to be the most important book dealing with the problem of numbers of mankind that has appeared since the days of Malthus."—PI.

CARVER, T. N. *The Present Economic Revolution in the United States*. Little, Brown. 1926. 270 pp.

"Professor Carver foresees the beginning of a new economic revolution in the world, which appears to be developing first in the United States of America, as the Industrial Revolution came first in England at the close of the eighteenth century. R. Boeckel and R. S. Brookings had already called attention to this movement, but this is the work of the Professor of Political Economy at Harvard. . . . 'It is just as possible [he writes] to attain equality under Capitalism as under any other system,' and in consequence, 'The apostles of discontent are being robbed of their thunder. . . .' This study of an Individualist society is one of the most suggestive writings on Individualism that exists."—PI.

CARVER, T. N. *Essays in Social Justice*. Harvard University Press. 1915. 429 pp.
———. *Principles of National Economy*. Ginn. 1921. 773 pp.

Other works which expound Professor Carver's vigorous individualistic free enterprise philosophy.

CASSEL, GUSTAV. *From Protectionism Through Planned Economy to Dictatorship.* London: Cobden-Sanderson. 1934. 26 pp.

This lecture, by an eminent Swedish economist who died in 1945, is included in this list (in violation of my general rule against including pamphlets) because it points out, with a persuasiveness, power and compactness surpassed by no other writer, how "planned economy," long enough continued, must lead to despotism. "The leadership of the State in economic affairs which advocates of Planned Economy want to establish is, as we have seen, necessarily connected with a bewildering mass of governmental interferences of a steadily cumulative nature. The arbitrariness, the mistakes and the inevitable contradictions of such policy will, as daily experience shows, only strengthen the demand for a more rational coordination of the different measures and, therefore, for unified leadership. For this reason Planned Economy will always tend to develop into Dictatorship." Cassel explains this process step by step. "If we allow economic freedom and self-reliance to be destroyed," he goes on to point out, "the powers standing for Liberty will have lost so much in strength that they will not be able to offer any effective resistance against a progressive extension of such destruction to constitutional and public life generally."

CATLIN, GEORGE. *The Story of the Political Philosophers.* Whittlesey. 1939. 802 pp.

Reviewing this book in *The New York Times* (Jan. 7, 1940) I wrote: "In dealing with successive political philosophers it presents their biographies and their theories in judicious proportions. It is written with wit and humor and contains some arresting characterizations. It is learned, crowded, discursive, allusive, but it is not always clear." Felix Morley calls it: "An encyclopedic study, gracefully written and useful to all who are interested in political theory."

CECIL, LORD HUGH. *Liberty and Authority.* London: Edward Arnold. 1910. 70 pp.

"A brief and thoughtful plea for ordered liberty; the ideal is a society held together not by coercion, but 'by the spontaneous cohesion of virtuous wills.' "—PI.

CHAMBERLIN, WILLIAM HENRY. *America's Second Crusade.* Regnery. 1950. 372 pp.

The author describes this work as an attempt "to examine without prejudice or favor the question why the peace was lost while the war was won." It is a brilliant and well-documented history of the blunders and misconceptions that were responsible for Teheran, Yalta and

Potsdam, and led to a "peace" that mainly realized the aims of Russian communism and totalitarianism at the expense of the aims, or of what should have been the aims, of a democratic and freedom-loving America.

CHAMBERLIN, WILLIAM HENRY. *Collectivism: A False Utopia*. Macmillan. 1937. 265 pp.

"Mr. Chamberlin comes vigorously to the defense of democratic institutions, with all their faults. He regards fascism and communism as similar examples of a collectivist state, and argues that progress is possible in the long run only on the basis of political liberty and wisely controlled individual enterprise."—*Springfield Republican*.

CHAMBERLIN, WILLIAM HENRY. *The Russian Revolution*. Macmillan. 1935. 2 vols. 511 pp. 556 pp.

"What Mr. Chamberlin, Moscow correspondent of *The Christian Science Monitor* from 1922 to 1934, has done with admirable clarity and scrupulous objectivity is not so much to offer sensational new judgments as to knit and co-ordinate a positively staggering amount of information based on source material, much of which had not previously been examined by scholars in this field, and to marshal the confused events of 1917-1921 in orderly fashion, giving chapter and verse for every important statement of fact or opinion."—*Books*.

CHAMBERS, WHITTAKER. *Witness*. Random House. 1952. 808 pp.

This is Whittaker Chambers' own account of his life, of the Hiss-Chambers trial, and of his connection with the Communist party and his repudiation of it. It is powerfully and eloquently written. Chambers joined the Communist party primarily for emotional and quasi-religious reasons and left it because of his religious conversion. This points to the one serious shortcoming of the book, which is its failure to understand or to explain adequately the *economic* case against communism and in favor of freedom.

"The name of the author, the theme of his work, the nature of our times all conspire to make this volume one of the most significant autobiographies of the twentieth century."—Sidney Hook, in *The New York Times*.

"This is a great book; one of the greatest written by a contemporary American. . . . Whittaker Chambers has composed an '*apologia pro vita sua*' . . . [and] also one of the best and most readable accounts of life both in the 'open' Communist Party and in its auxiliary underground organizations. . . . The Communist Party, in America as in every non-Communist country, is a criminal conspiracy, with its members pledged to stop at nothing, espionage or sabotage, murder or treason, which will advance the interests of the foreign power, the

Soviet Union, to which Communists everywhere are blindly subservient."—W. H. Chamberlin, in *Human Events*.

CHANCE, SIR WILLIAM. *The Better Administration of the Poor Law*. London: Sonnenschein. 1895. 260 pp.

"Sir William Chance has written several books on Poor Law administration, all from an emphatically Individualist standpoint. In the above he wrote: 'The principles which underlie the grant of Poor Relief which it—the Poor Law Relief Report of 1834—lays down are good for all time. Had the Poor Law been administered since 1834 strictly on those principles . . . pauperism would probably have been reduced to a negligible quantity.' "—PI.

CHODOROV, FRANK. *One Is a Crowd*. Devin-Adair. 1952. 176 pp. Reflections of an individualist.

CLAPHAM, J. H. *An Economic History of Modern Britain*. Cambridge University Press. 1926. 623 pp.

"An understanding of the *laissez-faire* and early industrial period is much needed. In this learned work Dr. Clapham, a leading authority, exposes 'the legend that everything was getting steadily worse for the working man down to some unspecified date between the drafting of the People's Charter and the Great Exhibition.' This legend seems to have been largely responsible for a tendency to a kind of unconscious Socialist bias in economic and social thinking, and it has, with a few exceptions, been spread by economic history textbooks. Knowles' *Industrial and Commercial Revolutions in the Nineteenth Century* is the most notable exception. Dr. Clapham's contribution represents the culmination of a reaction which has come in recent years as a result of modern historical research. (See also: GEORGE. *London Life in the 18th Century*. BUER. *Health, Wealth and Population* (1760-1815). TALBOT GRIFFITHS. *Population Problems in the Age of Malthus*. VAUGHAN WILKINS. *Sidelights on Industrial Evolution*.)"—PI.

(See also in this bibliography T. S. ASHTON, F. A. HAYEK, etc.)

CLARK, COLIN. *Welfare and Taxation*. Oxford: Catholic Social Guild. 1955. 80 pp.

Dr. Clark, the eminent Australian statistician and economist, now Director of the Institute of Research in Agricultural Economics at Oxford, argues in this little book that the tax rate in Britain is reducing incentives, productivity, and national income, and points out that even those with lower incomes are really paying for their own "free" social services. He concludes that we should "give the State, not the maximum, but the minimum of powers and duties. . . . Concentration of political power is always dangerous. . . . We should realize that, if we go on building up the power of the State . . . giving it more and more control over every detail of our lives . . . we create a State which will not merely tax us to excess but eventually enslave us completely."

CLARK, FRED G. *Magnificent Delusion*. Whittlesey. 1940. 152 pp.

An analysis of present economic and social ills in America, based on the thesis that we are in danger of losing our democracy through over-insistence on humanitarianism, the idea that the government owes all of us a living. "Mr. Clark has made an effective case."— Nicholas Roosevelt.

CLARK, F. G., AND RIMANOCZY, R. S. *How We Live*. Van Nostrand. 1944. 39 pp.

A short, clear, and vigorous primer on how the capitalist system works. The authors emphasize the importance of capital accumulation—the constant need for more and better tools to increase man's ability to utilize natural resources and so to increase his material welfare. The same authors have written other primers: *Money, How to Be Popular Though Conservative*, and *How to Think About Economics*.

CLARK, JOHN BATES. *The Distribution of Wealth*. Macmillan. 1899. 445 pp.

A work of epoch-making importance: a theory of wages, interest and profits which seeks to show that "free competition tends to give to labor what labor creates, to capitalists what capital creates, and to entrepreneurs what the coordinating function creates." It is thus indirectly an answer to the socialist contention that under competitive capitalism labor is "exploited" and "workmen are regularly robbed of what they produce." "It is not too much to say," wrote the economist Henry R. Seager in 1900, "that the publication of Professor Clark's *Distribution* marks an epoch in the history of economic thought in the United States. Its inspiration, its illustrations, even its independence of the opinions of others, are American; but its originality, the brilliancy of its reasoning and its completeness deserve and will surely obtain for it a place in world literature."

COBDEN, RICHARD. *Speeches on Questions of Public Policy*. London: Unwin. 1908. 2 vols.

"Cobden [1804-1865] was of all English statesmen the most powerful and persuasive exponent of the Individualistic view of Government. See his *Life* by John Morley."—PI.

COLE, FRANKLIN P. *They Preached Liberty*. Revell. 1941.

Significant excerpts from the sermons of New England ministers during the late Colonial period.

COLLINGWOOD, R. G. *The Idea of History*. Oxford University Press. 1946. 339 pp.

"With the death of R. G. Collingwood in 1943 British philosophy lost one of its most distinguished minds. His most original work grew out of his reflections on the special characteristics of historical thinking."—*Manchester Guardian*.

COMMUNIST INTERNATIONAL. *Blueprint for World Conquest*. Washington: Human Events. 1946. 263 pp.

This is designed to serve as a warning to anti-communists of the plans and tactics that they must learn to combat. It contains the theses and statutes of the Communist International, as adopted at the second world congress at Moscow in 1920; the program of the Communist International as adopted by the sixth world congress at Moscow on Sept. 1, 1928, and the constitution and rules of the Communist International. There is an introduction by William Henry Chamberlin.

CONSTANT, BENJAMIN. *De l'Esprit de Conquête*. 1813. Paris: Librairie de Médicis. 1947. 68 pp.

Benjamin Constant (1767-1830) was the author of a celebrated autobiographical novel, *Adolphe*. He was the lover of the famous Madame de Staël and later acquired an infatuation for Madame Récamier. The literary and amorous side of his career has unfortunately overshadowed his prophetic contributions in support of liberalism and freedom of the press, especially his *De l'esprit de conquête et de l'usurpation*, directed against Napoleon. In 1829 he wrote: "For forty years I have defended the same principle: liberty in everything, in religion, in philosophy, in literature, in industry, in politics; and by liberty I mean the triumph of individuality, as much over the authority that seeks to govern by despotism as over the masses who claim the right to enslave the minority to the majority." An English translation of *Conquest and Usurpation* was published by Reynal & Hitchcock in 1941.

CONSTITUTION OF THE UNITED STATES. 1787.

"The American Constitution," wrote Gladstone, "is the most wonderful work ever struck off at a given time by the brain and purpose of man." The first ten amendments, which constitute the Bill of Rights, are a charter of human liberties which has served as a model to mankind. (See HAMILTON, MADISON, FARRAND, NORTON.)

COOLEY, CHARLES HORTON. *Life and the Student*. Knopf. 1927. 273 pp.

A volume of aphoristic wisdom on human nature, society, and letters which deserves to be far more widely known than it is. It recalls the notebooks of Emerson and Thoreau, and will stand comparison with them. It is not a systematic defense or exposition of the philosophy of individualism, but every page breathes the spirit of that philosophy. Some individual paragraphs alone would justify including the book in the present bibliography. For example: "There are three irrefutable reasons why views that seem dangerous, unpatriotic or otherwise abominable should be freely expressed. 1: Discussion is the only way to modify or control them. 2: It is the only way to mobilize conservative views in order to combat them intelligently. 3: They may be right."

CORNUELLE, HERBERT C. *Mr. Anonymous*. Caldwell, Idaho: Caxton Printers. 1951. 212 pp.

A biography of William Volker, who rose from a penniless German immigrant in 1871 to a millionaire businessman in 1906. What was most remarkable about him, however, was not his rise from "rags to riches" but his determination to live according to the Golden Rule. "A man with money," he declared, "is to be pitied if he cannot give it away." So firm was his attitude against any sort of public recognition of his many selfless charities that it was not until after his death in 1947 that "Mr. Anonymous" could be identified as William Volker. Mr. Cornuelle's story is written with simple directness and has the readability and charm of an Horatio Alger novel. Indeed, the real hero of this story resembles in many respects—in diligence, industriousness, ambition, austere living, kindness, goodness, and belief in the American system of opportunity—one of Alger's fictional heroes.

CORTNEY, PHILIP. *The Economic Munich*. Philosophical Library. 1949. 262 pp.

Philip Cortney is a prominent businessman (president of Coty, Inc., and of Coty International) who has been a life-long student of economics. This book falls into three main parts. The first is an analysis and a rejection of the International Trade Organization Charter (signed by the United States at Havana) on the ground that its ratification would restrict international trade and undermine the individual competitive system. The second part is an illuminating analysis of the causes of the 1929 depression. The final part is an incisive refutation of Keynesian fallacies. The author is not only an eloquent defender of economic liberty but reveals a rare skill in dissecting the specific policies and ideas that constitute the greatest threat to it.

COUNTS, GEORGE S., AND LODGE, MRS. N. P. *Country of the Blind: The Soviet System of Mind Control.* Houghton Mifflin. 1949. 378 pp.

A study of the way in which the Central Committee of the All-Union Communist Party controls Russian cultural and intellectual life by rigid surveillance and direction of literature, drama, music, science, and education. Its long quotations from the actual texts of Committee resolutions and directives make it heavy going at times, but supply the authentic source material.

COWLING, DONALD J., AND DAVIDSON, CARTER. *Colleges for Freedom.* Harper. 1947. 180 pp.

A study of the purposes, practices and needs, and an evaluation of the place of the private liberal-arts college in American life, and a program for its independent survival.

COX, HAROLD. *The Capital Levy: Its Real Purpose.* Westminster: National Unionist Association. 1923. 71 pp.

"The Capital Levy has never been definitely renounced by the Labor Party as an item of its program. If a favorable opportunity arises in the future it may yet again become a live political issue. Mr. Harold Cox's book is largely a criticism of what is perhaps the most formidable defense of the levy, namely, that by Dr. Hugh Dalton. There is also a very useful chapter summarizing the experiences of six foreign countries. The author's conclusion is that 'All six countries tell the same story. In each case the levy was tried as a means of escaping from a financial debt which threatened the nation with bankruptcy. In no case have the results achieved justified the departure from sound methods of finance.' "—PI.

COX, HAROLD. *Economic Liberty.* Longmans, Green. 1920. 263 pp.

"A series of lucid essays by a thoroughgoing Individualist. The keynote is found in the preface. The essays, it is claimed, are all inspired by one purpose—the desire to defend economic liberty against the attacks made upon it by men and women who think they can secure progress by various schemes for curtailing freedom. 'Liberty,' it is admitted, 'can be abused, but it is the business of the community to prevent this abuse, not to destroy the liberty.' And 'It does not follow that the best form of restraint is the employment of the power of the State.' "—PI.

CREEL, GEORGE. *Russia's Race for Asia.* Bobbs-Merrill. 1949. 264 pp.

A warning—which proved to be completely in vain—that if the United States, by sins of omission or commission, allowed the Chinese communists to gain a victory over the National government of Chiang Kai-shek, it would put Russia in a position of mastery over half the world's population.

CROCE, BENEDETTO. *Historical Materialism and the Economics of Karl Marx*. Macmillan. 1914. 188 pp.

A collection of essays on the philosophical aspects of Marxism. Marx borrowed a great deal from Hegel, and yet reacted from him. The distinguished Italian philosopher here tries to separate the true from the false in Marx's particular form of Hegelianism and anti-Hegelianism.

CROCE, BENEDETTO. *Politics and Morals*. Philosophical Library. 1945. 204 pp.

A collection of essays by a distinguished Italian philosopher. Included are: *Liberalism as a Concept of Life, Free Enterprise and Liberalism,* and *The Bourgeoisie: An Ill-defined Historical Concept.* The last, a critique of a German book *The Bourgeois Mind in France,* is particularly instructive.

CROSSMAN, RICHARD (ed.). *The God that Failed*. Harper. 1949. 273 pp.

This is a collection of essays by former communists or communist sympathizers explaining the history of their disillusionment. The contributors include former "initiates"—Arthur Koestler, Ignazio Silone, Richard Wright—and former "worshippers from afar"—André Gide (presented by E. Starkie), Louis Fischer, and Stephen Spender. Some of the contributions are more interesting psychologically than for any light they throw on economic or political philosophy. Several of the disillusioned communists have remained socialists.

CROWTHER, SAMUEL. *Time to Inquire*. John Day. 1942. 353 pp.

This seeks to answer the question: "How can we restore the freedom, opportunity, and dignity of the average man?"

CUNNINGHAM, W. *The Growth of English Industry and Commerce.* Vol. 1: *Early and Middle Ages.* Fifth edition. 1922. Vol. 2: *Modern Times.* Sixth edition. 1922: Part 1, *Mercantile System;* Part 2, *Laissez-faire. The Industrial Revolution.* 1922. (A reprint of sections from the *Mercantile System* and *Laissez-faire.*) Cambridge University Press. 3 vols. 1,679 pp.

"Standard works on economic history. Archdeacon Cunningham was one of the founders of economic history as a regular branch of study in the Universities. The most important of his other works are: *Progress of Capitalism in England* (second impression, 1925); and

Western Civilization in Its Economic Aspects. (1924. Fourth impression. 2 vols.)"—PI.

CURTISS, WILLIAM MARSHALL. *The Tariff Idea.* Irvington, N. Y.: Foundation for Economic Education. 1953. 80 pp.

Dr. Curtiss carefully analyzes the principal arguments for protective tariffs and disposes of them. He also points out that the protective tariff philosophy is the source of a host of other political and economic errors.

DALLIN, DAVID J. *The Real Soviet Russia.* Yale University Press. 1944. 1947. 325 pp.

An acknowledged authority, who was himself a member of the Moscow soviet from 1918 to 1921, analyzes the communist tyranny. The first edition appeared in 1944, when Russia was still America's "ally" in the war against Germany. Dallin tries to show the workings of the huge apparatus of government, of the secret police, of the Army, and of the party within the party of peasants and workers. He emphasizes the contempt of the Russian leaders for human life and suffering.

DALLIN, DAVID J. *Soviet Espionage.* Yale University Press. 1955. 558 pp.

"Undoubtedly the major work on Soviet spy activities."—Igor Gouzenko, in *The New York Times.*

DALLIN, DAVID J., AND NICOLAEVSKY, BORIS I. *Forced Labor in Soviet Russia.* Yale University Press. 1947. 331 pp.

"A conscientiously documented and appalling report on slave labor in the corrective camps that the Soviet secret police runs for the government."—*New Yorker.*

DARK SIDE OF THE MOON. Anonymous. With a preface by T. S. Eliot. Scribner's. 1947. 299 pp.

An account, written anonymously, of what Soviet Russia did to the Polish people when, as a result of the 1939 pact with Germany, the NKVD entered Poland, arrested thousands, and deported them to labor camps in Siberia. "One of the most affecting and important books published in many years. . . . Revelation of how the Soviet pattern of life is imposed upon a conquered people."—Harry Schwartz, in the *Political Science Quarterly.*

DAVENPORT, H. J. *The Economics of Enterprise.* Macmillan. 1913. 544 pp.

"One may glean from this book only a moderate reflection of one of the greatest classroom teachers Cornell University ever had—one of those rare persons, able to use the Socratic method masterfully. Before concentrating on Economics, H. J. Davenport had first become accomplished in English, mathematics, law and logic—a rich background from which he taught.

"A jealous guardian of economic discipline founded in logic, his work strongly upheld the precepts of individualism. To him any such concept as the 'social organism' was anathema. And from that base he went on to develop the concept of the processes of the market at their best, in terms of human freedom. He defined the science of economics as 'little more than a study of price and of its causes and its corollaries.' Price was, to him, central to all economics. And that meant price freedom for *individuals*. Without freedom of pricing, therefore, economics was not operative. He therefore disclaimed all theoretical sympathies with the Socialists, whom he considered to be, in fact, the ultraconservatives."—F. A. Harper.

DE JAEGHER, RAYMOND J., AND KUHN, IRENE C. *The Enemy Within.* Doubleday. 1952. 314 pp.

An eyewitness account, by a Catholic priest, of the communist conquest of China, covering the period of their methodic climb to power in North China in the long years of war against Japan. "It makes a grisly story and will come as a surprise to those who have the notion that Reds of the Chinese species are less cruel than their cousins to the west; if anything, according to Father de Jaegher, they are worse. The book winds up with a discussion of the ill-fated Marshall mission to China, a chapter that is certainly as depressing as any in the book." —*New Yorker.*

DEWAR, HUGO. *Assassins at Large.* Beacon. 1952. 203 pp.

"This book sounds, in parts, like a collection of detective and mystery stories. Actually it is a well-documented, though far from complete, report on political murder and kidnapping cases perpetrated by Soviet secret agents all over the world that have become known during the last fifteen years."—Vladimir Petrov, in *Annals of the American Academy of Political and Social Science.*

DICEY, A. V. *The Law of the Constitution.* Oxford. 1885.

"A classic study of English constitutional law. The eighth (1915) edition (Macmillan), with its comprehensive and luminous introduction, should be utilized. The chapter on 'Parliamentary Sovereignty and Federalism' is especially important for American readers."—Felix Morley. "We are all servants of the laws," wrote Cicero, "in order that we may be free." Dicey called attention to the modern threat to freedom in the incursions that were being made into The Rule of Law.

DICEY, A. V. *Law and Public Opinion in England.* 1914. Macmillan. 1948. 506 pp.

"A work of fundamental importance. It traces the transition from the old Toryism or 'legislative quiescence' to Benthamism or Individualism, which was characteristic of the middle of the Nineteenth Century, and the subsequent gradual reaction to Collectivism, from about 1870 onwards."—PI. It also discusses such questions as judicial legislation and the right of association.

DODD, BELLA V. *School of Darkness.* P. J. Kenedy & Sons. 1955. 262 pp.

The repentant ex-communist teacher, Bella V. Dodd, calls communism a "school of darkness." "This volume of experiences and confession has more value than most books written by former Communists, because it gives the clearest picture yet of how communism was able to recruit intelligent, educated persons during the twenties and thirties."—Irene Corbally Kuhn, in *The Freeman.*

DOS PASSOS, JOHN. *The Grand Design.* Houghton Mifflin. 1949. 440 pp.

The final volume of a trilogy, the first two volumes of which were *Adventures of a Young Man* (1939) and *Number One* (1943). This novel tells the story of the New Deal years in American life. Some of the characters are evidently based on well-known figures. "*The Grand Design* is . . . respectful of the inner core of New-Deal idealism, contemptuous of the politics, confusion, jealousy, corruption, and inefficiency which accompanied it."—Orville Prescott in the *Yale Review.*

EAST, EDWARD M. *Mankind at the Crossroads.* Scribner's. 1923. 360 pp.

An authoritative study of the population problem.

EASTMAN, MAX. *Reflections on the Failure of Socialism.* Devin-Adair. 1955. 128 pp.

A lucid and brilliant analysis of the fallacies of Marxian and Fabian socialism. Mr. Eastman argues that socialism has failed over the last century in every nation and in every form in which it has been tried. He explains why political liberty depends upon a democratic competitive market and the price system. His arguments are all the more persuasive because of his personal history. He began as an extreme left-wing Socialist. As editor of the *Masses* and later of the *Liberator,* he "fought for the Bolsheviks on the battlefield of American opinion with all the influence my voice and magazine possessed." This book explains the reasons for his gradual disillusionment. The most powerful chapter is "The Religion of Immoralism," a devastating exposure of the peculiarly mystical but systematic rejection of morality which "is the one wholly original contribution of Karl Marx to man's heritage of ideas."

EASTMAN, MAX. *Marxism: Is It Science?* Norton. 1940. 394 pp.

Mr. Eastman, once a Marxist, here argues that scientific socialism, so-called, is not science but religion. "Max Eastman's book is, as readers of his earlier philosophical writings would expect, a work of art."—A. N. Holcombe, in *Books.*

EBON, MARTIN. *World Communism Today.* Whittlesey. 1948. 536 pp.

A useful reference work which attempts to give a survey of communism in every country in which it has been an important political factor.

ECONOMIC PRINCIPLES COMMISSION OF THE NATIONAL ASSOCIATION OF MANUFACTURERS. *The American Individual Enterprise System.* McGraw-Hill. 1946. 2 vols. 1119 pp.

These two volumes were prepared by a committee of fifteen authors, about evenly divided between professional economists and business executives. They were asked to submit to the National Association of Manufacturers "a thorough analysis of the philosophy, operations and achievements of the American economic system." There are chapters on the individual enterprise system, employment relations, agriculture, savings and capital formation, money and credit, profit and loss, the role of prices and price determination, competition and monopoly, government regulation, public finance, business fluctuations, etc. Among the authors were W. W. Cumberland, Willford I. King, Harley L. Lutz, Ludwig von Mises, Murray Shields, Bradford B. Smith, Rufus S. Tucker and Ray B. Westerfield.

EDMUNDS, STERLING. *The Struggle for Freedom.* Milwaukee: Bruce Publishing Co. 1946. 309 pp.

The history of Anglo-American liberty from the charter of Henry I to the present day. "The author was for many years a lecturer on constitutional law at St. Louis University. Professor Edmunds is convinced that the American people have been losing control over their lives and liberties. The Federal Government, in his opinion, with its increasing use of boards and administrative law, constitutes a threat to freedom. . . . Administrative boards rather than courts of law now direct the lives of the American people. . . . The background material which he presents in the field of constitutional law is perhaps unsurpassed by that found in any other book."—*The Commonweal.*

EINAUDI, LUIGI. *Greatness and Decline of Planned Economy in the Hellenistic World.* Bern, Switzerland: A. Franke. 1950. 48 pp.

Luigi Einaudi, the former President of Italy, is a distinguished liberal economist. Out of a dozen books written by him, this is the only one, to my knowledge, that has been made available in English,

EKIRCH, ARTHUR E., JR. *The Decline of American Liberalism.* Longmans, Green. 1955. 401 pp.

The author, Professor of History at the American University in Washington, argues that the main trend since the American Revolution has been to augment concentration of economic and state power and thus whittle away individual freedom.

ELLIOTT, W. Y., AND McDONALD, NEIL A. *The Western Political Heritage.* Prentice-Hall. 1949. 1027 pp.

"An excellent work of reference."—*Human Events.* "This book ought to find its way into the library of anyone who has any curiosity about the origins and development of the struggle between tyranny and freedom."—*San Francisco Chronicle.*

EMERSON, RALPH WALDO. Essays on *Wealth* and *Politics.* Many editions.

Emerson was not only a strong individualist in the broadest sense of the word, but a strong advocate of the free enterprise system (although it was not known under that name in his time) and a strong advocate of limited government. These two essays are outstanding illustrations, as the following excerpt from *Politics* will show:

"This is the history of governments—one man does something which is to bind another. A man who cannot be acquainted with me, taxes me; looking from afar at me ordains that a part of my labor shall go to this or that whimsical end—not as I, but as he happens to fancy. Behold the consequence. Of all debts men are least willing to pay the taxes. What a satire is this on government! Everywhere we think they get their money's worth, except for these. Hence the less government we have the better—the fewer laws, and the less confided power."

ERHARD, LUDWIG. *Germany's Comeback in the World Market.* Macmillan. 1955. 276 pp.

An exposition by the German Economics Minister of Germany's postwar economic policies. Dr. Erhard describes how the stabilization of the currency and the removal of price controls beginning in June of 1948 brought the "miracle" of German recovery. "It was the initiation of the market economy that awakened entrepreneurial impulses. The worker became ready to work, the trader to sell, and the economy in general to produce. In this way alone the conditions making possible a genuine foreign trade were provided."

ERNST, MORRIS L., AND LOTH, D. G. *Report on the American Communist.* Holt. 1952. 240 pp.

"The stated purpose of this book is to provide a better understanding of Communism in America and to prevent the growth of party membership. The authors interviewed nearly three hundred former Communists, asking why they joined and why they left the party."— *Library Journal.*

EUCKEN, RUDOLPH. *Socialism: An Analysis.* Scribner's. 1922. 188 pp.

"A philosophical analysis of Socialism by an eminent German philosopher. This book is in two parts. The first consists of an extraordinarily fair statement and explanation of Socialist ideals, and the second part of an examination and rejection of those ideals. The whole spirit as well as the methods of Socialism are here opposed." —PI.

EUCKEN, WALTER. *This Unsuccessful Age.* London: Hodge. 1951. 96 pp.

The author, a German thinker of stature, integrity and courage, summarizes the experiences of the first fifty years of the age of economic experiments. He points out the lessons that can be learned, in particular, from the lengthy experiments in planning, government direction, and price-fixing in Germany. He concludes that we can now know at least how *not* to attempt a solution of the problem of economic power, how *not* to try to achieve social security, and how *not* to "plan." He particularly stresses that a policy of full employment leads directly, through inflation, to a centrally planned and therefore totalitarian society. There is an introduction by John Jewkes of the University of Oxford.

EUCKEN, WALTER. *The Foundations of Economics.* London: Hodge. 1950. 358 pp.

The late Walter Eucken was, among German economists, the foremost opponent of the Historical School. He contributed greatly to the revival in Germany of interest in economic theory. The first German edition of this book appeared in 1940; the present English translation is based on the sixth German edition. The central theme is the dual aspect of economic problems, which has led to a dual approach to them—one historical, the other theoretical. The author attempts to clarify the respective roles of these two methods. The excesses of Nazism and of the early stringent controls in Germany after World War II led Eucken to emphasize more and more the advantages and urgency of a free market system.

FAIRCHILD, F. R., AND SHELLY, T. J. *Understanding Our Free Economy.* Van Nostrand. 1952. 589 pp.

Perhaps the best introduction to economics ever written for high school students, and certainly the best in existence now. Even many adults will find it an ideal elementary introduction to the subject. It is outspoken and unapologetic in its defense of free markets and free private enterprise as against government planning and socialism.

FAIRCHILD, FRED R., BUCK, W. S., AND SLESINGER, R. E. *Principles of Economics.* Macmillan. 1954. 780 pp.

A standard introductory college textbook. The 1954 edition has been "so thoroughly rewritten and revised that, in the opinion of the authors, it is virtually a new book. . . . It seeks understanding of the working of the modern free economy, while acquainting the student also with other economic systems and certain recent trends toward collectivism." Especially noteworthy are two chapters on "Government in Industry." These deal with such matters as price and wage controls, the Tennessee Valley Authority, and agricultural subsidies.

FARADAY, W. B. *Democracy and Capital.* London: Murray. 1921. 314 pp.

"A popular and exhaustive exposure of Socialism. It is argued that Socialist movements are definitely retrogressive, as the trend of social progress has been, in a juristic sense, away from status and towards freedom of contract, and that 'Our liberty has grown with the idea of the inviolability of property and the increased individuality of the man as opposed to the State.' "—PI.

FARRAND, MAX (ed.). *The Records of the Federal Convention.* Yale University Press. 1937. 4 vols.

"This is the definitive record of the Constitutional Convention, supplementing Madison's reports and correcting them wherever later evidence warrants; indispensable for thorough study of American governmental origins."—Felix Morley.

FAWCETT, HENRY. *Manual of Political Economy.* Macmillan. 1883. 631 pp.

"A textbook on the lines of Mill, but more severely individualistic."
—PI.

FEDERALIST, THE. (See HAMILTON.)

FEDERICI, FEDERICO. *Der Deutsche Liberalismus.* Zurich: Artemis-Verlag. 1946.

A study of German liberalism.

FERGUSON, ADAM. *An Essay on the History of Civil Society.* 1767.

"The spontaneous collaboration of free men often creates things which are greater than their individual minds can ever fully comprehend. This is the great theme of Josiah Tucker and Adam Smith, of Adam Ferguson and Edmund Burke, the great discovery of classical political economy which has become the basis of our understanding not only of economic life but of most truly social phenomena."— F. A. Hayek.

FERGUSON, JOHN M. *Landmarks of Economic Thought.* Longmans, Green. 1938. 295 pp.

A useful, readable and agreeable short history of economic thought, stressing the contributions of the leading thinkers. Reviewing it in *The New York Times* of Oct. 30, 1938, I wrote: "Professor Ferguson apparently intended his volume to serve both for the general reader and as a textbook. . . . It has the virtues of . . . straightforwardness, balance, impartiality."

FERRERO, GUGLIELMO. *The Principles of Power.* Putnam. 1942. 333 pp.

This is the last book of a trilogy by the eminent Italian historian of Rome. It contrasts "illegitimate" government, or government by fear (as represented by Bonapartism and Fascism), with "legitimate" government, or government in good faith (as represented by democracy and hereditary monarchy). Ferrero's thesis is that the "illegitimate" government must seek to keep itself in power by military adventures, neurotic activity, and coercion. Wilhelm Röpke calls this book "a true legacy to us."

FETTER, FRANK A. *Economics.* Vol. I: *Economic Principles.* 523 pp. Vol. II: *Modern Economic Problems.* 498 pp. Century. 1915. Revised ed., 1922.

Of Frank Fetter, Joseph Schumpeter writes: "Professor Frank A. Fetter rose to a leading position in the first decade of this century. He was primarily, though not exclusively, a theorist. . . . At that time all serious theoretical endeavor had to start from the bases laid by Jevons, Menger, and Walras . . . [but] Fetter erected a building that was his own, both as a whole and in many points of detail, such as the theory of 'psychic income.' The vivifying influence upon the American profession's interest in theory of his critical exploits cannot be evaluated too highly." Vol. II makes practical application of the theories treated in Vol. I to such matters as money, banking, international trade, labor organizations, agricultural economics, trusts, taxation, insurance, immigration, and similar topics.

FISHER, ALLAN G. B. *Economic Progress and Social Security.* Macmillan. 1945. 362 pp.

"Allan G. B. Fisher, well known New Zealand economist and professor at the Royal Institute of International Affairs in London, has set himself the difficult task of exploring the double impact of economic change and of the quest for security upon economic policy, national as well as international. . . . He shows that stability can be achieved amidst change and security without loss of freedom, but the stability as well as the security he offers are relative rather than absolute. He discards the security of slavery as well as the stability of immobility."—*Weekly Book Review*. "A polished and mature effort in the art of political economy."—John Jewkes, in the *Manchester Guardian*.

FISHER, ALLAN G. B. *The Clash of Progress and Security*. Macmillan. 1936. 234 pp.

"Professor Fisher's thesis is briefly this: Material progress means change, involving inconvenience and suffering for certain classes even though it may benefit others. Resistance is generated among those who suffer from change, so that the adjustments necessary, if progress is to develop smoothly, are not made rapidly enough. In short, there is a clash between progress and security."—*Pacific Affairs*. "An admirable and stimulating book, full of clear and concrete reasoning from start to finish."—London *Economist*.

FITE, WARNER. *Individualism*. Longmans, Green. 1924. 301 pp.

Four lectures which discuss the conception of the individual, the individual as a conscious agent, individuality and social unity, and individual rights and the social problem.

FLEMING, HAROLD. *Ten Thousand Commandments*. Prentice-Hall. 1951. (Paper-covered edition: Irvington, N. Y.: Foundation for Economic Education. 1952.) 206 pp.

The story of the antitrust laws, their history, their administration, their complexities and contradictions, and the amazing court decisions handed down about them. Mr. Fleming does not directly question either past or present need for antitrust legislation, but he shows by the record that within the framework of these laws there has operated an administrative instrument of arbitrary power and hostility threatening the very life of competitive enterprise in America. "The essential purpose of all the variegated attacks has been to hamper the more successful business for the benefit of the less successful business. . . . What is left is merely a rule that the bigger companies almost invariably are wrong on some count or other and the little companies almost invariably right. The result is that nobody knows what is legal and what isn't. The law is what the government lawyers say it is. And they are essentially interested not in *what* is done, but in *who does it*."

FLINT, ROBERT. *Socialism*. Lippincott. 1895. 1908. 512 pp.

Examining socialism in 1895, Professor Flint concluded that it "might prove the reverse of a blessing to working men although those who are pressing it on them may mean them well." Reviewing the first edition, the London *Athenaeum* declared: "It is impossible for anyone to have tried harder to be fair than Professor Flint." F. J. C. Hearnshaw declared it to be: "On the whole the ablest and most destructive criticism of socialism ever written. The two editions (first, 1895; second, 1908) differ considerably; both should be read and re-read."

FLYNN, JOHN T. *The Road Ahead: America's Creeping Revolution*. Devin-Adair. 1949. 160 pp.

John T. Flynn is one of America's most powerful pamphleteers. The central thesis of this book is that economic planning, social insurance, deficit financing, and the nationalization of credit lead step by step toward mass enslavement and the totalitarian state. This tendency, he believes, has been shown empirically by the British experience; it follows that the preservation of American freedoms and institutions is inseparable from the preservation of a free capitalism. The Americans for Democratic Action, he holds, are the present equivalent of the British Fabians. They sincerely consider themselves to be anti-communist; but their efforts to achieve the socialized state through a process of gradualism must lead, if successful, to dictatorship and the police state.

FLYNN, JOHN T. *As We Go Marching*. Doubleday. 1944. 272 pp.

"Mr. Flynn's thesis is that despite the many differences in the character, customs, laws, traditions, and resources of the people of Italy, Germany, and the United States, this country has been drifting on the same currents and experimenting with the same political and economic measures which resulted in the establishment of Fascism abroad. Two-thirds of his book is a scholarly, sober, valuable examination of the rise of Fascism in Italy and Germany, one-third is an attempt to support his thesis by trying to prove that it not only *can* happen here but already has happened."—*New Yorker*.

FLYNN, JOHN T. *The Epic of Freedom*. Philadelphia: Fireside Press. 1947. 127 pp.

The story of the growth of freedom told simply and briefly for young people of high-school age.

FLYNN, JOHN T. *The Decline of the American Republic*. Devin-Adair. 1955. 224 pp.

The American Republic, as the Founding Fathers conceived it, has been declining with special rapidity, according to the author, since

1930. A large part of this decline he attributes to the sapping of the Constitution by a modern semantics that has distorted the plain meaning of crucial clauses—so that the federal power to regulate commerce between the states may be interpreted to mean the federal power to regulate the pay and hours of an elevator operator who never leaves New York City. "A very necessary book."—John Chamberlain, in *The Freeman*.

FOERSTER, F. W. *Europe and the German Question*. Sheed. 1940. 474 pp.

An analysis of German history by a Prussian exiled from his native land long before World War I because of his unorthodox views. In his introductory chapter the author declares: "This book is above all intended to acquaint Germans living outside the Third Reich with Germany's authentic tradition and with its European mission. But it also looks forward to a not too remote day when the Germans of the Third Reich . . . may learn from it the chain of sin and doom in German history since Bismarck."

FOUNDATION FOR ECONOMIC EDUCATION. *Essays on Liberty*. Irvington, N. Y. Vol. I: 1952. 307 pp. Vol. II: 1954. 442 pp.

Essays on various aspects of liberty. The subjects include government, taxes, inflation, money, monopoly, price controls, subsidies, security, competition, etc. Among the authors are: Maxwell Anderson, Sir Ernest Benn, Arthur Bestor, Spruille Braden, Asa V. Call, Frank Chodorov, Russell J. Clinchy, W. M. Curtiss, Richard L. Evans, Ben Fairless, F. A. Harper, Henry Hazlitt, Bertrand de Jouvenel, Ed Lipscomb, Clarence Manion, Ludwig von Mises, Ben Moreell, W. C. Mullendore, Mario Pei, Sam Pettengill, Leonard E. Read, Dean Russell, Thomas J. Shelly, William Graham Sumner.

FOWLER, THOMAS. *Locke*. Macmillan. 1880. 205 pp.

"A concise biographical sketch. The author calls Locke, 'Perhaps the greatest, but certainly the most characteristic of English philosophers.' "—PI.

FRIEDMAN, WOLFGANG. *Law and Social Change*. London: Stevens & Sons. 1951. 322 pp.

A legal study from a libertarian point of view.

GANDIL, CHR (ed.). *Moderne Liberalisme*. Copenhagen: Rosenkilde og Bagger. 1948. 132 pp.

In this Danish book, Mr. Gandil has attempted to reply to the question: "What is liberalism?" (in the sense of individual liberty, as the word is still understood on the European continent). "He himself has written an introduction. Thereupon follows a chapter written by

Dr. Thorkil Kristensen, a former Danish Secretary of the Treasury. Then follows in reprint form two lectures which were broadcast by Professor Wilhelm Keilhau over the Norwegian radio immediately following the outbreak of the war. In the final chapters a number of young Danish political economists have taken extracts from neo-liberalist literature. . . . Mr. Gandil's introduction rates as one of the best chapters of the book."—Trygve J. B. Hoff, in *Farmand* (Oslo).

GARRETT, GARET. *The People's Pottage.* Caldwell, Idaho: Caxton Printers. 1953. 174 pp.

Garet Garrett, because of the accuracy of his knowledge, the quality of his thinking, and the rare distinction of his style, was one of the outstanding pamphleteers of our time. *The People's Pottage* is made up of three pamphlets bearing on the same theme. *The Revolution Was,* which appeared in 1944, propounded the thesis that under the New Deal the social revolution, depriving the individual of essential liberties and shifting power to the State, had already taken place. *Ex America,* which appeared in 1951, continued this thesis, and explained in particular how inflation is used to continue a statist regime in power, and how it affects the attitude of the people. *Rise of Empire,* which appeared in the following year, contends that the moral and constitutional restraints on political power which distinguish a republic from an empire have been all but obliterated. Despite this pessimistic theme, the author concludes: "The people know that they can have their Republic back if they want it enough to fight for it and to pay the price. The only point is that no leader has yet appeared with the courage to make them choose."

GARRETT, GARET. *The Wild Wheel.* Pantheon Books. 1952. 220 pp.

A fascinating but episodic account of the career of Henry Ford. The thesis of the book is that what Ford accomplished in the early decades of the twentieth century under a regime of *laissez faire* could not be duplicated today because of government interventionism.

"If in this country, for both good and evil, free private enterprise had its logical manifestations in a prodigious manner, so Henry Ford was its extreme and last pure event. . . . It is easier to imagine other Fords than it is to believe that another would be able to do in this regulated world what Henry Ford did in his free world. He would not be permitted to plow back his profits in that reckless manner as capital. . . . You may like it better this way. . . . [But] if *laissez-faire* had not begotten the richest world that ever existed there would have been much less for the welfare state to distribute."

GARRETT, GARET. *The American Story.* Regnery. 1955. 401 pp.

This was Garet Garrett's last book. It is a brilliant historical essay on America which lays special emphasis on the country's achievements in invention and productivity, but views the course of the last twenty-five years pessimistically, and despairs of the future of personal liberty and growth in the United States if recent political tendencies continue.

GÉBLER, ERNEST. *The Plymouth Adventure.* Doubleday. 1950. 377 pp.

A fictional account of the voyage of the Mayflower from England to Cape Cod and of the first winter spent by the Pilgrims in New England. The story is reconstructed from letters, journals and histories. This account of the first Americans who risked their lives for freedom of opinion will inspire all those who still believe in that ideal.

GEORGE, HENRY. *Protection or Free Trade.* 1886. Robert Schalkenbach Foundation. 1946. 335 pp.

The great majority of economists today regard the central tenet of Henry George—a single tax on land—as untenable. Yet what he *thought* he was doing is revealed in a sentence in his preface to the fourth edition of his famous *Progress and Poverty* (1879). It was "to unite the truth perceived by the school of Smith and Ricardo to the truth perceived by the schools of Proudhon and Lasalle; to show that *laissez-faire* (in its full meaning) opens the way to a realization of the noble dreams of socialism." His book *Protection or Free Trade,* which appeared seven years later, presents the case for free trade with great eloquence and power: "He who follows the principle of free trade to its logical conclusion can strike at the very root of protection; can answer every question and meet every objection. . . . He will see in free trade not a mere fiscal reform, but a movement which has for its aim and end nothing less than the abolition of poverty, and of the vice and crime and degradation that flow from it, by the restoration to the disinherited of their natural rights and the establishment of society upon the basis of justice. He will catch the inspiration of a cause great enough to live for and to die for, and be moved by an enthusiasm that he can evoke in others."

It is only fair to add that the present-day followers of Henry George, still numerous, are (apart from the implications of their single-tax-on-land theory) among the most zealous champions of a free capitalism.

GIDE, CHARLES, AND RIST, CHARLES. *A History of Economic Doctrines from the Time of the Physiocrats to the Present Day.* Heath. 1948. 800 pp.

A standard history by two French economists which first appeared in English in 1915 and has been brought down to date by successive editions and enlargements. Written with great lucidity in the original French, it has also been fortunate in its English translators. A full and very valuable history. Its excellent critical comments on various theories are written from a liberal point of view.

GIFFEN, SIR ROBERT. *Economic Inquiries and Studies*. London: George Bell. 1904. 461 pp.

"A large number of economic essays by a well-known authority. Some of them, such as *Protection for Manufacturers in New Countries* and *The Dream of a British Zollverein,* bear closely upon our subject. His point of view is strongly Individualistic."—PI.

GITLOW, BENJAMIN. *I Confess*. Dutton. 1940. 611 pp.

A disillusioned ex-leader of the Communist party in the United States gives a detailed account of its works, its personalities and its relations with Moscow. There is an introduction by Max Eastman. "A personal and political history of the utmost relevance for an understanding of the American Communist party. . . . A fascinating story for any one, and should be a positive boon for the annual crop of innocents who are drawn into Communist peripheral organizations under false pretenses."—Sidney Hook.

GITLOW, BENJAMIN. *The Whole of Their Lives*. Scribner's. 1948. 387 pp.

"A former prominent Communist (head of the American Communist Party in 1929), the author describes world Communism with especial emphasis on American Communism. Showing how it first started in this country among various rival factions, he then demonstrates its penetration of earlier liberal and Socialist groups and its emergence as a well-disciplined party. With considerable attention to personalities, he describes the American Communists, reveals their connection with Moscow, and flatly states that American Communism is directly controlled by Russia. Furthermore, he contends that it respects no American principles or traditions in its zeal to make our country a Soviet vassal."—*Library Journal.*

GLIKSMAN, JERZY. *Tell the West*. Gresham Press. 1948. 358 pp.

"Another eyewitness report on slave labor in the Soviet Union, this time by a Polish lawyer and Socialist who was arrested, for reasons he never fully understood, by the N.K.V.D. shortly after the invasion of Poland and shipped off to a concentration camp to be 'remolded' into a useful citizen by 'productive work and suitable educational approach.' The remolding, Mr. Gliksman says, consisted of nothing more than systematic starvation, ill treatment, and a losing battle to fill hopelessly high daily work quotas; it killed many of his fellows and would have killed him if amnesty had not been granted Poles willing to fight the Germans."—*New Yorker.*

GODWIN, WILLIAM. *An Enquiry Concerning Political Justice.* 1793. Numerous editions. (Knopf. 1926.) 2 vols. 554 pp.

"Godwin's book, coming at a time of revolution, created much revolutionary fervor. It was considered so dangerous that the authorities thought of prosecuting the author, but Pitt pointed out that 'a three-guinea book could never do much harm among those who had not three shillings to spare.' Godwin says: 'Since government even in its best state is an evil, the object principally to be aimed at is that we should have as little of it as the general peace of human society will permit.' Like many 'anarchists,' he believes in human perfectibility; the disappearance of government would be no evil, he thought, because the natural goodness of man, enhanced by progress, would serve to keep him in the right way. This theory of human perfectibility led him to demand the abolition of private property and the dissolution of all governments. To us, Godwin is now chiefly interesting for having inspired Shelley with his poetic dreams of innocent man, who has never been perverted and made miserable by the falsehood and tyranny of priests and kings, and who, if given freedom, will be once more happy and innocent."—PI.

GONZALEZ, VALENTIN R. *El Campesino.* Putnam. 218 pp.

" 'El Campesino' was a famous Communist Spanish general in Spain's Civil war. After the war he fled to Russia where he was at first lauded as a hero, later fell into disfavor with the authorities, and spent more than ten years in labor camps in Siberia before he made his escape."—*Book Review Digest.* "Campesino symbolized the highest reach of communism's romantic appeal. He suffered the worst horrors of its awful reality. The contrasts make his book an ugly and convincing testament."—Michael Straight, in the *New Republic.*

GORDON, MANYA. *Workers Before and After Lenin.* Dutton. 1941. 524 pp.

A detailed study of conditions among the laboring classes in Russia from the 1890's to the present, with statistics wherever they can be obtained. The author, born in Russia and educated in the United States, points out the fact that many Russian statistics are unreliable, and cites discrepancies. Among the subjects covered are insurance, wages, housing, dress, factory conditions, social security, education and the condition of the peasants. "Manya Gordon has performed a genuine service to the cause of historical truth by puncturing almost beyond the possibility of revival the legend that, whatever may be its defects, the Soviet regime represents a vast forward step, especially for the masses."—W. H. Chamberlin, in *The New York Times.*

GOUGH, G. W. *The Economic Consequences of Socialism*. London: Allan. 1926. 178 pp.

"A keen criticism of current Socialist proposals and particularly of the writings of Mr. and Mrs. Sidney Webb and Mr. Tawney. Mr. Gough merits the compliment of being compared with Mr. Hartley Withers in the power of dealing with economic complexities in a light and readable style. It is one of the best criticisms of Socialist theories that has appeared in recent years."—PI.

GOUZENKO, IGOR. *The Iron Curtain*. Dutton. 1948. 279 pp.

Autobiography of the young Russian code clerk, attached to the Canadian Soviet Embassy, who revealed to Canadian authorities the existence of a plot to turn over atomic bomb secrets to Russian spies. "The entire narrative is notable for its simplicity, humility, and candor. 'We have been impressed,' said the Royal Commission appointed in Canada to investigate this matter, 'with the sincerity of the man, and with the manner in which he gave his evidence.' "—Asher Brynes, in *The Saturday Review of Literature*.

GRAHAM, F. D. *Social Goals and Economic Institutions*. Princeton University Press. 1942. 273 pp.

An attempt to describe the ethical, political, and economic policies and institutions that would best embody liberal values.

GRAY, ALEXANDER. *The Socialist Tradition: Moses to Lenin*. Longmans, Green. 1946. 523 pp.

A scholarly, witty and unsympathetic survey, by the professor of political economy at the University of Edinburgh, of socialist thinking. "Professor Gray has made a unique contribution, even to the already voluminous literature about socialism and socialists. The book does not, as the author himself hastens to make clear in the prologue, 'aim at being a history of socialist thought.' Still less is it a history of the socialist movement. Rather, it is a series of studies of the ideas of certain individuals who stand high in the socialist tradition. . . . Students of socialist thought will be interested by the fresh viewpoint and the unquestionable depth of scholarship which Professor Gray brings to his consideration of even the familiar landmarks. His erudition is almost incredible, and he writes with grace and charm enlivened by frequent splashes of wit."—Hilden Gibson, in the *American Political Science Review*.

GRIFFIN, CLARE E. *Enterprise in a Free Society*. Chicago: Richard D. Irwin. 1949. 573 pp.

"This book is a timely and useful addition to the literature of American capitalism. Within its 573 closely printed pages of text, containing more than 250,000 words, Professor Griffin has given a systematic and scholarly treatment of enterprise in American society—its functions, motivations, consequences and the environmental conditions that facilitate it."—N. H. Jacoby, in the *American Economic Review*.

GROS, J. M. *Le Mouvement Littéraire Socialiste*. Paris. 1904.

"This well-written book, almost exclusively confining itself to France, deals with the aid which poets and other authors have given to Socialism since 1830."—PI.

GURIAN, WALDEMAR. *Bolshevism*. University of Notre Dame Press. 1952. 189 pp.

An introduction to Soviet communism. "Some excellent source material—verified citations from the writings of Lenin and Stalin—supplements and completes this highly valuable and instructive work, which is at once scholarly and unpretentious."—W. H. Chamberlin.

GUYOT, YVES. *Economic Prejudices*. London: Sonnenschein. 1910. 166 pp.

"To a superficial reader this book might leave an impression of M. Yves Guyot as a rather extreme doctrinaire free trader, but on its appearance it received a great deal of praise from the British Conservative Press. . . . The most valuable part of the book is its analysis of current Socialist and Labor fallacies. It is written in the form of a dialogue."—PI.

GUYOT, YVES. *La Démocratie Individualiste*. Paris: Giard & Brière. 1907.

"As a champion of liberty M. Yves Guyot is a worthy disciple and successor of Bastiat, although he is a little less optimistic than his master. *La Démocratie Individualiste* contains an excellent short account of the evolution of Individualism, and a brief statement and explanation of the doctrine."—PI.

GUYOT, YVES. *Principles of Social Economy*. Scribner's. 1892. 305 pp.

"A live and original introduction to the study of the subject. It is particularly valuable for its chapters on 'State Intervention in Economics' and 'The Province of the State.' "—PI.

HABERLER, GOTTFRIED VON. *The Theory of International Trade*. London: Hodge. 1936. 408 pp.

"This is a systematic treatise written primarily for the specialist. . . . The author makes the most devastating attack on the whole paraphernalia of tariffs, quotas, and exchange restrictions that has come from the pen of any living writer."—*Manchester Guardian.* "The most important and comprehensive study of the subject since Taussig's *International Trade.*"—*New Statesman and Nation.*

HACKER, LOUIS M. *The Triumph of American Capitalism.* Simon & Schuster. 1940. (Columbia University Press. 1947.) 460 pp.

A study of the development of forces in American history to the end of the nineteenth century. "Mr. Hacker has written a remarkable book. It is not a systematic history of the economic development of the American people . . . [but] an interpretive study, much of it brilliant and all of it suggestive. . . . At various points . . . the author is tempted into generalizations which will make all but the hardened economic determinist blench . . . but these passages . . . do not greatly impair the essential merit of his volume."—Allan Nevins.

HAHN, L. ALBERT. *The Economics of Illusion.* New York: Squier Publishing Co. 1949. 273 pp.

In my introduction to this book I wrote: "Dr. Hahn enjoys an enormous advantage as an analyst of Keynesian fallacies. As he has reminded us himself: 'All that is wrong and exaggerated in Keynes I said much earlier and more clearly.' . . . There is no more important task for the economic theorist today than to disentangle the network of confusion and error that now goes under the name of the Keynesian Revolution. Until this work has been thoroughly done, clarity and real progress in economics will not be possible. There is no more sophisticated, penetrating and thorough guide in this task than Albert Hahn."

HAHN, L. ALBERT. *Wirtschaftswissenschaft des gesunden Menschenverstandes.* Frankfurt-am-Main: Verlag Fritz Knapp. 1954. 280 pp.

The author describes a "model" of the economic process based on neo-classical as opposed to Keynesian thinking. It is written as an introduction to economics for students as well as a "minimum economics" for educated businessmen. A French translation has appeared under the title *Notions Pratiques d'Économie Politique.* (Paris: Librairie de Médicis. 1954.) An American edition is in preparation.

HALÉVY, ÉLIE. *L'Ère des Tyrannies.* Paris: Gallimard. 1938. 249 pp.

A discussion of "the era of despotisms." English versions of two of the most important essays in this volume will be found in *Economica,* February, 1941, and in *International Affairs,* 1934.

HAMILTON, ALEXANDER; MADISON, JAMES; AND JAY, JOHN. *The Federalist.* 1787. Many editions. (Random House. 1941.) 618 pp.

A collection of eighty-five articles in defense of the American Constitution. All but eight appeared originally in the New York press, between October 1787 and May 1788.

"It remains a classic commentary, not merely on American constitutional law, but on the principles of government generally. Guizot said of it that 'in its application of elementary principles of government to practical administration' it was the greatest work he knew, and Chancellor Kent declared it—quite justly—to be 'equally admirable in the depth of its wisdom, the comprehensiveness of its views, the sagacity of its reflections, and the fearlessness, patriotism, candor, simplicity and elegance with which its truths are uttered and recommended.' "—*Encyclopaedia Britannica.*

More than half of the articles were written by Hamilton. Madison's contributions "advocated a system of government in which democracy should be reconciled with the security of private rights. He saw that the central problem of democracy is not the maintenance of equality but the preservation of liberty."—William Carpenter in the *Encyclopaedia of the Social Sciences.*

HANEY, LEWIS H. *History of Economic Thought.* Macmillan. 1911, etc. 1949. 957 pp.

A critical account of the origin and development of the economic theories of leading thinkers in the leading nations. "Professor Haney, in addressing himself to the truly colossal task of writing of the totality of economic thought, has provided for the student by far the most comprehensive text for the study of this subject now available in the English language. By and large, the subject matter is well chosen and well arranged."—J. M. Ferguson, on third edition, in *American Economic Review,* 1936.

HANEY, LEWIS H. *How You Really Earn Your Living.* Prentice-Hall. 1952. 282 pp.

This is intended to be "Every Man's Guide to American Economics." It is an admirable introductory volume written with great clearness and simplicity. In addition to chapters on such central problems as market value, money, production and distribution, there is a chapter on public vs. private enterprise, and two chapters on "Seven Ways to Lose Freedom or Save It."

HANEY, LEWIS H. *Economics in a Nutshell.* Macmillan. 1933. 213 pp.

Most of these short discussions appeared originally in the author's column in the *New York Evening Journal.* They contain a condensed statement of the principles of economics as taught to Professor Haney's classes in New York University.

HARPER, F. A. *Crisis of the Free Market*. New York: National Industrial Conference Board. 1945. 83 pp.

This study, while aimed particularly at the policy of control during reconversion from a war to a peace basis, provides a simple exposition of some of the fundamental facts and principles that form the framework of a voluntary society and a free economy.

HARPER, F. A. *Liberty: A Path to Its Recovery*. Irvington, N. Y.: Foundation for Economic Education. 1949. 159 pp.

An analysis of the nature of individual liberty, a measurement of how much remains, and a program to regain what has been lost. The author explains how liberty in every other area rests on its preservation in the economic sphere.

HARRIS, S. HUTCHINSON. *Auberon Herbert: Crusader for Liberty*. London: Williams & Norgate. 1943. 382 pp.

The biography of an individualist whose works are discussed in the present bibliography.

HASKELL, HENRY J. *The New Deal in Old Rome*. Knopf. 1939. 269 pp.

In his preface the author, editor of the *Kansas City Star,* says: "To prevent any misconception let me say that this book is neither a criticism nor a defense of the New Deal. It is an attempt to provide an objective survey of instances of government intervention in the ancient world. Many of these were so like experiments tried in the United States in recent years that they may fairly be classed as New Deal measures. I have tried to show what these experiments were, why they were tried, and how they worked. Making allowance for the differences between ancient and modern society, I have ventured to call attention to certain warning signals from the past."

HAYEK, FRIEDRICH A. *The Road to Serfdom*. University of Chicago Press. 1944. 250 pp.

Reviewing this book in *The New York Times* of Sept. 23, 1944, I wrote: "In *The Road to Serfdom* Friedrich A. Hayek has written one of the most important books of our generation. It restates for our time the issue between liberty and authority with the power and rigor of reasoning that John Stuart Mill stated the issue for his own generation in his great essay, 'On Liberty.' It throws a brilliant light along the direction in which the world has been heading, first slowly, but now at an accelerative rate, for the last half-century. It is an arresting call to all well-intentioned planners and socialists, to all those who are sincere democrats and liberals at heart, to stop, look, and listen."

"Although," Hayek writes, "we had been warned by some of the greatest political thinkers of the nineteenth century, by de Tocqueville and Lord Acton, that socialism means slavery, we have steadily moved in the direction of socialism. . . . We are rapidly abandoning not the views merely of Cobden and Bright, of Adam Smith and Hume, or even of Locke and Milton, but one of the salient characteristics of Western civilization as it has grown from the foundations laid by Christianity and the Greeks and Romans. Not merely nineteenth- and eighteenth-century liberalism, but the basic individualism inherited by us from Erasmus and Montaigne, from Cicero and Tacitus, Pericles and Thucydides, is progressively relinquished."

HAYEK, FRIEDRICH A. *Individualism and Economic Order.* University of Chicago Press. 1948. 271 pp.

A collection of a dozen essays, some on various aspects of the philosophy of individualism, and others on technical economic subjects. For the purposes of this bibliography by far the most important essay is the first: "Individualism: True and False," which every individualist who desires to avoid or combat confusion should study. Other excellent essays deal with The Use of Knowledge in Society, The Meaning of Competition, "Free" Enterprise and Competitive Order, and Socialist Calculation. All of these essays bring great learning and intelligence to bear upon economic and social issues of central importance to our era. Every open-minded reader of this book will find his own understanding of these questions enriched, clarified and deepened.

HAYEK, FRIEDRICH A. *The Counter-Revolution of Science.* Glencoe, Ill.: Free Press. 1952. 255 pp.

This book is divided into two parts. The first is an acute and abstract study of the essential differences in method required in the study of the physical sciences on the one hand and the social sciences on the other. An uncritical and slavish imitation in the social studies of the methods, concepts and language of physics or engineering is condemned by Professor Hayek as "scientism." He goes on to show how "scientism" produces as its logical corollaries collectivism, Marxism and other forms of economic planning through centralized coercion.

The second part of the book is historical. It gives an amusing as well as enlightening account of the common origin of "scientism," positivism and socialism in the environment of the great engineering school of Paris, the *École polytechnique.* It traces the intellectual histories of Henri de Saint-Simon, Auguste Comte, and others, and shows how their ideas gave birth to "the religion of the engineers," merged with German Hegelianism, led to Karl Marx (who borrowed heavily from the Saint-Simonians as well as from Hegel), and is still seen in the engine-room outlook and pseudo-science which today threaten to reverse the historical trend toward greater freedom.

HAYEK, F. A. *John Stuart Mill and Harriet Taylor.* University of Chicago Press. 1951. 320 pp.

In his *Autobiography,* John Stuart Mill gave a highly extravagant account of the moral and intellectual qualities of Mrs. Harriet Taylor, who finally became his wife, and of her influence on his writings. Until quite recently, little has been known of the facts behind this tribute. But much of the correspondence between Mill and Mrs. Taylor came into the hands of various libraries in 1922 and 1927, and Professor Hayek (in 1951) gathered and published this material in the present book. It indicates that Mrs. Taylor did exercise considerable influence over the less technical aspects of Mill's thought. Whether this influence was on net balance for good or ill, the individual reader can decide for himself. But the evidence is clear that it was Harriet Taylor who was largely responsible for Mill's retraction of most of his opposition to socialism as expressed in the first edition of his *Political Economy,* and for his far more sympathetic attitude in the third edition. It was Michael St. John Packe's ability to draw heavily on the material in the present book that enabled him to add so much to our knowledge of Mill in his admirable *Life of John Stuart Mill* (q.v.) published in 1954.

HAYEK, F. A. *The Political Ideal of the Rule of Law.* Cairo: National Bank of Egypt. 1955. 79 pp.

Professor Hayek, although internationally best known as an economist, was by original training a lawyer. This book reprints lectures he delivered at the invitation of the National Bank of Egypt. They begin with an historical survey of the evolution of freedom and the Rule of Law in Britain, France, Germany, and America. They emphasize such safeguards of individual liberty as the generality, equality, and certainty of the law. The final lecture discusses the decline of the Rule of Law, particularly in England and the United States.

HAYEK, F. A. (ed.). *Capitalism and the Historians.* University of Chicago Press. 1954. 194 pp.

A provocative set of essays, several of which are brilliant, which argue that capitalism, even in the days of the Manchester slums and the child worker, was an immediate positive social good. The authors hold—from actual case studies of the English worker, his work, and his times—that the prevalent belief in the immediate evil of the Industrial Revolution is a myth, perpetuated by a few historians and intellectuals. The contributors are F. A. Hayek, T. S. Ashton, Louis Hacker, W. H. Hutt, and Bertrand de Jouvenel.

HAYEK, FRIEDRICH A. (ed.). *Collectivist Economic Planning*. London: Routledge. 1935. 293 pp.

This is a collection of critical studies on the possibilities of socialism by N. G. Pierson, Ludwig von Mises, George Halm, and Enrico Barone. A central subject is the possibility of economic calculation under socialism. Professor Hayek contributes an admirable introduction on the "Nature and History of the Problem" and a final chapter on the "Present State of the Debate."

HAZLITT, HENRY. *Economics in One Lesson*. Harper. 1946. (Paperbound edition: Irvington, N. Y.: Foundation for Economic Education. 1952.) 222 pp.

"Mr. Hazlitt writes strictly in terms of economics, urging upon his readers to look not merely at the immediate but also at the larger effects of an act or a policy. . . . [He] resents the travesty that many of his fellow economists have made of their profession. And so he has gone back patiently to first principles, proving once more that public works must be paid for by taxes, that taxes discourage production, that the invention of labor-saving machinery releases men to do other productive things, that soldiers and bureaucrats live off the rest of us, that tariffs make us collectively poorer, that exports must be paid for by imports, that 'parity' prices in agriculture do not solve the 'farm problem,' that you cannot produce for use except by producing for the profit that will enable you to buy other things for use, that government price-fixing increases the scarcity it is supposed to alleviate, that inflation is a form of taxation that exempts no one, that a still poverty-stricken world needs more 'saving' and not more 'spending,' that unions defeat themselves when they press for an uneconomic wage, and that the way to be sane is to look for the hidden long-term effects of a proposition on the whole social fabric as well as its effect here and now on Joe Doakes."—John Chamberlain, in *The New York Times*.

HAZLITT, HENRY. *The Great Idea*. Appleton-Century-Crofts. 1951. 374 pp.

This is written as a novel, set in the future, in a completely communized world, from which every trace of the former capitalist civilization has been removed; but in trying to solve their problems the people of this world rediscover democracy and the free enterprise system. I used this story-and-dialogue form because it seemed to me not only the most effective way to dramatize the contrast between communism and socialism on the one hand and capitalism or a free market economy on the other, but the most effective way to explain some of the fundamental and even abstruse problems involved in the choice.

The theme of the book might also be stated in the form: If capitalism did not exist, it would be necessary to invent it—and its discovery would be rightly regarded as one of the great triumphs of the human mind.

The title of the British edition of the book is *Time Will Run Back* (London: Ernest Benn).

HAZLITT, HENRY. *Will Dollars Save the World?* Irvington, N. Y.: Foundation for Economic Education. 1947. 95 pp.

A critical examination of the Marshall Plan, made when it was first proposed. It analyzes the fallacies behind most of the American intergovernmental "foreign-aid" programs, the controlist, statist or socialist assumptions implicit in them, and their consequent tendency to encourage and prolong controls, statism and socialism in the nations receiving aid. A 48-page pamphlet, also by the present author and under the imprint of the same publisher, makes a similar analysis of the *Illusions of Point Four* (1950).

HEARNSHAW, F. J. C. *A Survey of Socialism: Analytical, Historical, and Critical.* Macmillan. 1929. 473 pp.

"An unusually able student of the literature of liberty speaks of Hearnshaw's *A Survey of Socialism* as the only thing of its kind in existence. And were there many competitors, one would expect this to be acclaimed the best. Written by an outstanding British historian in a period when Britain had many and the United States had few, this is a reference book on socialism which anyone fortunate enough to possess a copy will want at his elbow. It treats persons, ideas, and programs from the earliest ancient times. Its depth and thoroughness reflect the forty years study of socialism which preceded its being written. Starting as a socialist sympathizer, his study radically altered his view to one of its most learned historical critics. He makes socialism a tragic drama on a literary stage where important personages from Moses onward take their places in the unfolding events and concepts."—F. A. Harper.

HEARNSHAW, F. J. C. *Democracy and Labor.* Macmillan. 1924. 274 pp.

"A vigorous attack on Socialism chiefly on the grounds that it is undemocratic. Democracy is held, rather optimistically, perhaps, to be the most effective means of securing freedom. The author, who is an eminent historian, is an Individualist of the Conservative school defending existing society on the grounds that it is based on Individualism. "It is becoming evident that the supreme issue of the day is the issue of Socialism versus Individualism: of Authority versus Freedom . . . of the maintenance of the Existing Order versus Utopian and Revolutionary Reconstruction." The book is a sequel to and in some respects a revision and abridgment of *Democracy at the Cross-Ways,* published in 1918. It is often witty and epigrammatic."—PI.

HECKSCHER, E. *Mercantilism.* Macmillan. 1935. 2 vols. 472 pp. 419 pp.

An effort has recently been made (e.g., by the late Lord Keynes and some of his disciples) to resuscitate mercantilism and to pretend that the mercantilists were more nearly right than Adam Smith and their other liberal critics. Anyone who is inclined to take this argument seriously, or to believe in modern State "planning" (which is little more than a revival of mercantilism) would do well to read this book by a Swedish economic historian. Here is a passage concerning French mercantilism during the seventeenth and eighteenth centuries (p. 173): "It is estimated that the economic measures taken in this connection cost the lives of some 16,000 people, partly through executions and partly through armed affrays, without reckoning the unknown but certainly much larger number of people who were sent to the galleys or punished in other ways. On one occasion in Valence, 77 were sent to the galleys, one was set free and none were pardoned. But even this vigorous action did not help to attain the desired end. Printed calicoes spread more and more widely among all classes of the population, in France as everywhere else."

HEILPERIN, MICHAEL A. *The Trade of Nations.* Knopf. 1947. 1952. 302 pp.

Intended as a book for the intelligent layman interested in the workings of the world economy, as well as a guide and reference for the professional economist. "In contemporary economic literature this book fills a niche that has been empty far too long. Michael Heilperin presents a spirited and intelligent defense of economic internationalism and its twin, free enterprise in international trade and investment, and a refutation of both the traditional and the new collectivist protectionism."—*Fortune.*

HENDERSON, H. D. *Supply and Demand.* Harcourt, Brace. 1922. 181 pp.

"The best short exposition of the standpoint of the modern 'Cambridge School' of economists. It is a very clearly written text-book, and the first chapter, 'The Economic World,' gets right to the heart of what may be called the *Laissez-faire*-Socialist controversy. The existence of an anti-Individualist bias may be suspected in his allusion to attempts by some persons to glorify the existing system of society whilst 'plastering over' such things as wastefulness in production, sweating, unemployment and slums. A reference to Bastiat suggests that Mr. Henderson has in mind those people who believe that the evils referred to are largely caused or aggravated by irrational government interferences with forces that he himself regards as fundamental."—PI.

HERBERT, AUBERON. *A Politician in Trouble About His Soul.* Chapman & Hall. 1884.

"This publicist, who (as will be acknowledged by all who had the good fortune to meet him) was one of the most charming personalities of his day, deserves considerably more attention than he has received. Accepting Herbert Spencer's strict Individualist creed, Herbert gave up his political career and devoted himself to its propagation in a form so thorough that to his contemporaries he appeared as a modern Don Quixote tilting at windmills. He long provided funds for a little journal called *Free Life,* whose main tenet was voluntary taxation. Auberon Herbert's proposals were derided as 'Anarchy plus a Policeman,' and they were too extreme for practical politics at a time when Socialism had not become formidable or very mischievous. It may be, however, that the spirit of Auberon Herbert will revive and inspire a new generation in England.

"*A Politician* is a charmingly written dialogue in which a Member of Parliament announces to his friends his intention of giving up his political career and entering upon a crusade for 'the perfect creed of liberty which he found in the writings of Herbert Spencer.' Doubtless, the zeal of the new convert went far beyond that of his master; Herbert admits this with his accustomed candor and urbanity. 'Would Mr. Spencer, do you think, agree to all these applications of his principle?' asked Argus. 'I fear that Mr. Spencer would dissent. You must not regard him as responsible for any corollaries which I have drawn.' "—PI.

HERBERT, AUBERON. *The Voluntarist Creed.* Oxford University Press. 1908. 107 pp.

"The swan-song of Auberon Herbert—the latter half was finished a few days before his death. The first, 'Mr. Spencer and the Great Machine,' was delivered in the Sheldonian Theatre at Oxford. The second, 'The Great Machine,' was addressed principally to the 'workers.' He entreated his audience: 'Don't believe in suppressing by force any form of evil—always excepting direct attacks upon person and property.' He declared that 'these new bonds and restrictions in which the nations of today have allowed themselves to be entangled' merely prepare 'docile and obedient State-material, ready-made for taxation, ready-made for conscription—ready-made for the ambitious aims and ends of the rulers.' He tells the wage-earners: 'Property is the great and good inducement that will call out your efforts and energies for the remaking of the present form of society.' No man has suffered more than Auberon Herbert from his contempt of the Time Spirit, and, undoubtedly, there was in his own day only a small audience for his creed. But the battle is not over, and he showed a way to success. The 'selfish' system of Bentham may repel sentimentalists and altruists. Auberon Herbert aimed at giving Individualism a noble spiritual significance. His writings are worthy of careful study, though he underestimated the value and possibilities of the modern State as a means of organizing public-spirited activity. In the eighteenth century the State was regarded, with considerable justification, as hostile to liberty. This was Herbert's view, and since his death the extension of State functions has made another revival of Individualism imperative in order to save Democracy from itself."—PI.

HERLING, ALBERT K. *The Soviet Slave Empire*. Funk. 1951. 230 pp.

An exposé of slave labor in the U.S.S.R. and its satellite countries. The report contains reprinted photostats of documents from the files of the Russian secret police. The author is a Unitarian minister who temporarily left his parish to devote himself to investigating this new slavery. He became director of research for the commission of inquiry into forced labor, which was set up in December 1948.

HERMANS, FERDINAND. *Democracy or Anarchy?* University of Chicago Press. 1940. (University of Notre Dame. 1951). 447 pp.

This study presents the arguments against proportional representation and in favor of majority rule. "What the conservatives have lacked up to now has been a well-documented scholarly analysis of the failure of proportional representation where it has been tried, and of the appalling contribution which this gadget has made to the growth of communism, fascism and other undemocratic phenomena. Professor Hermans, who has long since been regarded as a leading authority in this field, has now filled the gap by an excellent volume entitled *Democracy or Anarchy?*"—Robert Moses, in the *Political Science Quarterly*.

HEWART OF BURY, LORD. *The New Despotism*. London: Ernest Benn. 1929. 311 pp.

By the "new despotism" the author, who at the time of the appearance of this book in 1929 was Lord Chief Justice of England, means the danger which threatens the institutions of self-government through the steady encroachment of the executive upon the powers of the legislative and judiciary. His book is a strong argument against bureaucracy—the practice by which Parliament delegates wide powers of legislation to government departments and commissions. "Lord

Hewart's new book is a political event of first-rate importance."—*Saturday Review*. "Lord Hewart proves his case. He gives chapter and verse for all his accusations."—*Spectator*.

HEWES, THOMAS. *Decentralization for Liberty*. Dutton. 1947. 238 pp.

"Mr. Hewes' legal background, his obviously extensive studies of the literature on liberty, much experience in public service, and keen insight have enabled him to see clearly the great problem that Western Civilization must solve if it is to survive. In terms understandable to the layman he has described the principal features of this problem. That accomplishment alone is a meritorious public service."—American Institute for Economic Research.

HIRST, FRANCIS W. *Early Life and Letters of John Morley*. Macmillan. 1927. 2 vols. 327 pp. 285 pp.

Morley's "political doctrine," writes Hirst, "unites the traditions of the philosophical Radicals and of the Manchester School. Disciple of Mill, biographer of Cobden, friend of John Bright, favorite and most trusted colleague of Gladstone in his two last administrations, he held in later years a unique position as the philosophic guide of English Liberals." As Morley was the disciple of Mill, Hirst was the disciple of Morley; and Hirst has been himself described as "the most distinguished Cobdenite spokesman and political philosopher of his generation." He died in 1953, in his eightieth year. He was editor of the London *Economist* from 1907 to 1916, honorable fellow of Wadham College, Oxford, and governor of the London School of Economics.

HIRST, FRANCIS W. *Adam Smith*. Macmillan. 1904. 240 pp.

A standard biography.

HIRST, FRANCIS W. *Life and Letters of Thomas Jefferson*. Macmillan. 1926. 588 pp.

A full biography of a great individualist statesman.

HOFF, TRYGVE J. B. *Economic Calculation in the Socialist Society*. 1938. London: Hodge. 1949. 264 pp.

This book by a distinguished Norwegian economist and editor originally appeared in Norway in 1938 and was not translated into English until 1949. In it Dr. Hoff examines the crucial question whether economic calculation is or is not possible in a completely socialist society. He concludes, with Drs. Mises and Hayek, that it is not. "Very balanced and fair. . . . It is a pleasure to read such a scholarly, clear and patient exposition."—H. D. Dickenson, in *The Economic Journal*.

HOFF, TRYGVE J. B. *Fred og Fremtid. Liberokratiets vei.* Oslo: H. Aschehoug. 1945. 500 pp.

This is a book by an eminent Norwegian economist, editor of the magazine *Farmand,* published in Oslo. The book was written during World War II, the last chapter in a German concentration camp. It is a homage to Western culture and stresses the necessity of opposition to collectivist and Asiatic ideals, to the extent that the latter are fundamentally aggressive.

The book is also a plea for a new liberalism to which Mr. Hoff gives the name "liberocracy." In his own words: "Liberocracy is the name of an economic and political system representing the best in liberalism, in democracy and the aristocratic form of rule. It does not pretend to be something new; it is a new name for a new combination of old but revised ideas. Liberocracy means the rule of the free by the free. Its central idea is freedom—freedom for the individual, freedom of press, freedom for science and art, freedom to choose and exchange goods and services within and outside national borders."

The Norwegian title may be translated as *Peace and Future: The Way of Liberocracy.*

HOFFER, ERIC. *The True Believer.* Harper. 1951. 176 pp.

This carries the subtitle, "Thoughts on the Nature of Mass Movements." It is a scholarly, witty, epigrammatic, sometimes flippant but usually penetrating analysis of fanaticism, particularly in the political realm.

HOLYOAKE, G. J. *Self-Help a Hundred Years Ago.* London: Swan, Sonnenschein. 1888. 214 pp.

"Deals with the various elementary forms of self-help, in which the poor with the assistance of the well-to-do engaged during the darkest days of the Industrial Revolution. The spirit of the plucky, self-reliant man in adversity is still valuable, perhaps more necessary than ever. In our time we are too much inclined to scoff at thriftful industry. Yet may we not expect a finer character from one who rises by these means from poverty than from one who applies for the dole as soon as he sees the approach of trouble?"—PI.

HOOK, SIDNEY. *Heresy, Yes, Conspiracy, No.* Day. 1953. 283 pp.

A treatise on the nature of liberal thinking and its place in American life, particularly in academic circles. The author is opposed to communism because it is secret and conspiratorial, but holds that the outspoken leftist critic should not be silenced. "A balanced and incisive contribution."—E. N. Case, in *The New York Times.*

HOOVER, HERBERT. *American Individualism.* Doubleday. 1922. 72 pp.

A short but vigorous and important book, arguing for American individualism, "our most precious possession," and against governmental encroachment on personal freedom, initiative and enterprise.

HOOVER, HERBERT. *Challenge to Liberty.* Scribner's. 1934. 212 pp.

"The challenge to liberty is, briefly, regimentation. This, as Mr. Hoover points out, is close kin to Fascism, Communism, Nazism and Socialism in that it implies that the individual is the pawn of the state."—*Books.*

HOOVER, HERBERT. *Memoirs: The Great Depression.* Macmillan. 1951. 503 pp.

The third volume of ex-President Hoover's memoirs covers the years 1929 to 1941. In it he reviews the great depression era and gives his defense of his administration in Washington. "Mr. Hoover has turned his pen to a great penetrating analysis of the causes of the great depression, that economic catastrophe that nearly overwhelmed the Western world in 1929 and the years immediately after. Unthinking or malicious people have often dubbed this 'Hoover's depression,' one of the basest slanders of this century. The mountain of facts presented in this book should do much to sound the death knell of this calumny."—W. H. Baker, in the *San Francisco Chronicle.*

HOPKINSON, AUSTIN. *The Hope of the Workers.* London: Martin Hopkinson. 1923. 104 pp.

"The point of view of one who has himself been successful as an employer and is well known as an Individualist. In form a criticism of the Socialist attitude and an exposure of Socialist fallacies, the book is addressed as much to employers as to the work people of the country. Mr. Hopkinson believes that the survival of Socialist fallacies has been largely due to the fact that those who support the Individualist system have failed to show clearly that 'they do so, not for their own selfish ends, but because it is the one system under which prosperity and liberty can be secured to the people.' "—PI.

HUGHES, FRANK. *Prejudice and the Press.* Devin-Adair. 1950. 654 pp.

A restatement of the principle of freedom of the press with specific reference to the Hutchins-Luce commission. *"Prejudice and the Press* cannot be shrugged off. It presents a considerable body of authentic material, with citations and some documentation, which goes to the heart of the issues discussed in *A Free and Responsible Press* and which upsets many of the too facile generalizations of the group responsible for that 'report.' "—F. L. Mott, in the *New York Herald Tribune.*

HUME, DAVID. *Essays Moral, Political and Literary.* 1741-2. Numerous editions. 616 pp.

Although Adam Smith referred to David Hume in his *Wealth of Nations* as "by far the most illustrious philosopher and historian of the present age," even professional economists seldom seem to recognize the great intellectual debt that Smith owed to his older friend Hume, not merely in general philosophy but in the special realm of economics. These essays, published more than thirty years before *The Wealth of Nations,* embody many important ideas which Adam Smith later expanded and pushed further. The most important economic essays are Of Commerce, Of the Balance of Trade, Of the Jealousy of Trade, Of Money, Of Interest, Of Taxes, and Of Public Credit. In addition there are political essays, Of the Liberty of the Press, Of the Independence of Parliament, and Of Civil Liberty, that stand among the earlier developments of the modern philosophy of individualism. Hume was hardly less distinguished for the excellence of his literary style than for the originality and acuteness of his ideas.

HUNOLD, ALBERT (ed.). *Die Konvertibilität der europäischen Währungen.* Zurich: Eugen Rentsch. 1954. 336 pp.

An anthology on the measures that can be taken to bring about a return to freedom of currency convertibility. The contributors include G. Haberler, P. Jacobson, W. Röpke, G. Carli, F. Collin, H. Germain-Martin, H. Homberger, J. E. Meade, F. W. Meyer, S. Posthuma, and F. A. Lutz.

HUNT, R. N. CAREW. *Marxism: Past and Present.* Macmillan. 1955.

"It is a worthwhile endeavor to put the claims of Marxism through the wringer of factual analysis. This is what a British scholar, Mr. R. N. Carew Hunt, has now done with conspicuous success. . . . One Marxian dogma after another is fairly stated, examined and dismissed with the reasoned verdict: disproved or unprovable. From this searching examination a very deflated Marx emerges, stripped of all pretension to be recognized as a seer of the shape of things to come, or even as a reasonably accurate guesser."—William Henry Chamberlin.

The author pronounces this final judgment on utopianism in general and Marxism in particular: "It is easy enough to attack any economic system, as it is certain to contain features which are open to criticism, and to make large promises of replacing it by a new order of ideal harmony. But in an imperfect world no such order is attainable. 'It is a disease of the soul,' says a Grecian sage, 'to be in love with impossible things.'"

HUNT, R. N. CAREW. *The Theory and Practice of Communism*. Macmillan. 1951. 231 pp.

"The book falls into three sections. The first deals with the basis of Communist theory as laid down by Marx and Engels, which is still the official creed of the movement. The second covers the development of the European labor movement in the Nineteenth Century, with special reference to Marxist influence upon it and to the cross-currents of opinion which arose by way of reaction to his doctrines. . . . The third brings us to the period when the revolutionary movement begins to be shaped by Russia, which has since directed it, and deals with the attempts by Lenin and Stalin to apply Marxist principles to the changed conditions of the present century."—From the Foreword. "With a single demurrer, I recommend *The Theory and Practice of Communism* as a book that every man of politics, and every one prone to get into political arguments, ought to carry in his pocket."—Max Eastman, in *The New York Times*.

HUNTER, EDWARD. *Brain-Washing in Red China*. Vanguard Press. 1951. 311 pp.

The calculated destruction of men's minds. "One of the largest and most important jobs confronting the initial band of Chinese Communists was to subject their citizens to 'brainwashing' in order to rid them of 'imperialist poison' and to qualify them for their position in the 'new democracy.' . . . The author interviewed at length returnees from the mainland to Hongkong, and his story is a horribly incredible one of exploitation of human nature, destruction of individualism, and intellectual conquest."—*Library Journal*. "Mr. Hunter points up the basic issue of the struggle between Communism and democracy—that is, that Communism means the end of individual freedom. He says that we must find means of checking the psychological offensive of the Communist world if we ourselves are to be safe from brain washing and brain changing."—A. T. Steele, in the *New York Herald Tribune*.

HUTT, W. H. *The Theory of Collective Bargaining*. 1930. Glencoe, Ill.: Free Press. 1954. 150 pp.

This is a short but lucid and penetrating "history, analysis and criticism of the principal theories which have sought to explain the effects of trade unions and employers' associations upon the distribution of the product of industry." As Ludwig von Mises writes in his preface to the 1954 edition: "Professor Hutt's brilliant essay is not merely a contribution to the history of economic thought. It is rather a critical analysis of the arguments advanced by economists from Adam Smith down and by the spokesmen of the unions in favor of the thesis that unionism can raise wage rates above the market level without harm to anybody else than the 'exploiters.' As such it is of utmost use not only to every student of economics but to everybody who wants to form a well-founded opinion about one of the most vital as well as most controversial political issues of our age."

HUTT, W. H. *Plan for Reconstruction*. Oxford University Press. 1943. 328 pp.

Appearing during World War II, this presented Professor Hutt's project for victory in war and peace. "It is a careful and sound analysis of all forms of restrictionism, and it is a skilful discussion of some of the most important economic evils of our era."—B. F. Hoselitz, in the *American Journal of Sociology*.

HUXLEY, ALDOUS. *Brave New World*. Doubleday. 1932. 311 pp.

A chilling satirical novel on the "brave new world" of the future, when human liberty, dignity and individuality will have been systematically destroyed by "scientific conditioning."

HUXLEY, ALDOUS. *Ends and Means*. Harper. 1937. 386 pp.

This book, which combines lucidity and insight with mysticism and confusion, has a mixed value for the individualist. Reviewing it in *The New York Times* of Dec. 12, 1937, I wrote: *"Ends and Means* rests on the premise . . . that the end cannot justify the means, for the simple reason that the means employed inevitably determine the nature of the ends produced. Hence Huxley is opposed to all efforts to achieve a better world through the method of violence. . . . He is against the 'capitalistic system,' or at least he thinks he is. . . . Yet he fails to realize how much more opposed he is to the real alternative to capitalism. . . . 'State Socialism,' he recognizes explicitly at one point, 'tends to produce a single centralized, totalitarian dictatorship, wielding absolute authority over all its subjects through a hierarchy of bureaucratic agents.' The political road to a better society, he tells us, on the other hand, is 'the road of decentralization and responsible self-government.' But this comes pretty close to being a definition of private enterprise in the economic field."

HYDE, DOUGLAS. *I Believed*. Putnam. 1950. 312 pp.

Autobiographical account of how the author became a communist, worked hard for many years in the British Communist Party, and then left the party and became a convert to Catholicism. "This book is one of the most interesting and revealing of the score or so of confessions by ex-Communists."—Freda Utley, in the *Chicago Sunday Tribune*.

JEFFERSON, THOMAS. *The Declaration of Independence.* 1776. 1 p.

This is the most famous short statement in existence of the principles of political liberty (with the possible exception of Magna Charta [1215], if the two can be compared). Certainly, nothing bearing on those principles is more often quoted than the second paragraph of the Declaration, beginning: "We hold these truths to be self-evident, that all men are created equal, that they are endowed by their Creator with certain unalienable Rights, that among these are Life, Liberty and the pursuit of Happiness." Although Jefferson drew up the Declaration, it was slightly amended by Adams and Franklin.

JEFFERSON, THOMAS. *The Life and Selected Writings of.* Many editions. (Modern Library. 1944. 756 pp.)

Every student of human liberty should know something of the philosophy and writings of Jefferson (in addition to the Declaration of Independence, here listed separately). There are several collections and many selections. The volume listed above gives the *Notes on Virginia* and the *Autobiography* virtually complete, and allots the greatest amount of space to the letters. Jefferson was a staunch champion of limited government and the diffusion and decentralization of powers. He favored (p. 323) "a wise and frugal government, which shall restrain men from injuring one another, which shall leave them otherwise free to regulate their own pursuits of industry and improvement, and shall not take from the mouth of labor the bread it has earned. This is the sum of good government."

JEVONS, W. STANLEY. *The Theory of Political Economy.* 1871. Numerous editions.

A work of epoch-making importance. John Maynard Keynes writes of it: "Jevons's *Theory* is the first treatise to present in a finished form the theory of value based on subjective valuations, the marginal principle and the now familiar technique of the algebra and diagrams of the subject. The first modern book on economics, it has proved singularly attractive to all bright minds newly attacking the subject;— simple, lucid, unfaltering, chiselled in stone where Marshall knits in wool."

JEVONS, W. STANLEY. *The State in Relation to Labor.* 1882. Macmillan. 174 pp.

In this book Jevons takes a cautious, intermediate position regarding state intervention: "The all-important point," he explains in the preface, "is to explain if possible why, in general, we uphold the rule of *laisser-faire*, and yet in large classes of cases invoke the interference of local or central authorities. . . . The outcome of the inquiry is that we can lay down no hard-and-fast rules, but must treat every case in detail upon its merits." But in his *Primer on Political Economy,* published in 1878, he wrote, for example: "There is no reason whatever to think that trades unions have had any permanent effect in raising wages in the majority of trades."

JEVONS, W. STANLEY. *The Coal Question.* 1865. Macmillan. 383 pp.

This bears the subtitle: "An enquiry concerning the progress of the nation, and the probable exhaustion of our coal mines." It is significant as foreseeing far in advance a physical condition which, when it developed, was attributed to the wastefulness of private competition and led to Britain's futile nationalization of the coal mines.

JEWKES, JOHN. *Ordeal by Planning.* Macmillan. 1948. 248 pp.

The most forthright and powerful attack on government economic planning that has appeared in England since Hayek's *Road to Serfdom.* While it lacks some of the philosophic penetration and depth of Hayek's book, it is more explicit and concrete. Its style is lively, sparkling, and witty. Professor Jewkes was a wartime member of the British bureaucracy and has seen central economic planning from the inside. "The planned economy," he concludes, "must finally destroy the very instruments of free speech. . . . This is no accident. . . . It is due to the logical incompatibility of a planned economy and freedom for the individual. . . . There is no end to this process of seeking to cure the evils of planning by more planning except a totalitarian economy of the Russian type."

JOSEPH, H. W. B. *The Labor Theory of Value in Karl Marx.* Oxford University Press. 1923. 176 pp.

Professor Joseph holds that the theory which finds an objective measure of value for things in the labor embodied in them is fundamentally false. The author is well known as a logician. The late L. Susan Stebbing called his *Introduction to Logic* "by far the best systematic exposition of the traditional logic." James Bonar wrote of the present book in *The Economic Journal:* "It is not censure but commendation that in showing [that Marx's theory is false] Mr. Joseph follows the lines of many predecessors, especially Böhm-Bawerk, that model of conscientious thoroughness. . . . The book is sane and helpful. Its discussions give good training in Applied Logic."

JOUVENEL, BERTRAND DE. *The Ethics of Redistribution.* Cambridge University Press. 1951. 91 pp.

Deliberately putting aside the argument that current government efforts to redistribute incomes reduce or destroy incentives, Baron de Jouvenel seeks to deal with the subject on purely ethical grounds. Would total equalization of incomes, he asks, even if it did not reduce production, be good or desirable? Or does justice demand individual rewards proportionate to the value of individual services? In an acute and original discussion, de Jouvenel shows not only how disappointing (in Great Britain, for example) the results of a further redistribution of incomes would be, but how redistribution has turned out to mean in effect "far less a redistribution of free income from the richer to the poorer, as we imagined, than a redistribution of power from the individual to the State."

JOUVENEL, BERTRAND DE. *On Power*. Viking Press. 1949. 421 pp.

"M. de Jouvenel, a French journalist and historian, who finished this book in exile during the war, maintains that all power is corrupt, no matter what political philosophy it is dedicated to. Even revolutions, which break up special privilege in the name of the common good, are the products of a desire for power, he believes, and the iniquities of power cannot be prevented by putting philosophers, scientists, and 'men of good will' in high office, for as soon as they are on top, they become politicians. . . . The book is not a tract, but a fully considered line of thinking, and has caused a great deal of comment in Europe. An important book, brilliantly written."—*New Yorker*.

KALME, ALBERT. *Total Terror*. Appleton-Century-Crofts. 1951. 310 pp.

An account of the fate of the three Baltic countries—Estonia, Latvia and Lithuania—under the Nazis and the Russian communist regime.

KANTOROWICZ, HERMANN U. *The Spirit of British Policy, and the Myth of the Encirclement of Germany*. Oxford University Press. 1931. 541 pp.

The primary purpose of this scholarly and thorough book by an eminent German jurist is to disprove the notion of the "encirclement" of Germany through the operations of British diplomacy as a cause of World War I.

KAPLAN, A. D. H. *Big Enterprise in the Competitive System*. Brookings Institution. 1953. 269 pp.

A careful statistical study which throws a brilliant light on the question of bigness, monopoly, "oligopoly" and competition in American industry. Dr. Kaplan shows, for example, that of the 100 largest industrial firms in the United States in 1909 only 36 stayed in the list of the 100 largest for 1948. "The top is a slippery place," and no safeguard against the hazards of competition. Dr. Kaplan points out that the attitude of the American public toward "big business" is oddly inconsistent. Individually, as investors, employees, and consumers, the people support and promote the growth of big business enterprises. But collectively they regard "big business" with distrust.

KASENKINA, OKSANA. *Leap to Freedom.* Lippincott. 1949. 295 pp.

Autobiography of the Russian teacher, Oksana Kasenkina. "Her story of the first faint glimmering of the idea of breaking away from the soul-crushing tyranny which surrounded her, of the slow growth of her hope and determination, of her first abortive attempt to pull free and of her final desperate plunge from a window of the Soviet Consulate into the courtyard below, and into the welcoming arms of America, make up the best part of the book. Even though you know that she did escape, the suspense at the end is terrific."—Oriana Atkinson, in *The New York Times.*

KEETON, G. W. *The Passing of Parliament.* London: Ernest Benn. 1952. 208 pp.

G. W. Keeton is dean of the Faculty of Laws at University College, London. During the past seventy years, he points out, the British Parliament, although still nominally supreme, has conferred on government departments and agencies increasingly wide powers of lawmaking. The jurisdiction of the courts and the legislative powers of the House of Lords have been seriously curtailed. Party discipline has intensified, so that a government may rely upon a firm majority in the House of Commons to give legal force to almost any measure it proposes. The Rule of Law has been gravely undermined. It is Professor Keeton's thesis that, in consequence of these developments, the sovereignty of Parliament is in danger of becoming a fiction, and that all the necessary machinery for Cabinet dictatorship already exists. This scholarly and cogent book is a worthy successor to *The New Despotism* written by Lord Hewart (q.v.) more than twenty years ago.

KEEZER, DEXTER MERRIAM, and associates. *Making Capitalism Work.* McGraw-Hill. 1950. 316 pp.

A program for preserving freedom and stabilizing prosperity. The volume is the joint product of several members of the economics department of the McGraw-Hill Publishing Company. Its own declaration of purpose is: "This book is written from a definite point of view and with a clear-cut purpose. The point of view is that capitalism is the best way to economic life for the United States of America. The purpose is to explain that point of view and present a series of steps which, in the view of the authors, must be taken to give capitalism the promise of a prosperous future in the United States."

KELLER, THE REV. EDWARD A. *Christianity and American Capitalism.* Chicago: Heritage Foundation. 1954. 92 pp.

Father Keller examines socialism, capitalism, big government and big labor, and restates the case for the American economic system.

KELSEN, HANS. *The Political Theory of Bolshevism.* University of California Press. 1948. 60 pp.

A critical analysis of the political theory of bolshevism. "The purpose of this study is to show the paradoxical contradiction which exists within bolshevism between anarchism in theory and totalitarianism in practice, and to defend the true idea of democracy."—From the Introduction.

KELSEN, HANS. *The Communist Theory of Law.* Frederick A. Praeger. 1955. 203 pp.

"Hans Kelsen is one of the world's leading authorities on legal theory and international law. . . . He begins with an analysis of the Marx-Engels theory of state and law that is positively brilliant. . . . Kelsen's analysis of the logical contradictions in historical materialism and its application to state and law has, so far as I know, no equal." —Bertram D. Wolfe, in *The New York Times.*

KEMMERER, E. W. *The A B C of Inflation.* Whittlesey House. 1942. 174 pp.

An excellent little book on the causes and consequences of monetary inflation, although the threat of inflation to liberty was not as clear when this book was written as it has since become.

KIEKHOFER, WILLIAM H. *Economic Principles, Problems and Policies.* Appleton-Century-Crofts. 1951.

A standard college textbook.

KING, WILLFORD I. *The Keys to Prosperity.* Constitution and Free Enterprise Foundation. 1948. 242 pp.

Dr. King believes that most of the keys that unlock the gates to prosperity were found by Adam Smith in *The Wealth of Nations.* Additional "keys" have been discovered since that time. Yet "a great tangle of misconceptions and fallacies" has buried many of them "so deeply that it has required a trained eye to detect them." Dr. King attempts here to disentangle the fallacies from the economic truths in order that the reader may find the "keys to prosperity." He writes with lucidity and statistical authority.

KINTNER, WILLIAM R. *The Front Is Everywhere*. University of Oklahoma Press. 1950. 274 pp.

"The author, now at Fort Leavenworth, started research for this book while doing graduate work at Georgetown University. He believes that an overruling military purpose shapes every aspect of Communist organization. Kintner endeavors to prove his point by examining the history of the Marxist movement from origins to era of Lenin and Stalin. The volume contains some significant observations, based on wide acquaintance with Communist literature."—*Library Journal*.

KIRK, RUSSELL. *The Conservative Mind*. Regnery. 1953. 458 pp.

In my Introduction to this bibliography I call attention to the compatibility of an intelligent conservatism with a vigorous defense of freedom. Russell Kirk recognizes this. "Political liberalism before the middle of the nineteenth century," he writes, "was conservatism of a sort: it intended to conserve liberty." The present book analyzes the conservative spirit and philosophy as exemplified in a series of writers from Edmund Burke to George Santayana. "The author of *The Conservative Mind* is as relentless as his enemies, Karl Marx and Harold Laski, considerably more temperate and scholarly, and in passages of this very readable book, brilliant and even eloquent. . . . Against the Hegel-Marx-Laski axis he analyzes and describes the affirmative tradition of Burke, de Tocqueville and Irving Babbitt."— G. K. Chalmers, in *The New York Times*.

KNIGHT, FRANK H. *Risk, Uncertainty and Profit*. Houghton Mifflin. 1921. 381 pp.

In his preface, Professor Knight declares: "The particular technical contribution to the theory of free enterprise which this essay purports to make is a fuller and more careful examination of the role of the *entrepreneur* or enterpriser, the recognized 'central figure' of the system, and of the forces which fix the remuneration of his special function."

"The outstanding fact about Professor Knight's book is that the author has made a contribution to the theory of profit that no student of the subject can afford to neglect."—G. P. Watkins, in the *Quarterly Journal of Economics*.

KNIGHT, FRANK H. *The Ethics of Competition, and Other Essays*. Harper. 1935. 363 pp.

A collection of eleven important essays by Professor Knight, brought together by a group of his former students. It includes a bibliography of his writings from 1915 to 1935. "Professor Knight . . . manages in the course of this volume to throw original and arresting light on almost every corner of the contemporary economic problem. One page after another in his book is filled not merely with great wisdom and subtlety, but with constant aphoristic sentences that strike the reader at once with their pertinence and truth. . . . It is . . . because Professor Knight is an economic theorist of the first rank and a believer in personal and political liberty, that his criticism of the existing economic system is so extremely valuable. He also has the great merit of seeing the philosophical background clearly, and not falling back, like some economists, on philosophical solecisms while professing to eschew philosophy altogether."—London *Times Literary Supplement.*

KNIGHT, FRANK H. *Freedom and Reform.* Harper. 1947. 409 pp.

Essays in economic and social philosophy. "Knight's personal influence, through his teaching, exceeds even the influence of his writings. It is hardly an exaggeration to state that nearly all the younger American economists who really understand and advocate a competitive economic system, have at one time been Knight's students."—F. A. Hayek.

KNOWLES, LILIAN C. A. *Industrial and Commercial Revolutions in Great Britain during the Nineteenth Century.* Dutton. 1921. 420 pp.

"The best general economic history of England in the nineteenth and early twentieth centuries. On the question of the interpretation of State intervention during this period, its attitude may be described as 'neutral.' "—PI.

KOESTLER, ARTHUR. *Darkness at Noon.* Macmillan. 1941. 267 pp. (Also Modern Library. 1946.)

A powerful novel based on the famous Moscow trials. It centers about a former People's Commissar who has followed certain practices for a cause that seemed of supreme importance, and now finds himself victim of his own methods. In portraying the psychology of a loyal communist, the novel illuminates not only Russia but the conflict between the individual and the State.

KOESTLER, ARTHUR. *The Yogi and the Commissar.* Macmillan. 1945. 247 pp.

A collection of sixteen essays. These essays contain the shrewd and sometimes brilliant insights of a former communist—and the confusions of one who still remains a socialist.

KORNER, EMIL. *The Law of Freedom as the Remedy for War and Poverty.* London: Williams & Norgate. 1951. 2 vols. 562 pp. 663 pp.

This work, translated from the original German, contains much that seems to me confused and crotchety, but also much that is illuminating. "Korner offers stimulating viewpoints to those who adhere to L. Mises', F. A. Hayek's and L. Robbins' doctrines of economic freedom or to H. C. Simons' *Positive Program of Laissez-faire* and reject Marxism as well as Keynesian economics."—Theo Surányi-Unger, in *The American Economic Review*.

KRAVCHENKO, VICTOR. *I Chose Freedom*. Scribner's. 1946. 496 pp.

"About two months before D-Day on the beaches of Normandy, a frightened member of the Soviet Purchasing Commission deserted his post in Washington and placed himself under the protection of the people of the United States. He was Victor Kravchenko, long a member of the Communist party, an engineer, a factory director and for a time an official in the Council of Peoples Commissars of the Russian Soviet Federative Socialist Republic, by far the largest of the republics constituting the U.S.S.R. Kravchencko was not frightened of shell-fire but of the long arm of Soviet law dealing with a renegade. He escaped, however, and in *I Chose Freedom* he and his translator have described his life in the Soviet Union, his views of the Soviet régime and the events that prompted him to desert."—*Weekly Book Review*. "It is, I believe, the most remarkable and most revelatory report to have come out of the Soviet Union from any source whatsoever."—Dorothy Thompson, in the *Saturday Review of Literature*.

KRAVCHENKO, VICTOR. *I Chose Justice*. Scribner's. 1950. 458 pp.

"A sequel to *I Chose Freedom*. The author describes his successful libel suit against *Les Lettres Françaises*, a Parisian Communist magazine which had called his book a fake."—*The New York Times*. "The world is indebted to the author for material which should settle once for all every honest doubt as to the Kremlin's determination to destroy human liberties."—*Catholic World*.

KROPOTKIN, PRINCE. *Mutual Aid*. London: Heinemann. 1904. 348 pp.

"The Anarchists are Individualists of a somewhat perverse kind. So extreme an Individualist as Auberon Herbert was very careful to disclaim any connection with Anarchy. Kropotkin—who was considerably influenced by the farm-loving Fourier—advocated the extreme Individualism which threw off all restraint, and arrived, through Anarchy, at Communism. But the goal is 'free Communism untrammelled by the State.' In economics a good time is coming. . . . In social life and politics there is to be the enjoyment for all of the same liberty. All contracts—above all, marriage—are void unless 'voluntarily and frequently renewed.' With almost incredible optimism, the Anarchists held that sovereign Reason coupled with the inherited instinct of solidarity impelling men towards mutual aid (this seems to have been Kropotkin's own and comparatively commonsense contribution) would be sufficient to control human passions. Government would be quite unnecessary. There is a myth that the philosopher Empedocles, to prove some philosophical principle, threw himself into Etna and perished. Much the same fate befell poor Kropotkin. Believing that his principles had triumphed in Russia, he hurried to his native land in the expectation of seeing the world's great age begin anew. He soon discovered that, as the Jacobins were said to have no need of chemists, so the Leninites had no use for philosophers, and he died in poverty that almost amounted to starvation."—PI.

KRUTCH, JOSEPH WOOD. *The Measure of Man*. Bobbs-Merrill. 1954. 261 pp.

This is a well-written and closely reasoned book. It is a significant and hopeful sign that Joseph Wood Krutch, whose background has been mainly that of a literary and dramatic critic, and who has no special knowledge of economics and politics, should have arrived by an independent route at much the same conclusions as those of F. A. Hayek in *The Counter-Revolution of Science* (q.v.). Although the two writers show no knowledge of each other's work, Krutch, like Hayek, has become profoundly critical of the mechanistic, "conditioning" and "engineering" point of view toward man and society: he answers the arguments of the mechanists not on emotional or mystical, but on scientific and rational, grounds. Historically he shows how nineteenth century thought, under the influence of Darwin, Marx, Freud, and their followers, left us the heritage of materialism, mechanism and determinism that has played into the hands of the totalitarians. Krutch contends that man is capable of making independent choices and value judgments and of freely choosing what he will do.

KÜHNELT-LEDDIHN, ERIK MARIA VON. *Liberty or Equality*. Caldwell, Idaho: Caxton Printers. 1952. 395 pp.

"The book is an exploration of certain interconnected hypotheses, of varying generality, about contemporary politics. The first set of propositions to be examined is: That the impulse of 'democracy' (popular government) is the pursuit of equality, and that this leads unavoidably (and has in fact led) to collectivism and on to oppressive totalitarianism; and that 'liberalism' is the pursuit of liberty and is an incompatible mate for 'democracy.' . . . The second proposition: That 'monarchy' is a more serviceable manner of government than 'democracy' and likely to be more 'liberal.' . . . The third: That the political temper of Catholic nations is more 'liberal' than that of Protestant nations."—*Spectator*. "The book is uneven—sometimes naive, sometimes poorly thought out, and sometimes exasperatingly repetitious. But its genuine insights make it worth reading, despite its weaknesses."—W. P. Clancy, in *Commonweal*.

LACOUR-GAYET, JACQUES, and LACOUR-GAYET, ROBERT. *De Platon à la Terreur*. Paris: Éditions SPID. 1948. 268 pp.

This is a short history of the philosophy and practice of State economic planning and price controls "from Plato to the Terror." It contains chapters on Plato and the planned economy, the price-fixing edicts of the Roman Emperor Diocletian, reflections on the "just price" of medieval theory, the search for economic liberty in France from 1789 to 1791, the enormous inflation of the French currency, and its culmination in the dreadful Law of the Maximum (price control), which made the situation far worse and abolished liberty.

LACOUR-GAYET, JACQUES (ed.). *Vingt Ans de Capitalisme D'État*. Paris: Éditions SPID. 1951. 302 pp.

A critical examination by nine writers of "twenty years of State capitalism" in France. The authors show the deleterious consequences of the nationalization of various industries in the period from 1930 to 1950. The contributors are: André Armengaud, Louis Baudin, Jacques Chastenet, Pierre Fromont, Emile Mireaux, Marcel Pellenc, André Thiers, Daniel Villey and Jacques Lacour-Gayet.

LACOUR-GAYET, JACQUES (ed.). *Monnaie d'Hier et de Demain*. Paris: Éditions SPID. 1952. 226 pp.

Essays by five distinguished French economists on the vicissitudes of French money in recent years and on the necessity for returning to an international gold standard. Charles Rist writes on the experience of 1926 and the franc of today. Jacques Rueff writes on the reasons for returning to a gold standard. Alfred Pose writes on monetary stability and gold money. And Edmond Giscard d'Estaing writes on commerce and the need for an international money.

LACY, MARY G. *Food Control During Forty Centuries*. Scientific Monthly, June, 1923. 14 pp.

Mary G. Lacy was librarian of the Bureau of Agricultural Economics of the U.S. Department of Agriculture. This paper on the results of government efforts to control food prices through the centuries was reissued in pamphlet form by Swift & Co. in 1933. Although compact, it is remarkably comprehensive and carefully documented, and deserves to be far better known. Mary Lacy also compiled in 1926 (with Annie M. Hannay and Emily L. Day), *Price-fixing by Governments, 424 B.C. to 1926 A.D.*

LANE, ARTHUR BLISS. *I Saw Poland Betrayed*. Bobbs-Merrill. 1948. 344 pp.

The author was appointed United States ambassador to Poland in July 1944 and took up his duties while the Potsdam conference was still in session, July 1945. He retired in 1947, after nearly two years of frustration, to "tell the story as I had seen it." "For the sake of the American share in the history of the post-war years, one is sorry that the analysis of Soviet plans, the pattern for ideological conquest, were not presented to the public during the last days of the war. But since Lane was a career diplomat, that was impossible. He has done his best. It is very good."—Drew Middleton, in *The New York Times*.

LANE, ROSE WILDER. *The Discovery of Freedom*. John Day. 1943. 262 pp.

A discussion of man's struggle against authority. Mrs. Lane argues (1) that progress depends on a minimum of governmental control; and (2) that the only true control is individual and that individual control is in accord with religious faith. The book is eloquent and stimulating and covers a wide range of subjects.

LANE, ROSE WILDER. *Give Me Liberty*. Caldwell, Idaho: Caxton Printers. 1945. 56 pp.

An expansion of an article that originally appeared in *The Saturday Evening Post*. Mrs. Lane vividly describes her friendliness with communists in New York, her encounters with socialist bureaucracies in Europe, and her observations and discussions with simple villagers and primitive communists in Russia during the early years of the Soviet regime. She tells how she came to understand the rarity and the supremely precious values of personal freedom.

LE BON, GUSTAVE. *The Psychology of Socialism*. London: Unwin. 1909. 489 pp.

"This brilliant work by a convinced opponent of Socialism is based on the view that the best way to fight it and expose it is to make a scientific examination of it. . . . 'Hitherto psychologists has disdained to study it.' . . . The book abounds in epigrammatic apothegms. . . . 'All that has gone to make the greatness of civilization [he insists]: sciences, arts, philosophies, religions, military power, etc., has been the work of individuals, not of aggregates. . . . The peoples among whom Individualism is most highly developed are by this fact alone at the head of civilization, and today dominate the world.' . . . The theories of Socialism and its history are subjected to a penetrating analysis. Le Bon seems to fear that it will be victorious, and thus, he thinks, bring about the destruction of modern civilization. . . . Le Bon's other works are *The World in Revolt*, 1921; and *The Crowd*, 16th impression, 1926."—PI.

LECKY, W. E. H. *Democracy and Liberty*. Longmans, Green. 1896. 2 vols. 1169 pp.

"Of all English publicists Lecky was the most fit to take the place vacated by John Stuart Mill. He differed from Mill in most of his political and philosophical views, but he has the same candor and delight in learning. This discursive treatise is not one of his best works, but it has many wise comments on modern democracy, and the chapters on Socialism and Labor Questions should be studied. There is no systematic attack upon Socialism, but Lecky's intellectual attitude is Individualistic. He observes that 'Socialism is essentially opposed to Free Trade and international commerce.' As democracy is hasty and impatient, it may make changes in a collectivist direction. 'But proposed changes which conflict with the fundamental laws and elements of human nature can never, in the long run, succeed. The sense of right and wrong, which is the basis of the respect for property and for the obligation of contract; the feeling of family affection, on which the continuity of society depends, and out of which the system of heredity grows; the essential difference of men in aptitudes, capacities, and character, are things that never can be changed, and all schemes and policies that ignore them are doomed to ultimate failure.' "—PI.

LEVINE, ISAAC DON. *Stalin*. Cosmopolitan Book. 1931. 421 pp.

The first clear and complete account of the life of Stalin to appear in English, published when the Russian dictator was still an enigmatic figure to the Western world. The author's thesis is that "if it was Lenin who conceived the Communist party as a military order . . . it is to Stalin that is due the lion's share of the credit or onus of forging this order into an army of steel." The book gives a portrait of Stalin that is "vivid, graphic, intelligent and convincing. . . . Moreover, it portrays Bolshevism infinitely better than most of the books on Russia do."—Alexander Nazaroff, in *The New York Times*.

LHOSTE-LACHAUME, PIERRE. *Réhabilitation du Libéralisme*. 1950. Paris: Éditions SÉDIF. 320 pp.

The liberalism that this French economist wants to see restored is the traditional kind which demanded that the state should not encroach on "liberty of thought, of speech and of the press, private ownership of the means of production and a free market." Felix Morley writes: "The epic struggle of today, as M. Lhoste-Lachaume sees it, is between true liberalism and communism. The parliamentary socialists, among whom he includes many Americans who would resent the description, will in the long run be taken over by communism.

When people get the habit of living on subsidies, and expecting 'social security' from government, they tacitly become the fellow-travelers of the communists." The book is the first of a contemplated trilogy, and has not yet been translated into English.

LHOSTE-LACHAUME, PIERRE. *The Keystone of Liberty*. Paris: Éditions SÉDIF. 1954. 79 pp.

The French title of this book is *La Clef de Voute de la Liberté*. It presents the English text on each left-hand page, and the French on each right-hand page, of an article that appeared originally in the British quarterly, *The Owl*, in September 1953. The book discusses the liberal era of the nineteenth century, the gradual giving up of traditional liberal principles, and the necessity of a "liberal renovation" which would recognize the beneficial effects of the free market and avoid "the blind alley of democratic socialism." The author believes that the world's present choice is between either a "spiritualist liberalism" or a totalitarian materialism. There is an eight-page appendix presenting an extensive bibliography of recent books in French, German, Italian, Dutch, and English which support a free society and a free economy.

LIBRARY OF CONGRESS LEGISLATIVE REFERENCE SERVICE. *Communism in Action*. U. S. Government Printing Office. 1946. 141 pp.

A documented study and analysis of communism in operation in the Soviet Union. House Document No. 754. There is a foreword by Congressman Everett M. Dirksen.

LINDBLOM, CHARLES E. *Unions and Capitalism*. Yale University Press. 1949. 267 pp.

This is a strange book, written by an associate professor of economics at Yale University, a declared "liberal" (in the recent American sense, as opposed to "conservative"), yet which states the menace of present-day big unionism with far more power and clarity than most conservative economists have dared to state it. Professor Lindblom's thesis, in his own words, "is that unionism and the private enterprise economy are incompatible. . . . Unionism is destroying the competitive price system. . . . The strike . . . paralyzes production, and it is dramatic. But the real labor problem is its aftermath. . . . For if wage disputes call a halt to production temporarily, their settlement may disorganize it permanently. Unionism will destroy the price system by what it wins rather than by the struggle to win it. It sabotages the competitive order, not because the economy cannot weather the disturbance of work stoppages but because it cannot produce high output and employment at union wage rates." His grim conclusion is, in sum, that "union monopoly destroys the price system because it produces . . .

waste, unemployment, inflation, or all combined . . . to a degree which the economy cannot survive."

LINK, HENRY C. *The Rediscovery of Morals.* Dutton. 1947. 223 pp.

A discussion of what is wrong with the world of today and its people, and what can be done about it. Problems of race and class conflict are given special attention. The author takes our educational system to task for its lack of emphasis on morals, and advocates a return to Christian morality.

LIPPER, ELINOR. *Eleven Years in Soviet Prison Camps.* Regnery. 1951. 310 pp.

"A gently nurtured Dutch girl studying medicine in Berlin in 1931 was deeply touched by the miseries of the German unemployed, and at Hitler's ascendancy transferred her loyalties to the Soviet Union. From 1937-1948 she was a political prisoner held without trial for the bulk of her hideous, subhuman imprisonment at Kolyma in Siberia." —*Library Journal.*

LIPPMANN, WALTER. *The Good Society.* Little, Brown. 1937. 402 pp.

Reviewing this book in *The New York Times* of Sept. 26, 1937, I wrote: "No more powerful and thorough indictment" of the fallacies of collectivism and of a managed economy "has been written in America." The latter part of the book is marred by an inconsistent support of an apparently Keynesian type of "monetary management." But the first half is as penetrating as it is eloquent. Mr. Lippman contends that it is governmental coercion that is creating the very chaos it purports to conquer. He insists that a managed economy must mean a censored and managed opinion. He concludes that the consequences of collectivism must be regimentation, censorship, militarism, war, despotism, impoverishment, and barbarism, and that the only hope of mankind lies in the restoration of liberal doctrine.

LOCKE, JOHN. *Two Treatises of Civil Government.* 1690. Many editions. (Everyman's Library. 1924.) 242 pp.

The historical importance of these two works in the history of individualism is enormous. (For a discussion, see the introductory essay to this list, "Individualism in Politics and Economics.")

LOCKE, JOHN. *An Essay Concerning Human Understanding.* 1690. Many editions.

"This work, which is a landmark in the history of philosophy, does not bear directly upon Individualism; but some of the earlier chapters at least should be carefully studied, in order that the reader may grasp Locke's general principles, which guided politics in England and the

United States for some 200 years. It bases all knowledge and practice
on experience. . . . As Sir James Mackintosh said: 'Few books have
contributed more to rectify prejudice—to diffuse a just mode of thinking—to excite a fearless spirit of inquiry—and yet to contain it within
the boundaries which nature has prescribed to the human understanding.' This 'fearless spirit of inquiry' was subversive of the faith in
established laws and governments and was a necessary equipment for
those who, in the latter part of the eighteenth century, began their
attack upon obsolete institutions. It was thus a preliminary to Individualism, to voluntary instead of compulsory co-operation—to use
the phraseology of Herbert Spencer."—PI.

LOCKE, JOHN. *Considerations on the Lowering of Interest.* 1691.
Several editions. 138 pp.

"Here Locke anticipated many of the arguments of the better-known
work *On Usury* by Bentham, i.e., his position was *laissez-faire.*"—PI.

LUTZ, HARLEY L. *Guideposts to a Free Economy.* McGraw-Hill. 1945.
206 pp.

A series of essays on federal fiscal policy, taxation, and public ex-
penditures that give a rounded understanding of our journey along
two divergent roads of fiscal policy—one leading to a controlled economy and the other to the strengthening of the enterprise system and
individual freedom in a free economy. "Professor Lutz has written
such a book as will give true liberals no end of satisfaction and cause
the national planners acute anguish."—G. R. E., in the *Christian
Science Monitor.*

LUTZ, HARLEY L. *A Platform for the American Way.* Appleton-Century-Crofts. 1952. 114 pp.

The author, who was Professor of Public Finance at Princeton for
nearly twenty years, is distinguished for his clarity and logic and his
vigorous defense of the free enterprise system. His thesis in this book
is that "we are both drifting and being steered into some form of the
national socialist state." He regards the Right to Own as a basic
human right, and he here offers "a program and a way of life to all
who believe in freedom and who want to remain free here in America."

LUTZ, HARLEY L. *Public Finance.* Appleton-Century. 1936. 940 pp.

A solidly reasoned textbook pointing to the dangers in deficit financing and reaffirming the case for balanced budgets and other "orthodox" fiscal practices.

LYONS, EUGENE. *Assignment in Utopia.* Harcourt, Brace. 1937. 658 pp.

The author writes of his years of growing disillusionment in Russia, where he served as an American newspaper correspondent from 1928 to 1934. He describes among other things the famine of 1932-1933, and some of the causes of it. "An important book—vivid, sincere and full of factual and of psychological interest."—London *Times Literary Supplement.*

LYONS, EUGENE. *The Red Decade.* Bobbs-Merrill. 1941. 423 pp.

A study of the activities of communists and fellow-travelers in the United States during the decade from 1930 to 1940. "The facts are fabulous, and Lyons relates them with a gusto that rises at times almost to hilarity. He has a gift of slashing satire, and no fear of calling foolish acts and famous people by their exact names. But besides that, and somewhat surprisingly combined with it, he possesses sympathetic understanding."—Max Eastman, in *The New York Times.*

MACAULAY, LORD. *Selections from Writings and Speeches.* 1853. Many editions.

"Among Macaulay's Essays the most notable for our purposes is on Southey's *Colloquies on Society.* Among the speeches should be read that on the Ten Hours Bill (1846), in which he takes the modern view that in some cases it may be the duty of the State to protect labor. That on the Corn Laws (1845) is a vigorous statement of the Free Trade position. Another noteworthy speech is on the People's Charter in 1842. To Macaulay the Chartists appeared as the Communists appear to most people today. He was convinced that their object was the nationalization of the land and the abolition of private property. He says: "The doctrine of the Chartist philosophers is that it is the business of the government to support the people. It is supposed by many that our rulers possess, somewhere or other, an inexhaustible storehouse of all the necessaries and conveniences of life, and, from mere hard-heartedness, refuse to distribute the contents of this magazine among the people. . . . Is it possible to believe that the millions who have been so long and loudly told that the land is their estate and is wrongfully kept from them, should not, when they have supreme power, use that power to enforce what they think their rights? What could follow but one vast spoliation?' "—PI.

MCCARRAN, SISTER M. MARGARET PATRICIA. *Fabianism in the Political Life of Britain.* Chicago: Heritage Foundation. (Catholic University of America Press.) 1952. 612 pp.

The Fabian Society, which later, through the membership of Bernard Shaw, Beatrice and Sidney Webb, H. G. Wells and others, came to exercise an enormous intellectual influence for socialism out of all proportion to its numbers, was originally founded in 1883 by a few obscure young people in London with the object of "reconstructing society in accordance with the highest moral possibilities." This is a highly critical but encyclopedic reference work on the history of the society and its activities.

MACCUN, JOHN. *Six Radical Thinkers*. London: Arnold. 1907. 268 pp.

"The articles on Bentham and Cobden are worth notice."—PI.

MACEOIN, GARY AND ZOMBORY, AKOS. *The Communist War on Religion*. Devin-Adair. 1951. 264 pp.

"Today few Americans are complacent about the threat Communism constitutes to the things they hold dear . . . But we are still hazy about the essence of the Communist threat. The essential threat is to truth and freedom: that is, the freedom of men to be men, free to choose, free to move, to speak, to think—free to worship God. Wherever the Communists have seized power, they have destroyed these freedoms, wading through seas of human blood. . . . This book tells that story as illustrated in the persecution of religion in every Communist-controlled country."—From the Introduction.

MACINNES, HELEN. *Neither Five Nor Three*. Harcourt, Brace. 1951. 340 pp.

"A group of attractive, intelligent, well-intentioned New Yorkers who create, edit and publish an influential popular magazine called 'Trend' suddenly wake up to the fact that their magazine has been infiltrated, quietly and with devilish cleverness, that its columns are now being used subtly to disparage and undermine faith in everything American."—*New York Herald Tribune*. "It is good, exciting reading."—Edmund Fuller, in the *Saturday Review of Literature*.

MACKIEWICZ, JOSEPH. *The Katyn Wood Murders*. London: Hollis & Carter. 1951. 252 pp.

A former member of the Polish underground, who went to Katyn while the Polish Red Cross was investigating the discovery of the mass graves, describes his experiences and his beliefs about the crime. "The book is as fascinating as a detective story and deserves the widest possible audience as a final, conclusive exposure of Soviet responsibility for an atrocious butchery. This responsibility was hushed up far too long because of the supposed necessity of appeasing Stalin during the war years."—W. H. Chamberlin, in the *Chicago Sunday Tribune*.

MADISON, JAMES. *Reports of Debates in the Federal Convention.* 1787.
Several editions. 3 vols.

The basic source book on the actual framing of the American Constitution.

MAINE, SIR HENRY SUMNER. *Popular Government.* Holt. 1886. 261 pp.

"Including the famous essay on the 'Constitution of the United
States.' The careful student will also familiarize himself with Maine's
Ancient Law."—Felix Morley.

MALLOCK, W. H. *A Critical Examination of Socialism.* Harper. 1907.
303 pp.

"Mallock was a brilliant critic. This book in substance consists of
lectures delivered in the United States in 1907. It is an able attack
upon Socialism. He rightly begins with Marx, pointing out the main
error of his theory of labor—the leaving out of consideration *directive
ability.*"—PI.

MALLOCK, W. H. *Social Reform as Related to Realities and Delusions.*
Dutton. 1915. 391 pp.

"The primary purpose of this book is to illustrate the 'mischievous
delusions' by which popular opinion is vitiated in questions of social
reform owing to the general lack of knowledge and understanding of
the structure and functioning of the social system. . . . The immense
material advance which the nineteenth century has witnessed is constantly emphasized. Strangely enough, most of the specific delusions
to which Mallock drew attention in 1914 still seem to persist almost as
much as they did when the book was published."—PI (in 1927).

MALLOCK, W. H. *Democracy.* 1924. 213 pp.

"A ruthless exposure of the fallacies lurking in the term 'democracy.' The present edition is an abridgment of an earlier and very
much larger work entitled *The Limits of Pure Democracy.* [London:
Chapman & Hall. 1918. 397 pp.]"—PI.

MALLOCK, W. H. *Property and Progress.* Putnam. 1884. 248 pp.

"A criticism of Henry George's *Progress and Poverty* (1882). Also
somewhat out of date, even as George is out of date. But the Georgian
theory of land is historically important and still has its influence on
a certain type of Radical."—PI.

MALTHUS, THE REV. THOMAS R. *An Essay on Population.* 1798, etc.
Many editions. (Everyman's Library. 2 vols. 315 pp. 285 pp.)

This book has perhaps been "refuted" more often, and denounced
and ridiculed more often, than any other. Yet it is one of the world's

great seminal works. In the scientific field it helped to inspire Darwin's theory of evolution. And in the economic field, if its influence has been unfortunately less than it should have been, it has given birth to an enormous body of controversial literature. The form in which Malthus stated his theory in his first edition was certainly extreme and erroneous. Yet he was the first to seize and document a great and sobering truth. This is that, unless restrained, population tends to increase up to the limits of the means of subsistence. Because he overlooked many technical and scientific possibilities, Malthus's personal pessimism has not been justified by events. But it does not follow that his proposition, in its most general form, has been disproved by events, as it has been so often fashionable to believe. The rising standard of living in the Western world has been at least partly the result of deliberate population restraint (even if in the form of birth control rather than of the sexual "continence" that Malthus advocated). Where this population restraint still does not exist, as in India, China, and other parts of the Orient, the lesson of Malthus is only too plain today. An important corollary of his theory is that schemes of social reform and "redistribution of wealth" are not only futile but pernicious when they neglect the effect upon population growth.

MANDEVILLE, BERNARD. *The Fable of the Bees.* 1705. (Ed. by F. B. Kaye. Oxford. 1924.)

"The decisive importance of Mandeville in the history of economics, long overlooked or appreciated only by a few authors (particularly Edwin Cannan and Albert Schatz) is now beginning to be recognized, mainly thanks to the magnificent edition of the *Fable of the Bees* which we owe to the late F. B. Kaye. Although the fundamental ideas of Mandeville's work are already implied in the original poem of 1705, the decisive elaboration and especially his full account of the origin of the division of labor, of money, and of language occur only in Part II of the *Fable* which was published in 1728."—F. A. Hayek.

MANION, CLARENCE. *The Key to Peace.* Chicago: Heritage Foundation. 1950. 121 pp.

This bears the subtitle: "A Formula for the Perpetuation of Real Americanism." The author, dean of the law school of Notre Dame University, believes that the only possible formula for peace was discovered by the Founding Fathers when they wrote the Declaration of Independence and framed the American Constitutional system. The basic American principle, he declares, is "an uncompromising and uncompromised demand for the freedom and independence of the individual man."

MARKHAM, REUBEN HENRY. *Rumania Under the Soviet Yoke.* Meador. 1949. 601 pp.

"There is no better informed or more responsible writer on Balkan affairs than Mr. Markham. He was a European correspondent for the *Christian Science Monitor* for twenty years, and for *The Christian Century* for a shorter period, and during the war he served as deputy director of the Office of War Information. He knows the people, the languages, the history and (so far as anyone can) the present conditions in the Balkan states. In the 600 pages of this volume he surveys Rumania before and during the Hitler regime and recites in detail the course of events since the beginning of Soviet domination."—*The Christian Century.* "Mr. Markham's book is one of the strongest and best documented indictments of the system of political communism flourishing under the ever-lengthening shadow of Moscow."—*Christian Science Monitor.*

MARSHALL, ALFRED. *The Principles of Economics.* 1890. Often reprinted. Macmillan. Eighth edition, 1920. 871 pp.

"This book has had an immense influence and will remain a standard work for many years to come. It shows a pronounced reaction from the severe Individualism of most of the early economists, and, whilst no one would belittle its value in focussing and clarifying earlier thought, one may doubt whether the ultimate verdict of economists will regard the reaction that it heralded as entirely good."—PI.

MARTIN, EVERETT DEAN. *Liberty.* Norton. 1930. 307 pp.

The author seeks to arrive at the meaning of liberty partly through the method of historical survey. He discusses the Grecian conception, the contributions of Christianity and the Renaissance, of Rousseau, Voltaire, and others. In reviewing this book in *The Nation* of June 18, 1930, I wrote: "It is with misgivings that one approaches Everett Dean Martin's *Liberty.* These misgivings soon dissolve, however, before the flow of Mr. Martin's eloquence, his gift for felicitous and forcible statement, his attractive historical summaries, his broad, humane culture, his shrewd analysis and unfailing clarity. His *Liberty* is not perhaps a profound book or a remarkably original one, but it is none the less admirable. For in spite of the great existing classics, and of the fact that much of his argument is necessarily repetition, Mr. Martin has done a task that greatly needed to be done."

MENGER, KARL. *Principles of Economics.* Glencoe, Ill.: Free Press. 1950. 328 pp.

This epoch-making book, "one of the great landmarks in the development of economic thought," as Frank H. Knight calls it, had to wait seventy-nine years before it appeared in the present (or any other) English translation. The "Austrian School," of which Menger was the founder, was a fountainhead of classical liberalism on the European continent. F. A. Hayek, who calls Menger's *Principles* "the best introduction to the understanding of the theory of value which we possess," has also pointed out that Menger was "among the first in modern times consciously to revive the methodical individualism of Adam Smith and his school."

MIKOLAJCZYK, STANISLAW. *The Rape of Poland*. Whittlesey. 1948. 309 pp.

"The author, formerly Premier of Poland and head of the now suppressed Peasants' Party, witnessed what he calls the betrayal of his country from every political level, starting as a common soldier during the war in Poland. . . . After the war, he was helpless, even as a leader of one of the great parties, to avert the violent destruction of his country's democratic processes and finally had to flee in disguise. He believes that the Soviets were resolved from the first to annihilate Poland and says flatly that they killed fifteen thousand Polish officers in the woods around Katyn, near Smolensk, and that they purposely delayed giving help to General Bor during the Warsaw uprising until it was too late. . . . This book, heavily documented and written without fireworks, is a pretty powerful indictment."—*New Yorker*.

MILL, JOHN STUART. *Utilitarianism*. 1861. *On Liberty*. 1859. *Representative Government*. 1861. Many editions. (Dutton. 1950.) 532 pp.

"Three short but vital works. The first is outside our immediate purpose, being ethical, but it should be read; it reveals the mind of Mill perhaps better than any other of his works.

"*On Liberty* may be called the Individualist's textbook. It is a plea for allowing scope to individual character and action—even eccentricity is better than convention. Its whole argument should be carefully studied. There is also a concise and useful statement towards the end: 'The objections to government interference, when it is not such as to involve infringement of liberty, may be of three kinds. The first is when the thing to be done is likely to be better done by individuals than by the government. . . . The second . . . in many cases, though individuals may not do the particular thing so well, on the average, as the officers of government, it is nevertheless desirable that it should be done by them, rather than by the government, as a means to their own mental education.

"(Thus juries, 'free and popular local and municipal institutions,' and 'the conduct of industrial and philanthropical enterprises by voluntary associations,' are valuable on this principle as well as in themselves.)

" 'The third and most cogent reason for restricting the interference

of government is the great evil of adding unnecessarily to its power.'
Gladstone, with most of our Victorian statesmen, disliked increasing
the functions and expenditure of the State. He came to regard with
dismay the vigorous growth of the Income Tax, his own child, which
he had adopted from Peel, its actual father. He sometimes likens it to
a sword of excessive sharpness which is a dangerous weapon to en-
trust to a minister. He writes to Cobden in 1864 (Morley's *Gladstone*,
Book V, Chapter iv): 'I seriously doubt whether it [the spirit of ex-
penditure] will ever give place to the old spirit of economy, as long as
we have the income tax.' The income tax was then sevenpence in the
pound, and within fifteen months was to fall to fourpence, and a little
later to twopence!

"Mill's book *On Liberty* gives the pure doctrine of Individualism.
His excellent *Representative Government* does not bear so closely
upon our subject. The present Master of Balliol (Mr. A. D. Lindsay)
remarks: 'It reflects strikingly Mill's curious political position, com-
bining as it does, an enthusiastic belief in democratic government with
most pessimistic apprehensions as to what the democracy was likely to
do.' This is due to Mill's Individualism, for he saw that individual
freedom might incur great danger from majority rule in a Democracy.
It led him to attach much importance to such schemes as Hare's Proportional Representation, which he hoped would protect minorities
against tyrannical ignorance."—PI.

MILL, JOHN STUART. *Autobiography*. 1873. Many editions. (Columbia
    University Press. 1944. 240 pp.)

"All who study Individualism or any kind of economic or political
science must devote much careful consideration to Mill. This autobiographical masterpiece is too well known to require much comment.
It shows the influences to which Mill was subjected, his reactions, and
his invincible candor. It is pardonable to repeat that Mill's great object was not to found a sect but to discover truth, as far as it is dis-
coverable."—PI. (See also PACKE, MICHAEL ST. JOHN.)

MILL, JOHN STUART. *Principles of Political Economy*. 1848. Many
    editions. 1013 pp.

"Mill wrote this work at a time when Individualism had reached its
zenith, and its triumph was largely due to the efforts of his spiritual
and actual fathers, Bentham and James Mill. Thus this most important
work is, in the main, an exposition of Individualism. But J. S. Mill
here aims at stating his opponents' case, and so has given Socialists
the opportunity of citing him in their favor. In I, I, sec. 3, he makes an
amazing observation: 'If, therefore, the choice were to be made between Communism [Socialism] with all its chances, and the present
state of society with all its sufferings and injustices; if the institution of

private property necessarily carried with it as a consequence, that the produce of labor should be apportioned as we now see it, almost in an inverse ratio to the labor—the largest portions to those who have never worked at all, the next largest to those whose work is almost nominal, and so in a descending scale, the remuneration dwindling as the work grows harder and more disagreeable, until the most fatiguing and exhausting bodily labor cannot count with certainty on being able to earn even the necessaries of life; if this, or Communism, were the alternatives, all the difficulties, great or small, would be but as dust in the balance.'

"Again, Mill was so dominated by the Malthusian theory, that he was ready to adopt stringent Government measures to check over-population, e.g., by 'a great national measure of colonization.' (II, XIII, sec. 4.)

"Again we have his celebrated apology for occasional Protection when duties 'are imposed temporarily (especially in a young and rising nation) in hopes of naturalizing a foreign industry, in itself perfectly suitable to the circumstances of the country.' (V, X, sec. 1.)

"But the general spirit of the book is very strongly *laissez-faire*. The foregoing passages are exceptional. The following sentence is representative: 'The grounds of this truth are expressed with tolerable exactness in the popular dictum, that people understand their own business and their own interests better, and care for them more, than the government does, or can be expected to do.' (V, XI, sec. 5.) Throughout his life Mill believed, as he tersely expresses the truth in *Liberty,* that everyone ought to be allowed to do as he likes, provided that he does not make himself a nuisance to his neighbor. His candid mind brought forward numerous exceptions, but he steadily maintained his rule."—PI.

MILLAR, FREDERICK. *Socialism: Its Fallacies and Dangers.* London: Watts. 1907. 1923. 96 pp.

"This little shilling work was written to warn the public of the dangers of Socialism. It has chapters to show that it means material and national decay, the abolition of family life, its impossibility, etc. The writer has a healthy dislike of all kinds of Government interference. 'To attack wealth, to menace the free accumulation of private property, is like cutting open the bellows to see where the wind comes from. In this matter of wealth it comes from self-interest, and, therefore, the more you seek politically to prevent the free, unfraudulent, and unaggressive expression of self-interest, the less wind you will have to blow your fire, and consequently the worse off you will be."—PI.

MILTON, JOHN. *Areopagitica.* 1644. Many editions.

This written oration against censorship is the noblest of Milton's tracts, and one of the great documents on liberty. It is rich in magnificent sentences: "As good almost kill a man as kill a good book: who kills a man kills a reasonable creature, God's image; but he who destroys a good book kills reason itself." . . . "Who ever knew Truth put to the worse in a free and open encounter?" John Morley, in an article in the *Fortnightly Review* (August, 1873) wrote: "[John Stuart] Mill's memorable plea for social liberty was little more than an enlargement, though a very important enlargement, of the principles of the still more famous speech for liberty of unlicensed printing with which Milton enobled English literature two centuries before."

MISES, LUDWIG VON. *Human Action*. Yale University Press. 1949. 889 pp.

Reviewing this book in *Newsweek* of Sept. 19, 1949, I wrote: "*Human Action* is, in short, at once the most uncompromising and the most rigorously reasoned statement of the case for capitalism that has yet appeared. If any single book can turn the ideological tide that has been running in recent years so heavily toward statism, socialism and totalitarianism, *Human Action* is that book. It should become the leading text of everyone who believes in freedom, in individualism, and in the ability of a free-market economy not only to outdistance any government-planned system in the production of goods and services for the masses, but to promote and safeguard, as no collectivist tyranny can ever do, those intellectual, cultural, and moral values upon which all civilization ultimately rests."

MISES, LUDWIG VON. *Socialism*. 1936. Yale University Press. 1951. 599 pp.

Reviewing this book in *The New York Times* of Jan. 9, 1938, I wrote: "This book must rank as the most devastating analysis of socialism yet penned. Doubtless even some anti-socialist readers will feel that he occasionally overstates his case. On the other hand, even confirmed socialists will not be able to withhold admiration from the masterly fashion in which he conducts his argument. He has written an economic classic in our time."

MISES, LUDWIG VON. *The Theory of Money and Credit*. 1935. Yale University Press. 1953. 493 pp.

"In continental circles it has long been regarded as the standard textbook on the subject. . . . I know few works which convey a more profound impression of the logical unity and the power of modern economic analysis."—Lionel Robbins.

It may seem strange to include any work on money and credit in a bibliography concerned primarily with individual liberty. But Professor Mises shows here as elsewhere how mistaken monetary policies lead to the destruction of liberty. As F. A. Hayek has written, Mises "has been working since the early twenties on the reconstruction of a solid edifice of liberal thought in a more determined, systematic and successful way than anyone else."

MISES, LUDWIG VON. *Omnipotent Government*. Yale University Press. 1944. 291 pp.

In this book Professor von Mises provides an economic explanation of the international conflicts which caused both World Wars. He shows that economic nationalism and the trend toward economic self-sufficiency are the necessary outcome of present-day policies of government intervention in the private enterprises of citizens. He supports his analysis with an interpretation of the historical facts which both gave rise to Nazism and prevented Germany and the rest of the world from stopping until it was too late to do so without a frightful cost in blood and terror.

MISES, LUDWIG VON. *Bureaucracy*. Yale University Press. 1944. 125 pp.

Reviewing this book in *The New York Times* of Oct. 1, 1944, I wrote: "The main thesis of Professor von Mises is that bureaucracy is merely a symptom of the real disease with which we have to deal. That disease is excessive State domination and control. If the State seeks excessive control over the economic or other activities of the individual it is bound to need a bureaucracy to do it, and this bureaucracy is bound to function in a certain way. . . . Professor von Mises' penetrating analysis is closely reasoned. . . . Published on the day after F. A. Hayek's *The Road to Serfdom*, [it] once more calls attention to the ironic fact that the most eminent and uncompromising defenders of English liberty, and of the system of free enterprise which reached its highest development in America, should now be two Austrian exiles."

MISES, LUDWIG VON. *Planning for Freedom*. South Holland, Ill.: Libertarian Press. 1952. 174 pp.

This is a collection of twelve addresses and essays which supplement and present in simpler and shorter form the analyses of Professor von Mises in his great works on *Human Action* and *Socialism*. Readers without a special background in economic theory will find these essays not only rewarding in themselves but an excellent introduction to von Mises' work. The essays are: Planning for Freedom; Middle-of-the-Road Policy Leads to Socialism; Laissez-Faire or Dictatorship; Stones Into Bread, the Keynesian Miracle; Lord Keynes and Say's Law; Inflation and Price Control; Economic Aspects of the Pension Problem; Benjamin M. Anderson Challenges the Philosophy of the Pseudo-Progressives; Profit and Loss; Economic Teaching at the Universities; Trends Can Change; and The Political Chances of Genuine Liberalism.

MISES, LUDWIG VON. *Liberalismus.* Jena: Gustav Fischer. 1927. 175 pp.

This is a discussion of Liberalism (in the traditional sense of the term), of the political basis, economic policy and foreign policy appropriate to it, and of its probable future. There is an appendix on the literature of liberalism.

MISES, LUDWIG VON. *Kritik des Interventionismus.* Jena: Gustav Fischer. 1929. 136 pp.

Five collected essays discussing interventionism, restrictionism, price control, and the economic theories behind these policies.

MOLEY, RAYMOND. *How to Keep Our Liberty.* Knopf. 1952. 339 pp.

Raymond Moley, contributing editor of *Newsweek* magazine and professor of public law at Columbia University, created and headed the famous Brains Trust of Franklin D. Roosevelt's first campaign for the Presidency and later was a major architect of the early New Deal. His opposition to later developments in national policy culminated in this lucid and vigorous, but admirably organized and carefully thought-out, "conservative manifesto." "Today the people of this nation," he writes, "are presented with a choice between two forms of political and economic life. One form is that of our traditions, in which individual liberty prevails and is guarded by 'the long, still grasp of law.' The other is the dominance of the state in human affairs. My purpose here has been to present a plan for political action for those who do not wish to go down the road to socialism." Mr. Moley's book combines rich scholarship with the readability of first-rate journalism.

MONTESQUIEU, BARON DE. *The Spirit of Laws.* 1748. Many English and French editions. 2 vols.

The Baron de Montesquieu (1689-1755) published his famous *L'Esprit des Lois* in 1748. The *Encyclopaedia Britannica* declares that it "may be almost certainly ranked as the greatest book of the French Eighteenth Century." The political writer George Catlin thinks it "dull and prolix." To Montesquieu, however, is due the classical formulation of the doctrine of checks and balances, and of the division of powers.

Lytton Strachey writes of it in his *Landmarks in French Literature:* "It is enough to say that here all Montesquieu's qualities—his power of generalization, his freedom from prejudices, his rationalism, his love of liberty and hatred of fanaticism, his pointed, epigrammatic style—appear in their most characteristic form. Perhaps the chief fault of the book is that it is too brilliant. . . . Montesquieu's generalizations are always bold, always original, always fine; unfortunately, they are too often unsound into the bargain. . . . He believed he had found in [the English constitution] a signal instance of his favorite theory of the beneficial effects produced by the separation of the three powers of government—the judicial, the legislative, and the executive; but he was wrong. In England, as a matter of fact, the powers of the legislative and the executive were intertwined. This particular error has had a curious history. Montesquieu's great reputation led to his view of the constitution of England being widely accepted as the true one; as such it was adopted by the American leaders after the War of Independence; and its influence is plainly visible in the present constitution of the United States. Such is the strange power of good writing over the affairs of men!"

MONTGOMERY, GEORGE S., JR. *The Return of Adam Smith*. Caldwell, Idaho: Caxton Printers. 1949. 160 pp.

"This book is intended to serve as a little prayer for the awakening or—symbolically—for the return of Adam Smith." And it speculates upon how Adam Smith would probably feel and think about our present institutions. Mr. Montgomery discusses the merits and demerits of government-run business and re-evaluates such terms as "reactionary," "laissez faire," and "robber baron." He also points out vigorously the socialist and collectivist implications in many present-day textbooks, and particularly in some articles in the fifteen-volume *Encyclopaedia of the Social Sciences*.

MORGAN, CHARLES. *Liberties of the Mind*. Macmillan. 1951. 252 pp.

A collection of essays and addresses, some previously published elsewhere, several in the London *Times Literary Supplement*. The theme of the essays is what the author sees as the imminent danger of the loss of freedom of mind and moral choice, of individuality and identity, by the majority of mankind. "There can be scarcely a more important task than that which this book attempts, and perhaps no more encouraging and hopeful sign than that one of the greatest contemporary masters of English prose should be impelled to undertake it. . . . All that the mere student of these problems can do is to testify to the importance of the book and to acknowledge that here certainly the artist sees much to which the expert tends to be blind."—F. A. Hayek.

MORLEY, FELIX. *The Power in the People*. Van Nostrand. 1949. 293 pp.

In this scholarly, thoughtful and often brilliant book, Mr. Morley attempts to present a unified study of the origin of the political ideas on which our nation was founded, and how they have developed. "This is a remarkable book, nobly written and profoundly thought out. It is also, at least to this reviewer, sui generis, an account of the founding and development and significance of the American Republic which is unique as far as my acquaintance with the literature on the subject goes. . . . There is a fire in it which no survey of the past as the past could kindle. *The Power in the People* is a Tract for the Times, concerned with what is of paramount importance for us today, at this precise moment in our history."—Edith Hamilton, in *The Saturday Review of Literature.*

MORLEY, JOHN (VISCOUNT). *The Life of Richard Cobden.* 1881. London: Unwin. 1903. 985 pp.

The outstanding biography of the great Free Trader and leader of the Manchester School.

MORLEY, JOHN (VISCOUNT). *The Life of William Ewart Gladstone.* Macmillan. 1911. 3 vols.

A masterly biography of the great nineteenth century liberal statesman.

MORLEY, JOHN (VISCOUNT). *Voltaire.* Macmillan. 1872. 365 pp.

"Morley's *Voltaire* fully appreciates the influence of Locke and English Individualism upon Voltaire."—PI.

MOSCA, GAETANO. *The Ruling Class.* McGraw-Hill. 1939. 514 pp.

This is an English translation, with some reorganization of the material, from the 1923 edition of the work of the eminent Italian political philosopher first published in 1895. The Italian title is *Elementi di Scienza Politica.* It contains an illuminating chapter on the political character of collectivism. "This work, already a classic in Europe, deserves the widest attention in America."—*Foreign Affairs.* "The picture Mosca gives of the ruling class, of politics and of political behavior is one which students in these fields cannot afford to neglect." —A. T. Mason, in the *Survey Graphic.*

MUSSATTI, JAMES. *The Constitution of the United States.* Van Nostrand. 1956. 173 pp.

A short, simple and admirably organized statement of the basic principles of the American Constitution. Its intent is to explain to the layman the philosophies, motives, and actions of the framers of that great document. It is accompanied by full bibliographic references, and a study guide prepared by Thomas J. Shelly.

MUTHESIUS, VOLKMAR. *Müssen wir arm bleiben?* Frankfurt a. M., Germany. 1952.

A discussion by a courageous and outspoken German liberal, who is devoted to the principles of the free market, of the postwar problems of his country.

NEWBURY, FRANK D. *The American Economic System.* McGraw-Hill. 1950.

Designed as a textbook on the basic institutions and principles of the American economic system. Among those institutions and principles the author stresses private property; individual freedom of choice and action; individual responsibility for success or failure; free and active competition; and the principle of economic rewards proportional to economic contribution.

NEWCOMB, SIMON. *Principles of Political Economy.* Harper. 1886.

Schumpeter says of Simon Newcomb: "He was an eminent astronomer who also taught, and wrote on, economics but not enough to acquire the influence he deserved. His *Principles of Political Economy* is the outstanding performance of American general economics in the pre-Clark-Fisher-Taussig epoch. His presentation was masterly and highly suggestive, also original in several points."

His rugged individualism and his vivid illustrations are often reminiscent of Bastiat. He emphasizes the "let-alone principle" and the "keep-out principle": "The one claims that the government should not stop the citizen from acting; the other that it should keep out of certain fields of action."

NICHOLSON, J. S. *The Revival of Marxism.* Dutton. 1921. 145 pp.

"A ruthless criticism and exposure of Marxism. Marx's writings are shown to have contributed nothing of tangible value to the world's knowledge. Insofar as they are original they are false."—PI.

NOCK, ALBERT J. *Our Enemy, the State.* 1935. (Caldwell, Idaho: Caxton Printers. 1946.) 209 pp.

The author develops the theme that the State is founded on conquest and confiscation and tends to devour civilization. He foresaw "ever-increasing corruption, inefficiency and prodigality" under State domination which will lead us to impoverishment and "a system of forced labor." Some of Nock's ideas were extreme and tended toward anarchism. But his style combined urbanity with vigor.

NORTH, SIR DUDLEY. *Discourses upon Trade.* London. 1691.

"He exposes the fallacies of the Mercantile Theory and is an advocate—one of the earliest—of Free Trade. . . . 'A nation in the world, as to trade, is in all respects like a citizen in a kingdom, or a family in a city.' Therefore trade between nations ought to be left free and not loaded with restrictions, as is the present practice of rulers. The following sentence might have been written by Fawcett or any of his fellow economists: 'There can be no trade unprofitable to the public, for if any prove so, men leave it off, and whenever traders thrive, the public, of which they are a part, thrive also."—PI.

NORTON, THOMAS J. *The Constitution of the United States.* 1922. (New York: America's Future. 1951.) 319 pp.

An elementary reference work, designed not for the legal profession but "to make accessible to the citizen . . . such a knowledge of the Constitution of the United States as will serve in emergency as a 'first line of defense.' " The text of the Constitution is printed in boldface type, followed by a note to every line or clause "that has a historical story or drama back of it" or that otherwise calls for interpretation in the light of court decisions. The book has been kept up-to-date by numerous printings. "I know of no book which so completely and coherently explains our form of government."—James M. Beck, former Solicitor General of the United States.

NORTON, THOMAS J. *Undermining the Constitution.* Devin-Adair. 1950. 351 pp.

"The author, who in the twenties published a standard commentary on the constitution, calls his new commentary a 'history of lawless government' and cites case after case to support his charge that 'clever, irresponsible men' have been doing their best to demolish the Constitution and popular government along with it. As examples of how the intent of the writers of the Constitution has been 'demolished,' Mr. Norton discusses such matters as the TVA, the agricultural adjustment act, the national labor relations act, the child labor law, the assumption by Washington of much police power originally held by the several states, the influence of the Supreme Court in creating new laws, and the loss of congressional power to the executive."—*Springfield Republican.*

NUTTER, G. WARREN. *The Extent of Enterprise Monopoly in the United States, 1899-1939.* University of Chicago Press. 1951. 169 pp.

A careful and detailed statistical study. Professor Nutter concludes that there is no basis for the impression that there has been a significant increase in monopoly in the United States since about 1900.

NYARADI, NICHOLAS. *My Ringside Seat in Moscow.* Crowell. 1952. 307 pp.

"A report on a most melancholy mission to Moscow, written by the last non-Communist Finance Minister of Hungary. Mr. Nyaradi went to Russia in 1947 to negotiate with the Kremlin a two-hundred-million-dollar Russian claim against his government. . . . He got it reduced, but it took him seven months to do so, and by that time the Communists had infested his government and the claim had become academic."—*New Yorker.* "From one point of view this book can be read as a rollicking account of Moscow life, with its strange contrasts between the abysmal poverty of the many and the sybaritic life of the rulers . . . More important, however, Nyaradi gives us a glimpse of some key figures in the Politburo and near Politburo levels of Soviet life."—Harry Schwartz, in *The New York Times.*

ONEAL, JAMES, AND WERNER, G. A. *American Communism.* Dutton. 1947. 416 pp.

"A revision and extension of Oneal's same title published in 1927 by the Rand School. To the original thirteen chapters now slightly revised, Werner adds nine, covering events since original publication. . . . The original sections are careful and judicious, the latter, somewhat less so; but the documented whole adds up to a clear picture of the development of Communism in the United States which the authors insist is not a political party in our sense but an agency of the Russian Dictatorship."—*Library Journal.*

OPPENHEIMER, FRANZ. *The State.* Huebsch. 1922. 302 pp.

"This brilliant political study is simultaneously readable, brief and profound."—Felix Morley.

ORME, ALEXANDREA. *Comes the Comrade.* Morrow. 1950. 376 pp.

Beginning with Dec. 22, 1944, this diary of a Polish woman, "Lida," married to a Hungarian aristocrat, covers the days to March 28, 1945. During that time the Russians were supposed to have "liberated" that section of Hungary. At first Lida had welcomed the Russians, but as it became apparent that their ideas of liberation were very crude, she devoted all her time and intelligence to the task of keeping one step ahead of them. "If one can imagine a group of Roman patricians caught by an invading flood of Goths and Vandals one can appreciate the situation which Mrs. Orme describes with courage, wit and vivacity. . . . There could hardly be a better close-up view of the Soviet overrunning of Eastern Europe."—W. H. Chamberlin, in the *Chicago Sunday Tribune.*

ORTON, WILLIAM AYLOTT. *The Liberal Tradition.* Yale University Press. 1945. 317 pp.

This bears the subtitle: "A Study of the Social and Spiritual Conditions of Freedom." "In an era that speaks so glibly and so hopelessly of the inevitability of collectivization, Professor Orton casts a favorite-son vote for freedom."—H. T. Maguire, in *Commonweal.*

ORTON, WILLIAM AYLOTT. *The Economic Role of the State*. University of Chicago Press. 1950. 192 pp.

A discussion of the basis and limitations of government action. John Chamberlain writes: "Orton's view is that the best society is the one in which people put their reliance on the voluntary action of autonomous non-state social groups. He brings us back to the central lack of modern man, which is philosophy. He himself is evidently in accord with the Catholic philosophy of economics and government. But he is so persistently oblique in his phraseology that he often leaves the reader in doubt as to how he would apply Catholic philosophy in given instances."

ORWELL, GEORGE. *Nineteen Eighty-Four*. Harcourt, Brace. 1949. 314 pp.

A satirical novel about a future time when men and women living in a collectivist society are constantly spied upon through "tele-screens," and drilled by a Thought Police into thinking that war is peace, that ignorance is strength, and that freedom is slavery. Orwell was the foremost satirist of our time. *Nineteen Eighty-Four* portrays with classic power and finality the intellectual paralysis and spiritual depravity that a totalitarian regime imposes. But except for its vivid picture of the dreadful end-results for consumers, it leaves the determining *economic* aspect of such a totalitarian society virtually blank.

Orwell in an earlier book (*The Lion and the Unicorn: Socialism and the English Genius;* Secker & Warburg: 1941) had argued for a special "English socialism." With his increasing disillusionment he ceased to be a communist sympathizer, and, in the end (some time after writing *Animal Farm*), even to be a socialist. In *Nineteen Eighty-Four* he ridiculed his own former ideas by his sarcastic references to "Ingsoc" (the short name in his collectivist society for English socialism). But so bitter and complete had been Orwell's previous hatred of "capitalism" that he never came to understand the real nature and effects of free private enterprise. This, I think, is why *Nineteen Eighty-Four* could only end on a note of utter despair. Yet the book presents an unforgettable picture of what collectivism leads to.

ORWELL, GEORGE. *Animal Farm*. Harcourt, Brace. 1946. 118 pp.

The animals on Mr. Jones's farm stage a successful revolution and take the place over. The revolution begins to go wrong—yet ingenious excuses are always forthcoming for each perversion of the original doctrine. This fable is the vehicle for a brilliant satire on the actual course of the Russian communist revolution up to the time when *Animal Farm* appeared. Unfortunately, much in this satire implies the familiar socialist view that the Russian revolution was perhaps a necessary method of putting a great ideal into effect, but that the revolution was "betrayed" by Stalin through selfishness and abuse of power and a return to capitalist ideals. These implications spoil the satire for individualists and believers in free enterprise. In *Nineteen Eighty-Four* Orwell was to become far more disillusioned with socialism than he is here.

PACKE, MICHAEL ST. JOHN. *The Life of John Stuart Mill.* Macmillan. 1954. 567 pp.

An admirable biography of the great nineteenth century liberal economist and philosopher. It carries the reader along like a first-rate novel, yet Mr. Packe never invents conversations or inner thoughts, but supplies documentation for all his statements. Readers of Mill's *Autobiography* will find Mr. Packe's book an almost indispensable supplement; it throws entirely new light on Mill's life and character, and supplements the material in the *Autobiography* at a hundred points, while repeating surprisingly little. "For eighty years after his death," writes F. A. Hayek in a preface, "no satisfactory biography of Mill has been available. In many ways, the unique value of his own description of his intellectual development has increased rather than diminished the need for a more comprehensive account of the setting against which it ought to be seen. Until recently, the material on which such a picture could be based was not available. . . . There may still be details to be filled in here and there; but on the whole I feel that Mr. Packe has given us the definitive biography of Mill for which we have so long been waiting."

PAINE, THOMAS. *Common Sense.* 1776. Many editions. 129 pp.
———. *The Rights of Man.* 1791. Many editions. 389 pp.

"Paine's *Common Sense* helped to inspire the Declaration of Independence, while *The Rights of Man* raised a great outcry among the admirers of the British Constitution. He was a bold champion of individual as well as of national independence."—PI.

PAINE, THOMAS. *The Complete Writings of Thomas Paine.* Edited by Philip S. Foner. New York: The Citadel Press. 1945. 2 vols.

These two volumes contain, among other writings, both *Common Sense* and *The Rights of Man.* "At once the fullest, the most inexpensive, and the most usable edition of Paine that has yet been published."—Allan Nevins, in *The New York Times.*

PALGRAVE, R. H. INGLIS (ed.). *Dictionary of Political Economy.* Macmillan. 1918. 3 vols. 2,525 pp.

"An indispensable work of reference. The article on Individualism should be studied."—PI.

PALMER, CECIL. *The British Socialist Ill-fare State*. Caldwell, Idaho: Caxton Printers. 1952. 656 pp.

A study of the shortcomings of the British welfare state, which examines the State's challenge to individual liberties, nationalized medicine, and the nationalization of industries and utilities. The author was a former British publisher and lecturer, and was the organizer of the Society of Individualists. He died in January 1952.

PALYI, MELCHIOR. *The Dollar Dilemma*. Regnery. 1954. 208 pp.

In this vigorous, well-informed and penetrating book, the author argues that American dollar aid to Europe and elsewhere has done more harm than good. He contends that it has financed socialism, planned and directed economies, excessive social security and wealth distribution systems, the destruction of incentives and the promotion of inefficiency. Dr. Palyi was born in Hungary but since 1933 has lived in America, where he has been active as a research economist.

PALYI, MELCHIOR. *Compulsory Medical Care and the Welfare State*. Chicago: National Institution of Professional Services. 1949. 156 pp.

An analysis based on a special study of governmentalized medical care systems on the continent of Europe and in England.

PARKES, HENRY BAMFORD. *Marxism: An Autopsy*. Houghton Mifflin. 1939. 300 pp.

Reviewing this book in *The New York Times* of April 7, 1940, I wrote: "Mr. Parkes's autopsy . . . cannot compare in depth, penetration and rigor of thought with von Mises' masterly refutation of socialism, to the extent that the two volumes cover similar ground. But it is an important volume and one of the ablest direct replies to Marxism ever to appear in America. . . . In his attempt to formulate a constructive program Mr. Parkes is less happy."

PATERSON, ISABEL. *The God of the Machine*. Putnam. 1943. 292 pp.

The author argues that only free men, in a free economy of private property, can maintain "the long circuit of energy" that makes civilization work. Collectivism, she contends, does not and cannot work. The book is acute, pungent, epigrammatic, full of original insights and sometimes powerfully eloquent. (The chapter "The Humanitarian with the Guillotine" is an outstanding example.) But much of the thinking and style of the work are marred by a persistent and obsessive effort to write of man's economic, political and moral problems on the analogy and in the vocabulary of the flow of electrical energy.

PATON, WILLIAM A. *Shirtsleeve Economics.* Appleton-Century-Crofts. 1952. 460 pp.

A highly successful effort, by an eminent accountant and professor of economics at the University of Michigan, to present "a common sense survey" of economics in easily understandable terms. "The central proposition of this book," declares the author, "is very simple: We can't consume any more than we produce and only through increased production is a higher standard of living possible. This has an important corollary: We must be everlastingly on our guard to check those influences and developments that tend to limit and discourage production. Among such is 'social legislation' which emphasizes diversion only, without regard to what happens to output."

PERCY OF NEWCASTLE, LORD. *The Heresy of Democracy.* Regnery. 1955.

The author, a British statesman and scholar, shows how democracy, in the sense of a temporary majority sentiment, may be corrupted and frozen into totalitarian forms. His book deals with such basic questions as the growth of state power, the relation of the individual to the state, and the dangers of demagogic mass manipulation. "It is possible," he warns, "for multiplied legislation, whether by Act of Parliament or dictatorial decree, to destroy the very conception of law. . . . Under the best laws much governed men are less free than lightly governed men. For, whenever the law converts (as it often must) an obligation to a fellow-citizen into an obligation to the state it substitutes a claim to obedience for the give-and-take of mutual rights and duties between individuals."

PETROV, VLADIMIR. *Soviet Gold.* Farrar, Straus & Young. 1949. 426 pp.

"A sixteen-year-old boy writes his political thoughts into a diary. Three years later a lady friend turns against him and plants anti-Soviet books in his room. The young fellow is caught in the net of the vast purges of the mid-1930's. Terror-stricken ex-friends denounce him. It all adds up to a fat NKVD dossier, a six-year sentence to heavy labor, and an odyssey that leads through the prisons of Leningrad to the labor camps and gold mines of Siberia. That's what happened to Vladimir Petrov. That is the story he tells."—*Saturday Review of Literature.*

PETROV, VLADIMIR. *My Retreat from Russia.* Yale University Press. 1950. 357 pp.

In his earlier book, *Soviet Gold,* the author gave an account of his six years in the forced labor camps in Siberia. In the present volume he describes his activities after his release at the time of the outbreak of the war. He worked his way back to his home in Russia proper, where he discovered that as an ex-prisoner he was no longer considered a trusted citizen. Thence he fled through Central Europe into American-occupied Italy.

PETTENGILL, S. B. *Jefferson, the Forgotten Man.* America's Future, Inc. 1938. 249 pp.

"Mr. Pettengill is a member of Congress from Indiana and one of those Democrats who, enthusiastic in their support of the first New Deal, looked with misgiving on the second; his attitude toward the third New Deal is one of dismay. In a vigorous style, with ample reference to Jefferson's principles and precepts and to those of other eminent mentors, including the President himself, he explains this." —W. M. Houghton, in *Books.*

PETTY, SIR WILLIAM. *A Treatise on Taxes.* 1662. Many editions. 75 pp.

"This and Petty's other works are of much historical interest. Like North, later in the century, Petty anticipated Adam Smith in his exposition of Free Trade."—PI.

PHILBRICK, HERBERT A. *I Led Three Lives.* McGraw-Hill. 1952. 323 pp.

"The now-it-can-be-told story of Herbert Philbrick, 'Citizen, Communist, Counterspy,' who testified before Judge Medina against The Eleven after nine years of conspiracy, uncertainty, and deliberate penetration into the Communist Party."—Virginia Kirkus. "The real significance lies in the clarification it brings to Communist purposes and achievements through indirect infiltration."—E. B. Canham, in the *New York Herald Tribune.*

PICK, FRANZ. *Black Market Yearbook.* 1951, etc. Pick's World Currency Report. 160 pp.

Since 1951 Dr. Franz Pick has published a yearbook on world black-market prices and trading in currencies and gold. His book is dedicated "to the more than 2,000,000,000 victims of inflation, who, for obeying the law, have been punished by the law." He declares in his foreword: "Distrust of every system of planned economy, fictional official values of gold, currency, and government bonds cannot be wiped out. People cannot and will not accept arbitrary confiscation through inflation, as practiced by every government in the world today." In his 1954 edition he points out: "At the beginning of 1954, nine-tenths of the world's population were legally denied freedom to transfer their assets into less diseased monies."

PILAT, OLIVER RAMSEY. *The Atom Spies.* Putnam. 1952. 312 pp.

"An exhaustive account of how the Communist spy network succeeded, with disturbing ease, in relieving the United States of the

biggest military secret in history. It is a complicated story, dealing not
only with the machinations of the spies but also with their motives
. . . Mr. Pilat focusses attention on this ideological aspect of the case,
and on the clear and continuing danger of having among us an amor-
phous group of people who can be persuaded at any time to betray
their country for what they are told are super-patriotic reasons."—
New Yorker.

POIROT, PAUL LEWIS. *The Pension Idea*. Irvington, N. Y.: Foundation
for Economic Education. 1950.

The author points out that there is not nearly enough total capital
or savings in any nation to support in retirement all citizens over 65,
and hence there cannot be a fully funded pension plan covering
everybody. The unfunded "social security" promises can only mean
either further inflation, taxes upon private savings, or further attempts to tax the earnings of future citizens.

POLANYI, MICHAEL. *The Contempt of Freedom*. London: Watts. 1940.
116 pp.

Essays about the Russian experiment and its consequences. It includes: *The Rights and Duties of Science* (1939); *Collectivist Planning* (1940); *Soviet Economics—Fact and Theory* (1935); *Truth and
Propaganda* (1936).

POPPER, K. R. *The Open Society and Its Enemies*. Vol. I: *The Spell of
Plato*. Vol. II: *The High Tide of Prophecy: Hegel, Marx and the
Aftermath*. London: Routledge. 1945. 2 vols. 268 pp. 352 pp.
(Princeton University Press. 1950. 744 pp.)

The author, Reader in Logic and Scientific Method in the University of London, demonstrates that Plato, Hegel, and Marx formu-
lated ideas in political philosophy inimical to the "Open Society,"
i.e., to a society based on reason and not on myth. The encomiums
with which this book was greeted on its British publication in 1945
were for the most part fully deserved. Certainly we can agree with
Sir Ernest Barker that "There is an abundance of riches in the book
—classical scholarship, scientific acumen, logical subtlety, philosophic
sweep." Bertrand Russell thought it: "A work of first class importance
. . . which ought to be widely read for its masterly criticism of
the . . . enemies of democracy, ancient and modern. . . . His attack
on Plato, while unorthodox, is in my opinion thoroughly justified.
. . . His analysis of Hegel is deadly. . . . Marx is dissected with equal
acumen."

The book is weak, however, on the economic side. Dr. Popper gives
Marx undeserved credit for his alleged services to "social justice." He
is himself capable of saying that Marx was "right in asserting that

increasing misery tends to be the result of *laissez-faire* capitalism."
This is because Dr. Popper has in his own mind a mere caricature
called *"laissez-faire* capitalism," as Marx had. In spite of this weakness
there are so many merits in the book that we must set it down as
powerful and important.

POSSONY, STEFAN THOMAS. *Century of Conflict*. Regnery. 1953. 439 pp.

"The author, Professor of International Politics at Georgetown University, traces the Communist techniques in revolution from 1848. Beginning with Marx, he depicts the story of Communist efforts in Western Europe, the Russian Revolution, Communist tactics between the
wars, and Communist internal and external aggression since the war.
He outlines the methods, both from without and from within, by
which he believes the Communists hope to win a war with the United
States."—*Current History.* "An invaluable storehouse of first-hand
information."—W. H. Chamberlin, in the *Chicago Sunday Tribune.*

POUND, ROSCOE. *The Rise of the Service State and Its Consequences.*
New Wilmington, Pa.: The Economic and Business Foundation.
1949. 34 pp.

This is a devastating analysis, by the former dean of the Harvard
Law School and one of the world's great authorities on jurisprudence,
of "the service state, the state which, instead of preserving peace and
order and employing itself with maintaining the general security,
takes the whole domain of human welfare for its province and would
solve all economic and social ills through its administrative activities."

Dean Pound's pamphlet is included in this list, in violation of my
announced general rule against including pamphlets, in the hope that
some publisher may be inspired to publish it in book form, together
with a score of the same author's other pamphlets and articles on
kindred topics, now scattered in the files of a dozen legal journals.
These would include such articles as *The Disappearance of Law,
Dangers in Administrative Absolutism,* and *Administrative Agencies
and the Law.*

POUND, ROSCOE. *Justice According to Law*. Yale University Press. 1951.
98 pp.

This small book consists of three lectures by Roscoe Pound, dean
emeritus of the Harvard Law School, on What Is Justice?, What Is
Law?, and Judicial Justice. The book is a wise, scholarly and compact survey of the philosophy of law, a plea for the rule of law rather
than for widened administrative discretion, and a defense of the justice of the courts as against that of administrative or other substitute
agencies. Dean Pound defends the rule of law also as the guardian
of individual liberty. "The real foe of [governmental] absolutism is

law. It presupposes a life measured by reason, a legal order measured by reason, and a judicial process carried on by applying a reasoned technique to experience developed by reason and reason tested by experience."

POUND, ROSCOE. *Administrative Law*. University of Pittsburgh Press. 1942. 138 pp.

"To the growing attacks on current developments in administrative justice, Roscoe Pound adds the weight of history and philosophy in a volume that is one of the more succinct and reasoned analyses of the shortcomings of administrative justice unrestrained by the traditions and processes of the common law as administered by regularly constituted courts. Proceeding from the assumption that the common law is a taught tradition of the supremacy of law, of individual rights, and of adjudication instead of administration, Dean Pound denies the idea that 'whatever is done officially is law.' Administrative law, so-called, is, therefore, but a species of justice without law, lacking the restraints of judicial procedure and the techniques of decision inherent in that 'artificial reason' of the law."—*American Political Science Review*.

POUND, ROSCOE. *New Paths of The Law*. University of Nebraska Press. 1950. 69 pp.

Three lectures delivered at the University of Nebraska in 1950, which marked the opening of a lectureship established in honor of Roscoe Pound. The lectures discuss, respectively, "The Path of Liberty," "The Humanitarian Path," and "The Authoritarian Path."

PROTHERO, MICHAEL. *Political Economy*. London: George Bell. 1895. 266 pp.

"This is meant for beginners, who will find it most useful. Two chapters, 'Alternative Schemes to Private Property,' and, especially, 'Theoretic Ideas about Economic Facts,' give more serviceable information than perhaps will be found, in a concise form, in any other book."—PI.

QUEENY, EDGAR M. *The Spirit of Enterprise*. Scribner's. 1943. 267 pp.

It is the spirit of enterprise exercised by individuals and voluntary groups, according to the author, who is chairman of the board of the Monsanto Chemical Company, that has made America grow. The kind of social planning advocated by New Dealers, he contends, can lead only to a lower standard of living and a loss of liberty. "This book is a magnificent indication that business is finding its voice. In the public debate over what kind of social and economic system the U. S.

should have, the professional theorists on the left have done most of the talking during the past decade. Now comes a businessman with a fluent pen and a vigorous set of convictions to take up the cudgels for free enterprise."—Claude Robinson.

QUESNAY, FRANÇOIS. *Tableau économique.* 1758. 216 pp.

"A man of great importance among French Physiocrats; he was physician to Louis XV, and a man of noble character; he had much influence on Turgot, the wise minister of Louis XVI. Accounts of him and his school are given in all economic histories. His doctrine, which was carefully studied by Adam Smith, is briefly: Let entire freedom of commerce be maintained; for the regulation of commerce, both internal and external, the most sure, the most exact, the most profitable to the nation, and to the State, consists in entire freedom of competition."—PI.

RAE, JOHN. *Contemporary Socialism.* 1884. Scribner's. 1905. 555 pp.

"A very useful and fairly full history of modern Socialism beginning with Lassalle and Marx. The point of view is strongly Individualistic, but the writer sees the necessity of constructive action. He remarks: "Free institutions run continual risk of shipwreck when power is in the possession of the many, but property—from whatever cause—the enjoyment of the few. With the advance of democracy a diffusion of wealth becomes almost a necessity of State."—PI.

RAND, AYN. *Anthem.* 1938. (Caldwell, Idaho: Caxton Press. 1946.) 105 pp.

This book, first published in England in 1938, is a striking predecessor of Orwell's *Nineteen Eighty-Four.* "*Anthem* records the life of a rebel against the totalitarian order, a man named Equality 7-2521, who rejects the collectivist Utopia. He dwells in a society which, by deliberately destroying independence of mind, has laid waste all the achievement of earlier civilizations—a world which has banned as criminal the singular pronoun and all talk of 'The Unmentionable Times.' The Council of Vocations . . . proclaims him a street-sweeper. Secretly working underground in the shafts of former days, he rediscovers electricity. He defies the world of State-planned eugenics and State-directed mating and discovers a personal love. Among a people which exists to serve a soulless State, he discovers that the pursuit of his own happiness conjointly advances the happiness of his fellows. He is denounced, imprisoned and tortured, but his spirit cannot be conquered. *Anthem* is at once an exaltation of liberty and an exhortation to the counter-attack."—Deryck Abel.

RAND, AYN. *The Fountainhead.* Bobbs-Merrill. 1943. 754 pp.

This novel about an uncompromising architect is based on a belief in "the importance of selfishness." Its theme is that man's ego is the fountainhead of human progress. Many will think the author's intransigent type of individualism extreme, but the novel is exciting and impressive.

RANDALL, CLARENCE B. *A Creed for Free Enterprise.* Little, Brown. 1952. 177 pp.

An admirable book on American business and businessmen by the president of the Inland Steel Company. "Should do much in counteracting the untruthful and insidious propaganda of the socialists against free enterprise."—The Rev. A. Keller, in *The Freeman.*

RANDALL, CLARENCE B. *A Foreign Economic Policy for the United States.* University of Chicago Press. 1954. 83 pp.

A plea for the removal of barriers and the liberalization of international trade by a distinguished businessman who is also a vigorous thinker and writer.

RAPPARD, WILLIAM E. *The Secret of American Prosperity.* Greenberg. 1955. 124 pp.

This book originally appeared in French as an attempt by an eminent Swiss economist to explain the secret of American prosperity to other Europeans. In my foreword to the American edition I wrote: "Among the qualities that make it remarkable . . . are not only the generosity with which it acknowledges and insists upon the economic superiority of the United States, but the still rarer generosity with which it attributes this superiority not merely to good luck—such as great natural resources or escape from the direct destruction of the two world wars (the usual European explanation)—but primarily to the character and the free economic institutions of the American people, to our greater efficiency and to our greater competitive spirit." The book is lucid and admirably organized. It may serve as an indirect reminder to Americans that their own economic achievement has been the result, above all, of a free, dynamic, private, competitive economy, and can be preserved only by preserving this type of economy.

RAPPARD, WILLIAM E. *The Crisis of Democracy.* University of Chicago Press. 1938. 288 pp.

An analysis of democracy: its definition, sources, and probable longevity. While he "does not despair of modern democracy, [the author] rather questions the solidity and the longevity of modern dictatorships."—From the Foreword.

RAVINES, EUDOCIO. *The Yenan Way*. Scribner's. 1951. 319 pp.

"A sort of *mea culpa* by a man who was until recently one of the top Communist organizers in South America. Mr. Ravines, a Peruvian, studied his peculiar art in the same Comintern schools in Moscow that Klement Gottwald and Mao Tse-tung attended. He was one of the major figures in the South American Bureau of the Comintern and was very active in the Spanish Civil War. It was while he was on Comintern duty in Spain that he began to lose faith in the world revolution and in revolutionists, and began to see Stalin for what he is, rather than as the workers' messiah. Altogether, an important, instructive, and astonishingly specific book."—*New Yorker*.

READ, LEONARD E. *Government—An Ideal Concept*. Irvington, N. Y.: Foundation for Economic Education. 1954. 149 pp.

Leonard Read argues that the purpose of government is to use "defensive force" to neutralize "aggressive force"; and that government can have no legitimate function beyond that. He applies this principle to such subjects as socialism, taxation, conscription, world government, efforts to increase trade or prevent depressions, money, public housing, foreign aid, education and religion.

READ, LEONARD E. *Outlook for Freedom*. Irvington, N. Y.: Foundation for Economic Education. 1951.

This small volume contains an allegorical report of the ideas and experiences, failures and successes, of many associates and friends of the author during the last two decades, and relates it to the concept of individual liberty. "The substance for a thorough-going, twentieth century intellectual revolution," he writes, "is in the making, and is showing a vitality that can be accounted for only by the inextinguishable spirit of individualism—the insistence of man to complete his own creation. That this spirit at present is evident among only a minority need not necessarily deject the devotee of liberty. Everything begins with a minority of one, extends to a few, and then to many."

RICARDO, DAVID. *Principles of Political Economy and Taxation*. 1817. Many editions. 538 pp.

The work of this brilliant deductive thinker has been used to draw such corollaries as extreme *laissez faire,* the single tax, and Marxism! In 1952 *The Works and Correspondence of David Ricardo* were published in nine volumes under the careful and scholarly editorship of Piero Sraffa with the collaboration of M. H. Dobb. "Ricardo is more the father of Victorian Political Economy (hated by Ruskin and Carlyle) than either Adam Smith or John Stuart Mill."—PI.

RICHTER, EUGENE. *Pictures of the Socialistic Future.* 1893. London: Jarrolds. 1925. 134 pp.

"A satirical account of an imaginary Socialist regime by an eminent German. It is very interesting when read in conjunction with the earlier works of Robert Blatchford. Sir Ernest Benn writes in the introduction: 'The really extraordinary thing about this book is that it was written and first published more than thirty years ago, in 1893. It is not, however, published afresh now on account of its interest as a piece of prophecy, but rather because of the remarkable way in which it fits in every detail the problem of Socialism as it presents itself to us in 1925.' "—PI.

RIST, CHARLES. *Défense de l'Or.* Paris: Recueil Sirey. 1953. 120 pp.

A collection of articles appearing over eight years in favor of a return to the international gold standard in place of present "managed" paper money systems.

ROBBINS, LIONEL. *The Great Depression.* Macmillan. 1934. 238 pp.

In reviewing this book in *The New York Times* of Nov. 18, 1934, I wrote: "If Mr. Robbins's economic philosophy is 'discredited' and 'outmoded,' it is not because he is a bleary old man with an ossified brain. He is, to be sure, a professor, and his acquaintance with the work of the classical economists has no doubt poisoned his mind, but he is still only 35, and writes with as much clarity and vigor as J. M. Keynes or John Strachey. What he himself is sometimes pleased to call his 'orthodox' economics, indeed, will seem very unorthodox to those who are fairly well acquainted with contemporary British economic thought."

ROBBINS, LIONEL. *Economic Planning and International Order.* Macmillan. 1937. 330 pp.

Reviewing this volume in *The New York Times* of Aug. 1, 1937, I wrote: "Altogether, Mr. Robbins's short volume is one of the ablest and most vigorous statements in recent years of the orthodox liberal position, as it is one of the most uncompromising and damaging analyses of the whole philosophy of planning. Professor Robbins is deeply grounded; he uses the tools of classical economic analysis like a fine surgeon; he moves deliberately from step to step with relentless logic; and he writes a lucid and compact prose."

ROBBINS, LIONEL. *The Theory of Economic Policy in English Classical Political Economy.* Macmillan. 1952. 217 pp.

Professor Robbins here presents in broad outline the theory of economic policy held by the leading English classical economists—notably Hume, Adam Smith, Bentham, Malthus, Ricardo, Senior, Torrens,

McCulloch and the two Mills. It is the author's conviction that the views of the classical economists on economic policy have been gravely misrepresented in contemporary discussion, on the one hand by presenting them as being callous to or neglectful of humane considerations, such as the problems of unemployment and poverty, on the other hand as carrying the doctrine of *laissez faire* further than they actually did. But Dr. Robbins does emphasize their general adherence to "the System of Economic Freedom." This "was not just a detached recommendation not to interfere," but "an urgent demand that . . . hampering and anti-social impediments should be removed and that the immense potential of free pioneering individual initiative should be released." Dr. Robbins's book is written with great lucidity and charm, out of a rich and accurate scholarship. It contains an excellent index.

ROBBINS, LIONEL. *The Economic Basis of Class Conflict*. Macmillan. 1939. 277 pp.

A collection of essays united by a common theme—an analysis of the way in which forms of organization facilitating group exclusiveness may be the cause of social disharmony. The author contends that the real modern tendency of the West is not so much "collectivism" as syndicalism or corporativism. The book also discusses the causes of increased protectionism, the consequences of agricultural planning, and the general vices of restrictionism. In reviewing it in *The New York Times* of Oct. 22, 1939, I wrote: "Readers of Professor Robbins will find here, as in his previous volumes, vigor of style, rigor of thought and an uncompromising liberalism."

ROBBINS, LIONEL. *The Economic Causes of War*. London: Cape. 1939. 124 pp.

"The chief British exponent of neo-classical economics writes in his usual lucid and suave way about war. He carries on his long standing feud with Marxian theory, and rejects any basic connection between war and capitalist imperialism."—*The New Republic*. "A masterpiece of sound analysis and clear exposition by a professor of economics at the University of London."—*Foreign Affairs*.

ROBBINS, LIONEL. *Wages*. London: Jarrolds. 1925. 94 pp.

"A modest but valuable essay. It is a lucid discussion of the economics of wage determination. Although written primarily for those who have no economic training, it is a work which might well be read with profit by all students of social problems, for although its language is simple, it is much more than a mere elementary tract. One would like to feel that a means could be found of persuading all intelligent workmen to read this book."—PI.

ROBBINS, LIONEL. *The Economic Problem in Peace and War*. London: Macmillan. 1947. 86 pp.

Some reflections on objectives and mechanisms. "This authoritative recapitulation of the case for individualism by an illustrious economist, with a philosophical background, is most timely."—London *Times Literary Supplement*.

ROBERTSON, D. H. *The Control of Industry*. London: Nisbet. 1924. 169 pp.

"A compact study of the physiology of modern industry and the forms of control to which it can be subjected by the capitalist, the State, the consumer and the worker. Mr. Robertson writes with toleration and detachment, although his conclusions do not favor undiluted Individualism. He believes that for some years to come 'private enterprise will be the dominant form of industrial organization,' but that 'by its side there is plenty of room for collectivism in selected cases.' Further, that as in the case of an alternative creed, the 'philosophy of the academic Individualists does not fit all the facts.' Written in an entertaining style, this book should be read by all Individualists because it is probably the fairest criticism of extreme Individualism that exists and deals directly with the difficulties involved."—PI.

RÖPKE, WILHELM. *International Economic Disintegration*. Macmillan. 1942. 283 pp.

This book, a diagnosis of the long-run crisis in international economic relations, was finished in 1942, when World War II was still going on. It begins with a careful examination of the state of affairs at the time, and goes on to explain the powerful forces which created it—the disintegration of the framework of world economy, the military aspect of economic nationalism, the effort of industrial countries to "agrarianize," the effort of agricultural countries to "industrialize," the disturbances in the monetary and financial mechanism of the world economy, and the influence of policies that aim at national economic "stabilization." It is the most thorough and penetrating analysis of international economic disintegration up to the time of its appearance, and is particularly impressive because it sees the problem in its wider implications.

RÖPKE, WILHELM. *The Social Crisis of Our Time*. University of Chicago Press. 1950. 260 pp.

This book, first published in Switzerland under the title *Die Gesellschaftskrisis der Gegenwart,* is the first volume of a trilogy (though each of the volumes is self-contained), and it is the most available to

American readers. Röpke is outstanding, not merely for the acuteness of his analysis, but for the breadth of his learning and the breadth of his view, which go much beyond the purely economic field.

Some readers are likely to have difficulties because Professor Röpke repudiates not only "collectivism," but "capitalism," and advocates a course that he has called "The Third Way." This, however, does not mean a "middle-of-the-road policy" as commonly understood. When Röpke comes to specific issues he nearly always advocates the solution of "the free market economy." But he makes a sharp distinction between a free market economy as an ideal, and its actual historical embodiment in "capitalism." This seems to me a semantic separation which, in face of the established usage of the words, is likely to be more confusing than clarifying. Röpke quite properly contends that while economic liberty is a *necessary* condition of "the Good Society" it is not always a *sufficient* condition. This in itself is true enough, but it sometimes leads him into irrelevant or dubious recommendations. Yet every individualist and true liberal will profit from reading him. Frank H. Knight has rightly called this "a tremendously impressive book."

RÖPKE, WILHELM. *Civitas Humana.* London: Hodge. 1948. 235 pp.

This is the second volume of the Röpke trilogy. It seeks to outline the requirements of "a humane order of society." It discusses such questions as moral foundations, the place of science, the criteria of the healthy and the sick government, counterweights to the power of the State, the problem of "decongestion" and "deproletarianization," the decentralization of industry, and the elimination of business-cycle fluctuations. It pleads for the maintenance of a "peasant agriculture" and briefly outlines the requirements of a new international order.

RÖPKE, WILHELM. *Internationale Ordnung.* Erlenbach-Zürich: Eugen Rentsch Verlag. 1945. 337 pp.

Although this volume has been translated into French under the title *La Communauté Internationale* (Geneva: Éditions du Cheval Ailé), no English translation is available. It is concerned, as its title implies, with international economic problems. It discusses the decay of a world economy, the general fear of competition, the fear of a "passive balance" of payments, and the steps necessary to establish a new world economy. Among these steps the author puts courageous emphasis, in view of present fashionable Keynesism, on the need of restoring an international gold standard. "If the existence of a neo-liberal movement is known far beyond the narrow circles of experts, the credit belongs mainly to Röpke, at least so far as the German-speaking public is concerned."—F. A. Hayek.

ROGERS, JAMES E. THOROLD. *The Economic Interpretation of History.* London: Unwin. 1888. 548 pp.

"Thorold Rogers was, perhaps, the most broad-minded of the Victorian economists who followed Adam Smith and John Stuart Mill; he refused to be tied by the abstractions of Ricardo, and unlike the majority of the economists, he had a command of pure and vigorous English. . . . The above work is most valuable. . . . The preface will repay careful study. It is the work of a strong Individualist. . . . The chapter on *Laissez-faire* (XVI) should be especially noted."—PI.

ROGERS, SHERMAN. *Why Kill the Goose?* Irvington, N. Y.: Foundation for Economic Education. 1947. 78 pp.

A former socialist, converted to the benefits of the free private enterprise system, argues that we have in it a goose which lays golden eggs, and will continue to produce in abundance the economic necessities of life—if we do not kill it through impatient and ignorant policies. He presents a long list of popular misconceptions and fallacies and of the facts which correct them. Elementary, simple and very readable.

ROOT, E. MERRILL. *Collectivism on the Campus.* Devin-Adair. 1955.

The theme of this book is "the battle for the mind in American colleges." Professor Root argues that American college faculties today are dominated by collectivists—whom he calls "State liberals"—and that conservatives, libertarians, or true individualists on those faculties are not only in a minority but have a difficult time.

ROSENBERG, ARTHUR. *A History of Bolshevism.* Oxford University Press. 1934. 250 pp.

This is a translation from the German. Dr. Rosenberg wrote the book as a disillusioned communist. "Theory dominates Russian politics to an extent almost incomprehensible to the ordinary, practical Englishman; and Professor Rosenberg analyzes, with skill and knowledge, the theoretical foundations of the struggles of the past seventeen years. They revolve, of course, round the interpretation of Marxism." —John Hallett, in *The Spectator.* "One of the most instructive books yet published on the history of bolshevism."—W. L. Langer, in *Foreign Affairs.*

ROSSI, ANGELO. *The Communist Party in Action.* Yale University Press. 1950. 301 pp.

"This analytical study of the French Communist Party is one of the most important books on political theory and practice that have appeared in recent years. . . . Professor Kendall is to be congratulated not only for his translation but for his thoughtful introduction which challenges some of the premises of Rossi's own alternative position as well as those of its critics."—Sidney Hook, in *Annals of the American Academy.*

ROSTOVTZEFF, MICHAEL IVANOVICH. *Social and Economic History of the Roman Empire.* Oxford University Press. 1926. 696 pp.

Not a history in the ordinary sense, but a study of the social and economic life of the Roman Empire. "Unquestionably the most solid and also the most brilliant contribution which has ever been made toward the interpretation of the Roman Empire."—R. P. Blake, in the *American Political Science Review.* "Professor Rostovtzeff's book will probably rank among the most notable contributions to the subject since Gibbon's."—A. J. Toynbee, in the *Nation and Athenaeum.*

ROUGIER, LOUIS. *Les Mystiques Économiques.* Paris: Librairie de Médicis. 1938. 1949. 278 pp.

This is a penetrating study of the steps by which liberal democracies have been or can be transformed into totalitarian states. By *"mystiques"* the author refers to economic doctrines that are mere rationalizations of prejudice, passion or sentimentality, and rest neither on reason nor experience. Special chapters are devoted to an examination of the older liberal *mystique,* the *mystique* of a planned economy, of the corporative state, of Marxism, etc. M. Rougier advocates what he calls *"le libéralisme constructeur,"* which implies liberty within a carefully constructed framework of law, constantly safeguarding competition, and "is not to be confused with the theory of *laisser faire, laisser passer,* which ends in the suppression of liberty through the very excess of liberty."

ROUSSEAU, JEAN JACQUES. *The Social Contract.* 1762. Many editions. 227 pp.

There is a discussion of the great influence of Rousseau in the introductory essay to this list, "Individualism in Politics and Economics." Although Rousseau's ideas deeply colored subsequent development of the philosophy of individualism, his peculiar type of rationalistic individualism, as F. A. Hayek has pointed out, mainly led to the opposite of true individualism—i.e., socialism or collectivism.

RUEFF, JACQUES. *L'Ordre Social.* Paris: Recueil Sirey. 1945. 2 vols. 747 pp.

A profound and original book, which makes a searching analysis of fundamental economic, political, legal and moral concepts. It draws a constant contrast between a regime of economic liberalism with true rights, and a statist, socialist or authoritarian regime with its system of "false rights." It is especially effective in demonstrating the demoralizing economic and political effects of the cycle of deficit financing, monetary inflation, exchange control and price control that has marked the policies of so many "free" countries of the West since World War II.

RUEFF, JACQUES. *Épître aux Dirigistes.* Paris: Gallimard. 1949. 120 pp.

This is a "letter" addressed in a conciliatory tone to the Economic Planners, and more particularly to those who think that they can halt inflation or control an economy largely through the control of prices. M. Rueff shows the many evils to which attempts at price-fixing lead, and points on the other hand to the benefits brought about by freedom of the markets and a policy of economic liberalism.

RUEFF, JACQUES. *The Fallacies of Lord Keynes' General Theory. Quarterly Journal of Economics.* May, 1947. 24 pp.

An important analysis.

RUGGIERO, GUIDO DE. *The History of European Liberalism.* Oxford University Press. 1928. 476 pp.

The author defines liberalism as neither democracy, in the sense of the rule of the mere majority, nor authoritarianism, in the sense of the irresponsible rule of those who happen to be in power. "An excellent exposition of modern liberalism."—*Boston Transcript.*

RUSSELL, DEAN. *The TVA Idea.* Irvington, N. Y.: Foundation for Economic Education. 1949. 108 pp.

"With surgical skill, Dean Russell dissects not only the Tennessee Valley Authority in operation, but the philosophy of industry socialization, which the TVA represents. In a mere 100 pages, packed with supporting data, Russell thoroughly debunks the blatant claims made for TVA by its starry-eyed supporters. He then raises a warning that the TVA is more than just dams and power plants—it's an idea, the extension of which involves loss of individual freedom and drastic political, social and economic consequences."—John Fisher, in the *Chicago Tribune.*

SALTER, F. R. *Karl Marx and Modern Socialism.* Macmillan. 1921. 260 pp.

"In some ways this is the most useful account and criticism of Karl Marx that we have. Prof. J. Shield Nicholson in his *Revival of Marxism* can hardly hide his complete contempt for Marx's inconsistencies and confusions, and he admits that he finds him 'hopeless and depressing.' But *Das Kapital* has had an immense influence, and Mr. Salter is more sympathetic. In fact, one might almost say that he is clearly out to paint as favorable a picture of Marx as his conscience will allow. In spite of this and his constant attempts to explain away or minimize errors, he cannot avoid exposing the false assumptions and the structure of false reasoning on which Marxian theories are built."—PI (1927).

SAMUELSON, BERNARD. *Socialism Rejected*. London: Smith, Elder. 1913. 330 pp.

"A satirical examination of Socialism, written in a mock heroic style."—PI. The author considers "art" socialism, "Christian" socialism, political and ethical socialism, utopian socialism, "natural" socialism, and syndicalist socialism, and rejects them all.

SANBORN, FREDERIC ROCKWELL. *Design for War*. Devin-Adair. 1951. 607 pp.

A study of secret power politics from 1937 to 1941. "The basic contention of the book is that a President of the United States ought to consult freely and publicly with the Cabinet and Congress before making foreign engagements of any consequence. The author expresses the belief that the U. S. should follow more nearly the pattern of Britain, where foreign policy decisions generally are made only after a thorough airing in Commons, and where the Prime Minister is always directly accountable to the elected representatives of the people. The book is heavily documented."—*Springfield Republican*.

SAY, JEAN BAPTISTE. *Treatise on Political Economy*. 1803. (Philadelphia: Grigg & Eliot. 1834.)

Jean Baptiste Say (1767-1832) was the founder of the classical school in France. Although an ardent disciple of Adam Smith, he made it his mission to reduce the "vast chaos" of Smith's ideas to more orderly and simplified form. Among his original contributions were the introduction of the famous term *entrepreneur* into economic terminology, his emphasis on and explanation of the role of the entrepreneur, and his theory of markets. Say was the originator of "Say's Law," which points out that ultimately goods and services must be bought and paid for with other goods and services. This is a truism. But many errors resulted from ignoring it, as Malthus and others did, in their theory that depressions are caused by a *general* overproduction. And many present-day fallacies result from actually *denying* Say's Law, as the Keynesians do. In short—although this truth must, of course, be understood with the proper qualifications—supply creates its own demand.

SCHAPIRO, J. SALWYN. *Liberalism and the Challenge of Fascism*. McGraw-Hill. 1949. 421 pp.

An admirable history of social and intellectual forces in England and France from 1815 to 1870. The book is unsatisfactory in its inter-

pretation and understanding of economic developments and the contribution of the classical economists; but it is excellent in its shrewd
and balanced judgments of the political, philosophical and literary
currents of the period. It is distinguished by a ripe scholarship and
is very well written.

"This book is devoted to a study of the formation of the pattern
of liberalism in England and France, where its ideals and policies became a model, followed more or less by the other nations of Europe.
It also treats of the origins of fascist ideology in these countries . . .
Chapters 13 to 15, dealing with the Heralds of Fascism, aim to throw
a new light on Louis Napoleon, Proudhon, and Carlyle—the light
of the present on the past. The system established in France by the
strange and enigmatic Emperor cannot be understood without its
being seen as a historic preview of the fascist state with its popular,
even socialist, appeals cloaking a ruthless personal dictatorship."—
From the Preface.

SCHATZ, ALBERT. *L'Individualisme économique et social*. Paris: A.
Colin. 1907. 590 pp.

"This great work of 590 pages is one of the most exhaustive studies
of Individualism that exists and probably the most complete history."
—PI. "An excellent survey of the history of individualist theories.
. . . Deserves to be much more widely known as a contribution not
only to the subject indicated by its title but to the history of economic theory in general."—F. A. Hayek.

SCHNABEL, F. *Deutsche Geschichte im 19. Jahrhundert*. Freiburg i.B.
4 vols. 1929-37.

"A remarkable recent work on the modern history of Germany
which is not so well known abroad as it deserves."—F. A. Hayek.

SCHUMPETER, JOSEPH A. *Capitalism, Socialism and Democracy*. Harper.
1942. 381 pp.

An attempt to compare the relative merits and defects of capitalism
and socialism, explain their respective relations to democracy, and
indicate the type of society probable or possible in the future. I include this book in the present list with misgivings. Much of it is
deliberately paradoxical. Professor Schumpeter seems to me unduly
pessimistic about the future prospects of capitalism. He airily grants
to socialism a practicability that no complete socialism could possess;
and he never seriously comes to grips with the main economic argument against it. Yet this is nonetheless a remarkable book, rich in
scholarship, witty, and often penetrating and profound. At least one
college professor of my acquaintance, who himself ardently supports
the principles of free enterprise, tells me that this book more than

any other has shaken some of his students out of previous pro-socialist leanings. It can probably be recommended, therefore, to advanced economic students already acquainted with the work of von Mises, and possessing analytical powers of their own.

SCHUMPETER, JOSEPH A. *History of Economic Analysis*. Oxford University Press. 1954. 1,260 pp.

"A monumental achievement of scholarship, without equal in its field. . . . Readers of this journal will probably be irritated by the unnecessary condescending, if not contemptuous, manner in which Schumpeter usually refers to nineteenth-century liberalism and *laissez-faire*. But they should remember that it comes from an author who knew as well as anybody 'that capitalist evolution tends to peter out because the modern state may crush or paralyze its motive force,' yet who seems to have had an irrepressible urge *pour épater les bourgeois*."—F. A. Hayek, in *The Freeman*.

SCHWARTZ, HARRY. *Russia's Soviet Economy*. Prentice-Hall. 1950. 592 pp.

A careful description of the historical and ideological background of Soviet Russia, its economic plan, its industry, agriculture, and transportation. "The true value of this book lies in its solidly informative presentation of the Soviet economic machine and its pernicious effects upon the individual human Russian. A lucid introductory essay is contributed by William Henry Chamberlin."—David Hecht, in the *Saturday Review of Literature*.

SCHWARZ, SOLOMON M. *The Jews in the Soviet Union*. Syracuse University Press. 1951. 380 pp.

"In the first part of the book Dr. Schwarz exhaustively analyzes Communist doctrine on minority nationalities in general, and on the Jewish people in particular; the history of the Soviet treatment of the Jewish community since the coming to power of the Bolsheviks in 1917; the successive Soviet programs for solving the Jewish problem; the story of the province of Birobidzhan; and the present situation of the Jews in the Soviet Union. In the second part of the book, the author makes a study of the evidences of antisemitism in the USSR from the first years of Communist rule until today."—From the Publisher's Note. "For the time being, it can be called the definitive study on the subject."—Hans Kohn, in *The New Republic*.

SCHWARZSCHILD, LEOPOLD. *The Red Prussian*. Scribner's. 1947. 422 pp.

"A biography of Karl Marx, mostly based on the enormous Marx-Engels correspondence, along with a critique of Marx's *Capital* and of the Marxian theory of value. Mr. Schwarzschild does not present a kindly portrait of his subject; he convicts Marx, by quoting him, of virulent anti-semitism, and makes him out to be a petty, dishonest, completely unscrupulous and opportunistic man, a loose thinker, and a very bad prophet—in other words, the archetype of the totalitarian exponent of power who has become such a common figure in our times. . . . In holding the Marxian economic theory up to a strong light, the author uncovers some grave flaws in it, which have been noted by other critics but rarely so sharply illuminated. An important and well-presented book."—*New Yorker*.

Scoville, John W. *Labor Monopolies or Freedom.* Committee for Constitutional Government. 1946. 167 pp.

A vigorous criticism of "collective bargaining" as commonly interpreted in practice. The author contends that competition will ensure fair wages. His final conclusion is: "Employers and employees should be free to make voluntary agreements with each other. The employer should be free. The worker should be free. Neither should be subject to coercion, intimidation, or compulsion from any source."

Scoville, John W., and Sargent, Noel. *Fact and Fancy in the T. N. E. C. Monographs.* National Association of Manufacturers. 1942. 812 pp.

During the administrations of President Franklin D. Roosevelt, the Temporary National Economic Committee was set up, held hearings, and published forty-three monographs, running to 12,400 pages, which attempted to prove the existence of great concentration of economic power. This is a documented answer. The authors declare: "Many, but not all, of these monographs are impregnated with hostility to corporations and individuals of wealth. These reviews expose those statements and conclusions which, in the opinion of the reviewers, are fallacious or unsupported by evidence. . . . The monographs vary greatly in quality; they run the gamut from scholarly and comprehensive exposition to political claptrap."

Sennholz, Hans F. *How Can Europe Survive?* Van Nostrand. 1955. 336 pp.

This is one of the very few books of recent years to give a realistic analysis of the numerous schemes for European and Western unification, and to show how virtually all of these schemes have been rendered futile by internal interventionist and socialist policies that inevitably intensify and perpetuate nationalism. The author points out that the only feasible alternative is international cooperation based on individual liberty and free enterprise.

SENNHOLZ, MARY (ed.). *On Freedom and Free Enterprise.* Van Nostrand. 1956. 333 pp.

Essays in honor of Ludwig von Mises, on subjects ranging from "The Road to Totalitariansm" to "Progressive Taxation Reconsidered," by nineteen authors from the United States, South Africa, Switzerland, Italy, Mexico, and France: Jacques Rueff, William E. Rappard, Henry Hazlitt, Bertrand de Jouvenel, Hans F. Sennholz, F. A. Harper, Wilhelm Röpke, Faustino Ballvé, Carlo Antoni, Louis M. Spadaro, Fritz Machlup, L. M. Lachmann, Leonard E. Read, W. H. Hutt, William H. Peterson, Murray N. Rothbard, F. A. Hayek, Percy L. Greaves, Jr., and Louis Baudin.

SERGE, VICTOR. *The Case of Comrade Tulayev.* Doubleday. 1950. 306 pp.

On a cold winter's night a young clerk, on impulse, shot and killed a highly placed member of the Communist party in Russia, Comrade Tulayev. The young man escapes, but, in the far-flung investigations of the "plot," three other men, of far greater importance, are pursued to their death, men who are not guilty of this crime, at least, but men who have roused the distrust and enmity of the rulers of Russia. The author, who died in 1947, was an old revolutionary who had lived in exile, in France and Mexico, after the mid-thirties. "This is a novel in the great Russian tradition. Its theme is the modern tragedy of the old Bolsheviks, faced with the insoluble problem of reconciling their abiding faith in the original Communist ideal with acceptance of the tyranny, injustice and misery of the Soviet world they made."— Freda Utley, in *Human Events.*

SHADWELL, ARTHUR. *The Socialist Movement, 1824-1924.* London: Allan. 1925. 2 vols.

"Dr. Shadwell has been described as 'the greatest authority on the Socialist movement,' and outside the Socialist camp this is probably true. These volumes constitute the best short history of the movement, and the only one which brings the account up to 1924. . . . The work includes an excellent refutation of Marxism, and the errors and illusions of Socialism are constantly indicated."—PI (1927).

SHADWELL, ARTHUR. *The Breakdown of Socialism.* Little, Brown. 1926. 272 pp.

"A valuable study of recent Socialist experiments in Europe."—PI.

SHUB, DAVID. *Lenin: a Biography.* Doubleday. 1948. 438 pp.

"Mr. Shub's biography is the book you must read if you want to know what Communism is. . . . You will learn that Lenin's superiority as a politician lay in the fact that he alone realized that social democracy is not the ultimate state of liberalism, but its antithesis; and you will learn by that token—though not directly from Mr. Shub, who sticks to his job as the biographer of a doctrine—how to deal with Communism effectively."—Asher Brynes, in *The Saturday Review of Literature.*

SIDGWICK, HENRY. *The Principles of Political Economy.* Macmillan. 1883. 592 pp.

"In economics Sidgwick tends to follow John Stuart Mill; but his was an independent type of mind and he is always anxious to unearth new truths. . . . In the second . . . section . . . he begins by referring to the 'sweeping doctrine,' mainly derived from the Physiocrats, that 'the sole function of an ideal government in relation to industry is simply to leave it alone.' While giving this a certain general approval, he holds that it postulates a large amount of human virtue and unselfishness, and that there must be cases 'in which its optimistic conclusion is inadmissible.' Monopolies, for instance, are often urgent matters for Government interference. He gives a list of the familiar exceptions, e.g., Government must interfere for the purpose of national defense, the preservation of public health, etc., etc. Much of what he lays down is too well recognized to need recapitulation."—PI.

SIDGWICK, HENRY. *The Elements of Politics.* Macmillan. 1891. 665 pp.

"Henry Sidgwick was a thinker of very high ability; possibly his influence is below his merits, because he possessed a cautious and noncommittal mind which did not favor vivid and popular treatment of his subjects; and further, his style is dry. This book from Chapters III to XII has much to say about the respective provinces of the Government and the individual. He is too cautious to go much beyond empiric methods, and is content to allow the questions to be determined largely by the circumstances of each particular case. However, his bias is towards Individualism. He points out several dangers in Government interference—(1) That of overburdening the governmental machinery with work. (2) That of increasing the power capable of being used by governing persons oppressively or corruptly. (3) The danger that the delicate economic functions of government will be hampered by the desire to gratify certain specially influential sections of the community. He adds: 'When, along with these dangers, we take into account that the work of Government must be done by persons who—even with the best arrangement for effective supervision and promotion of merit—can only have a part of the stimulus and enterprise which the independent worker feels, it will be easily understood that we are not justified in concluding that governmental interference is always expedient, even where *laissez-faire* leads to a manifestly unsatisfactory result; its expediency has to be decided in any particular case by a careful estimate of advantages and drawbacks, requiring data obtained from special experience.' "—PI.

SIMONS, HENRY C. *Economic Policy for a Free Society.* University of Chicago Press. 1948. 353 pp.

Reviewing this book in *The New York Times* of Aug. 1, 1948, I wrote: "As an economic theorist Simons was far from first-rate; his originality lay in the realm of phrase-making rather than in that of thought; and while his style was vigorous, epigrammatic and witty, it was also interrupted, discursive and often pedantic. . . . [But] no one could deny Simons' disinterestedness, or the depth of his desire for a better and freer society. Though many of his ideas were eccentric and crotchety, and neither adopted nor expounded with the patient, step-by-step reasoning which mark the work of Adam Smith, Mill, Marshall and most of the others to whom he felt himself to belong, he shared with these great figures their deep concern for freedom and a suspicion everywhere of concentrated power."

A more favorable verdict is given by F. A. Hayek: "One need not agree with the whole of this work and one may even regard some of the suggestions made in it as incompatible with a free society, and yet recognize it as one of the most important contributions made in recent times."

SIMONSON, GUSTAVE. *A Plain Examination of Socialism.* London: Swan Sonnenschein. 1900. 155 pp.

"A short and handy criticism, written by an American, of the general Socialist position. The writer contends that it is based upon absurd postulates. It rests on the undemonstrable and untenable assumptions that we can possibly right in the present supposed wrongs of the past; that each one who is born has a 'natural right to the free use of the instruments of production which others may own; that labor is the sole cause of the value of anything and everything produced; that all values in property are not founded on demand-and-supply; and that a large share of these values has been produced by, and wrongly withheld from, those who have created them—in other words, that most of the present private property is the accumulated plunder from unrewarded past labor, and that this plunder must go on forever as long as the instruments of production are in private ownership.' "—PI.

SMITH, ADAM. *The Wealth of Nations.* 1776. Many editions. (London: Methuen. Edited by Edwin Cannan. 1904.) (Modern Library. 1937.) 2 vols. 462 pp. 506 pp.

Adam Smith is not merely the founder of political economy, but the father of economic liberty. In the 180 years since *The Wealth of Nations* appeared, the case for free trade, for example, has been stated thousands of times, but probably never with more direct simplicity and force than in that volume.

Gide and Rist, in their *History of Economic Doctrines,* have admirably summarized the qualities that make *The Wealth of Nations* unique: It "instantly eclipsed the tentative efforts of [Smith's] predecessors. . . . His discussion of . . . questions is marked by such mastery of detail and such balance of judgment that he convinces without effort. His facts are intermixed with reasoning, his illustrations with argument. He is instructive as well as persuasive. Withal there is no trace of pedantry, no monotonous reiteration in the work, and the reader is not burdened with the presence of a cumbersome logical apparatus. All is elegantly simple. . . . In addition to this, Smith has been successful in borrowing from his predecessors all their more important ideas and welding them into a more general system. He superseded them because he rendered their work useless. A true social and economic philosophy was substituted for their fragmentary studies, and an entirely new value given to their contributions."

SMITH, BRADFORD B. *Liberty and Taxes.* Irvington, N. Y.: Foundation for Economic Education. 1947. 20 pp.

The author argues against the progressive income tax and in favor of proportional taxation. "The one thing always to dread is the laying of a tax burden on minorities by majorities which the majority itself escapes. That is tax despoliation."

SMITH, WALTER BEDELL. *My Three Years in Moscow.* Lippincott. 1950. 346 pp.

An account of three years of the cold war in Russia as viewed by the former United States ambassador to Moscow in the period from March 1946 to March 1949. Among the subjects discussed are Soviet industry and agriculture, the cultural purge, slave labor, anti-Semitism, the Berlin blockade, the Yugoslav situation, and the possibility of war.

SNYDER, CARL. *Capitalism the Creator.* Macmillan. 1940. 473 pp.

"The thesis here presented," writes the author, "is that there is one way, and only one way, that any people, in all history, have ever risen from barbarism and poverty to affluence and culture; and that is by that concentrated and highly organized system of production and exchange which we call capitalistic."

In reviewing this book in *The New York Times,* I wrote: "It is frankly and belligerently a defense of capitalism, and as such it is one of the most original and interesting this reviewer has ever seen. Mr. Snyder is one of the country's best known statisticians; he is full of all sorts of miscellaneous learning. . . . He uses epithets freely and he has a habit of deliberately leaving out the verbs in most of his sentences, so that the reader is bumped and jolted rather than carried along.

"Mr. Snyder has a profound faith in the probative value of statistics . . . Impressive are the statistics and reasoning by which Mr. Snyder contends that wages are determined primarily by the product per worker; and that the product per worker is determined in the long run by the capital investment per worker, which makes possible the use of new machinery, new processes and new methods of production."

SOLOVIEV, MIKHAIL. *When the Gods Are Silent*. McKay. 1953. 506 pp.

"The author, a former editor of *Izvestia*, tells a moving story of the development of the Russian revolutionary movement from its beginnings before World War I until a period just after World War II. It depicts, through the eyes of members of a Russian peasant family deeply involved in the whole movement, the growing blind obedience and the final realization that Russia must be saved but cannot be by the Communists."—*Library Journal*.

SOMARY, FELIX. *Democracy at Bay*. Knopf. 1952. 171 pp.

William Henry Chamberlin calls this "a profound and searching little book" which "deserves a place on the same shelf with Hayek's *Road to Serfdom*." Somary measures the ills of the modern world against the standards of old-fashioned liberal individualism. He condemns the contemporary erosion of property rights, the tendency of direct taxation to reach confiscatory levels, and the general abandonment of the gold standard for unlimited paper inflation. "The more functions the state assumes," he contends, "the less it is possible to control the administration."

SOUVARINE, BORIS. *Stalin: A Critical Survey of Bolshevism*. Alliance. 1939. 690 pp.

"This book is one of the most remarkable biographies of our times. . . . It is the best critical history of Bolshevism from Lenin to Stalin that has been written to date. . . . Lesser men would have been borne down by the weight of M. Souvarine's vast erudition, but the author has a keen mind, a delightful sense of humor, and knows how to etch in acid."—Sidney Hook, in *Books*.

SPENCER, HERBERT. *The Man Versus the State*. 1884. Many editions. (Caldwell, Idaho: Caxton Printers. 1940.) 213 pp.

One of the most powerful and influential arguments for limited government, *laissez faire* and individualism ever written. The prophe-

tic insight of such essays as "The Coming Slavery," pointing out the
then unrecognized threat of socialism to the freedom of the individual,
has led to a strong revival of interest in Spencer after long neglect.

"Dictatorial measures, rapidly multiplied," he wrote in the preface
to this volume in 1884, "have tended continually to narrow the liberties of individuals. . . . Regulations have been made in yearly-
growing numbers, restraining the citizen in directions where his actions were previously unchecked, and compelling actions which previously he might perform or not as he liked; and at the same time
heavier public burdens . . . have further restricted his freedom, by
lessening that portion of his earnings which he can spend as he
pleases, and augmenting the portion taken from him to be spent as
public agents please."

Spencer contended that the sphere of government should be "confined to the duty of preventing aggressions of individuals upon each
other, and protecting the nation at large against external enemies." It
should, in other words, be confined to maintaining security of life
and property, and the freedom of the individual to exercise his
faculties. He warned against all efforts by the State to confer positive
benefits upon citizens. He objected even to sanitary supervision. Even
most individualists today would regard Spencer's individualism as in
many respects extreme. Yet no one concerned with individual freedom
can afford to ignore his work. Every student of the subject should be
familiar with it.

Hardly less important in its bearing on individualism is Spencer's
Social Statics, published in 1850. But the theme of individualism runs
through all his writings—through *The Study of Sociology, The Principles of Ethics,* and the *Autobiography.*

SPERBER, MANES. *The Burned Bramble.* Doubleday. 1951. 405 pp.

A novel about the Communist party in Europe in the 1930's. "An
impassioned and profound picture of Communist experience in the
years before Stalinism had fully shown its face—of the faith and
exaltation; the monstrous erasure of human decency and truth; the
incredible loyalty and self-sacrifice whose eventual reward was a disillusioned soul, a cheated mind, and a bullet in the neck."—C. J. Rolo,
in *The Atlantic.*

SPITZBERGEN, HENRY E. (HENRY PLOWDEEPER). *"Liberals" and the
Constitution.* Washington, D. C.: Liberty & Freedom Press. 1950.
301 pp.

A defense of free enterprise, private ownership of property, limited
government, and the doctrine of constitutional "separation of powers."

SPRADING, CHARLES T. (ed.). *Liberty and the Great Libertarians.* Los Angeles: The author. 1913. 540 pp.

An anthology on liberty. Among the authors from whom passages have been selected are: Edmund Burke, Thomas Paine, Thomas Jefferson, John Stuart Mill, Emerson, Thoreau, Ingersoll, Henry George, Bernard Shaw, Olive Shreiner, and Maria Montessori.

STAMP, SIR JOSIAH. *Wealth and Taxable Capacity.* London: King. 1922. 195 pp.

"An analysis of the fundamental factors determining the relation of price, taxation and public debt to the total national income and capital. . . . Like Prof. Bowley's works on national income, this is a book with which all who are seriously concerned about the problem of distribution ought to be acquainted."—PI.

STAMP, SIR JOSIAH. *Inheritance as an Economic Factor. Economic Journal.* September 1926.

"The best analysis of the economic significance of inheritance that has yet been made. Of the conclusions, the following is of fundamental importance in modern controversy. 'I think it probable that, through the inequalities due to the system in which inheritance has a part, the average man has a slightly smaller proportionate share of the aggregate than he would have had if there had been no inheritance system, but a substantially larger *absolute* amount because he shares a larger aggregate. . . . Whether under the circumstances he is justified in having a sense of injustice . . . is a matter lying beyond economics.'"—PI.

STANNARD, HAROLD MARTIN. *Two Constitutions.* Van Nostrand. 1949. 210 pp.

A comparative study of the written American constitution and the unwritten British one. It attempts to show a unity of purpose underlying the two.

STEINBERG, JULIEN. *Verdict of Three Decades.* Duell, Sloan & Pearce. 1950. 634 pp.

"An integrated and well-edited collection of writings about Soviet Communism, drawn mostly from the works of men and women who have revolted against it and believe that Lenin and Stalin cynically betrayed a revolution that they did not start in the first place. . . . If there are any people around who still do not believe the accusations made against Lenin and Stalin, this book should dispel their doubts."—*New Yorker.*

STEPHEN, SIR JAMES FITZJAMES. *Liberty, Equality, Fraternity*. London: Smith, Elder. 1873. 350 pp.

"A considerable portion of the book is devoted to J. S. Mill's essay *On Liberty*. Stephen was a utilitarian and an admirer of Mill's earlier writings. Mill, he says, 'is the only modern author who has handled the subject with whom I agree sufficiently to differ from him profitably.' Stephen delights in logical controversy. Here is an example: 'To force an unwilling person to contribute to the British Museum is as distinct a violation of Mr. Mill's principle as religious persecution.' Stephen emphasized the necessity for definitions and the difficulty of finding a satisfactory definition for liberty. It is an interesting and useful book by a clever and vigorous writer with a good legal brain, who leans to the individualistic side and despises sentimentalism in economics and politics."—PI. There are chapters on "Equality," "Fraternity," and "The Doctrine of Liberty in Its Application to Morals."

STEPHEN, SIR LESLIE. *History of English Thought in the Eighteenth Century*. 1876. London School of Economics. 1950. 3 vols. 1,233 pp.

"No single work quoted will be more useful to a beginner than this. Chapter X, 'Political Theories,' and Chapter XI, 'Political Economics,' are indispensable, but the whole is very valuable, because a knowledge of the intellectual conditions of the eighteenth century is all important for an understanding of English Individualism."—PI.

STEPHEN, SIR LESLIE. *The English Utilitarians*. Putnam. 1900. 3 vols. 326 pp. 382 pp. 525 pp.

"Written when Stephen's health was failing, these volumes have less vigor and merit than the previous work. But almost every chapter bears on our subject, and much useful information and criticism may be extracted."—PI.

STEPHEN, SIR LESLIE. *The Life of Sir James Fitzjames Stephen, Bart.* London: Smith, Elder. 1893. 504 pp.

"Stephen, who in later life became a judge, was long a busy journalist, writing much for the *Saturday Review* and *Pall Mall Gazette*. His brother and biographer says: 'He had sat at the feet of Bentham and Austin, and had found the most congenial philosophy in Hobbes.' He had two counts against Mill— (1) That he had forsaken the straightforward principles of utilitarianism and *laissez-faire*. (2) That though he had diverged into a sort of sentimental Socialism, he would not permit the State to use the force it had at its disposal, for the purpose of restraining evil. Stephen was a convinced Individualist. His creed was to allow as much scope as possible to liberty and the individual, under the protection of a strong Government for purposes of police and security."—PI.

STIGLER, GEORGE J. *Five Lectures on Economic Problems*. Longmans, Green. 1949. 65 pp.

These lectures, delivered before the London School of Economics by a professor of economics at Columbia University, are distinguished for pithy wisdom and shrewd analysis. They discuss "equality," monopolistic competition, classical economics, mathematical economics, and the status of competition in the United States. This last lecture is particularly notable for the deftness with which it punctures the popular myth that competition has been declining steadily (and in many versions, drastically) for a half century or more. Professor Stigler estimates that competitive industries were producing seven-tenths of the national income in 1939, and utilizing more than four-fifths of the labor force. In his lecture on the classical economists he shows how much more they knew, and how much more humane and realistic they were, than it has been fashionable for our generation to believe.

STOWE, LELAND. *Conquest by Terror*. Random House. 1952. 300 pp.

A study of the countries behind the Iron Curtain: Rumania, Czechoslovakia, Poland, Hungary and Bulgaria. The author, an American newspaperman, bases his work on his own knowledge, plus material gained from journalists in exile, recent refugees, former officers, specialists of various kinds, and the underground. "Mr. Stowe has written a book to alarm the West, to make it aware of the important changes which five to seven years of Soviet control have already produced, not in the satellites alone but also in the balance between East and West in Europe. It is a grim story and one which needs to be widely reflected on."—Philip Mosely, in the *New York Herald Tribune*.

STRAUSZ-HUPÉ, ROBERT, AND POSSONY, STEFAN T. *International Relations in the Age of the Conflict Between Democracy and Dictatorship*. McGraw-Hill. 1950. 947 pp.

"The long title of this book suggests its massive character. The almost unlimited subject of international relations is examined in almost one thousand pages of text, buttressed with vast erudition and illuminated by many flashes of perceptive wisdom. The authors are scholars connected respectively with the University of Pennsylvania and Georgetown University. . . . However, the book is far from being a colorless collection of undisputed facts. It should be, but probably will not be, required reading for all utopians. For much learning has made the authors profoundly skeptical about the value of one-idea panaceas. And they are ruthless with attempts to make platitudes a substitute for policy."—W. H. Chamberlin, in *Human Events*.

STRIPLING, ROBERT E. *Red Plot Against America*. Drexel Hill, Pa.: Bell Publications. 1950. 282 pp.

"The author of this book was the chief investigator for the House Committee on Un-American Activities from 1938 to 1948. Mr. Bob Considine has 'edited' the story of Mr. Stripling's adventures first for a newspaper syndicate, then for publication in the present book. The final 113 pages are lifted, by permission, from 'primers' against communism published by the committee in 1948 and obtainable from the Government Printing Office."—*The New York Times*.

STRUNSKY, SIMEON. *Two Came to Town*. Dutton. 1947. 219 pp.

A fantasy, speculating on what Alexander Hamilton and Thomas Jefferson, respectively (introduced under the thin disguises of "Mr. Alexander" and "Mr. Thomas"), would say and think about New York and the ideology of present-day America if they could pay us a visit from the grave. Under a surface of playful humor, the author conveys a wise and penetrating message on how recent fashionable ideas and phrases could cause us to surrender our liberties.

STYPULKOWSKI, ZBIGNIEW F. *Invitation to Moscow*. McKay. 1951. 359 pp.

The author, a Polish lawyer and political prisoner, describes his long session in the notorious Soviet Lubianka prison, and the methods used to obtain a confession of his non-guilt. "It would be unfortunate if this volume were catalogued as merely another book on Soviet political terror. It is much more than that. An important half of the book is devoted to the author's experience in the Polish underground, fighting against the German invaders. . . . Finally, this book is valuable because it gives the detailed story of Soviet perfidy toward the Polish underground in the closing days of World War II."—Harry Schwartz, in *The New York Times*.

SULLIVAN, LAWRENCE. *Bureaucracy Runs Amuck*. Bobbs-Merrill. 1944. 318 pp.

A study of the confusion and overlapping in hundreds of the United States war emergency bureaus and agencies.

SULZBACH, WALTER. *National Consciousness*. Washington, D. C.: American Council on Public Affairs. 1943. 168 pp.

"Whoever reads it should have a more lively and discerning understanding of contemporary nationalism."—Garland Downum, in the *American Political Science Review*.

SULZBACH, WALTER. *"Capitalistic Warmongers."* University of Chicago Press. 1942.

Punctures with facts and economic analysis the socialist superstition that "capitalism creates war."

SUMNER, WILLIAM GRAHAM. *What Social Classes Owe to Each Other.* 1883. (Yale University Press. 1927.) 169 pp.

Few men have ever exposed the fallacies of state paternalism with more gusto and devastating logic than the American sociologist and economist, William Graham Sumner (1840-1910). The lucidity of his style and the humor of his illustrations are comparable to those of Bastiat. This little book contains among others the famous essay on "The Forgotten Man"—a phrase later perverted by politicians to mean exactly the opposite of what Sumner meant by it: "The type and formula of most schemes of philanthropy or humanitarianism is this: A and B put their heads together to decide what C shall be made to do for D. . . . I call C the Forgotten Man. . . . The state cannot get a cent for any man without taking it from some other man, and this latter must be a man who has produced and saved it. This latter is the Forgotten Man."

Sumner also wrote valuable essays on free trade, protectionism and *laissez faire.* He was more celebrated in his own lifetime for his sociological work—his *Folkways* (1907), and his monumental four-volume study, *The Science of Society,* with A. G. Keller, which appeared in 1927.

SWANSON, ERNST W., AND SCHMIDT, EMERSON P. *Economic Stagnation or Progress.* McGraw-Hill. 1946. 212 pp.

A critique of recent doctrines on the mature economy, oversavings, and deficit spending. It is also a critique of the Keynes-Hansen school of economic stabilization—which held that the American economy was stagnant because of "lack of investment opportunities," and that therefore deficit spending by government on a more or less continuous basis was necessary to sustain prosperity. Basically, this is a book of readings from other economists, but these are linked together by commentaries and supplemented by the authors' own summaries and conclusions. The book covers much of the same ground as George Terborgh's *The Bogey of Economic Maturity* (q.v.).

TALMON, L. J. *The Rise of Totalitarian Democracy.* Beacon Press. 1952. 366 pp.

This study seeks to show how totalitarian ideas grew out of utopianism, and how the extreme democrats of the French Revolution turned into the most ruthless dictators. "A book of great wisdom which I recommend to anyone who not only wants to broaden his basic knowledge of the French Revolution but also wishes to understand the basic—that is the intellectual—causes of the modern world crisis. Dr. Talmon's work meets the highest academic standards."—S. T. Possony, in the *Annals of the American Academy*.

TANSILL, CHARLES CALLAN. *America Goes to War*. Little, Brown. 1938. 731 pp.

A study of the reasons why America went to war in 1917. "The great value of Professor Tansill's book is that it shows with incontestable detail just how independent of Congressional check is the President's control of foreign affairs, and how this control can lead to war."—John Chamberlain, in *Books*. "Mr. Tansill's book . . . is critical, searching and judicious. . . . It is presented in a style that is always vigorous and sometimes brilliant. It is the most valuable contribution to the history of the pre-war years in our literature, and one of the notable achievements of historical scholarship of this generation."—H. S. Commager, in *The Yale Review*.

TANSILL, CHARLES CALLAN. *Back Door to War*. Regnery. 1952. 690 pp.

The author is professor of American diplomatic history at Georgetown University. This volume on the origins of World War II is based on extensive research, including access to the confidential files of the State Department. "Prof. Tansill sketches briefly American foreign policy from Versailles to 1933, then gives many details and biting comments on the actions and attitudes of F. D. Roosevelt, Hull, Stimson, Ambassador Dodd, etc."—*Library Journal*. "When he is at his best, he is unfolding a diplomatic narrative with considerable skill, and with an excellent command of his sources."—Dexter Perkins, in *The New York Times*.

TAUSSIG, F. W. *Principles of Economics*. Macmillan. 1911, etc. 2 vols. 545 pp. 576 pp.

"Characterized by an exquisite sanity. We do not recall any work in which these subjects are discussed with an equal degree of lucidity. Professor Taussig's book from beginning to end is intensely readable."—*The New York Times*, in 1925. "The reviewer is impressed anew with the maturity and breadth, as well as with the literary style, which are outstanding characteristics of Taussig's *Principles*."—R. T. Bye, in the *Annals of the American Academy*, 1940. "A fine picture of classical doctrines. . . . All in all, Professor Taussig's *Principles* remains an important part of economic literature—as it has been for over a quarter of a century. That is a distinguished record, almost unique for textbook writers in the field."—T. F. Haygood, in the *Southern Economic Journal*, 1940.

TAUSSIG, F. W. *International Trade*. Macmillan. 1927. 425 pp.

The outstanding exposition, after the period of Bastable, of the "classical" theory of international trade. "What gives this book its great value—apart from gifts of exposition which recall the seductive clarity of the best pages of Stuart Mill—is the analysis and description of a multitude of facts drawn from his practical experience and which, even if one does not accept his general theory, have a special flavor and provide rich information of all sorts."—Charles Rist. "Clarity of exposition is perhaps the first of the characteristics that will make the book supersede other treatises on the subject."—London *Times Literary Supplement*.

TAYLOR, REGINALD. *The Socialist Illusion*. 1920.

"A study of the illusions and delusions from which Socialists suffer. Ideas such as 'surplus value' and the 'something for nothing attitude' are attacked. It is pointed out how much worse off all classes would be under a Socialist regime than under one which is primarily individualist."—PI.

TCHERNAVIN, MME. TAT'YANA. *Escape from the Soviets*. London: Hamilton. 1934. 320 pp.

"By all odds the most vivid and inspiring—and compassionate—human document that has come out of the whole Bolshevik Revolution and the subsequent regime."—F. H. Britten, in *Books*.

TCHERNAVIN, VLADIMIR. *I Speak for the Silent Prisoners of the Soviets*. Boston: Hale, Cushman & Flint. 1935. 368 pp.

In *Escape from the Soviets* Mme. Tchernavin told the story of her escape to Finland with her husband and her young son. In this book Vladimir Tchernavin recounts what happened before the escape, of his work as a scientist in a northern fishing center, of his arrest and the long months during which the GPU tried to wring a "confession" out of him, of his sentence to five years hard labor, and of the conditions of the prisons and concentration camps in which he was held. "It is a book which no lover of human liberty can read without being moved to horror and indignation."—J. D. Adams, in *The New York Times*.

TENNIEN, MARK A. *No Secret Is Safe*. Farrar, Straus, 1952. 270 pp.

"No book has yet appeared which compels more belief than does Father Mark Tennien's account of the ordeal of contemporary China. Speaking as both observer and victim, Father Tennien, a Maryknoll priest, provides us with a model of dispassionate reporting."—Julien Steinberg, in *The Saturday Review*.

TERBORGH, GEORGE. *The Bogey of Economic Maturity.* Chicago: Machinery & Allied Products Institute. 1945. 263 pp.

The doctrine of economic maturity was born in the depression years of the thirties. It held that the passing of the frontier, the tapering off of population growth, the improbability of any further revolutionary inventions, left a dearth of opportunity for private investment, and that therefore the government must either expand "public investment" through deficit financing, or tax out of existence the excess savings poisoning the economy. Reviewing this book in *The New York Times* of Aug. 27, 1945, I wrote: "One by one, with closely reasoned arguments, with historic illustrations, and with a wealth of statistical documentation, the author kicks all the props from under the mature economy doctrine. . . . A first-rate contribution."

THOMAS, IVOR. *The Socialist Tragedy.* Macmillan. 1951. 254 pp.

"Mr. Ivor Thomas is a former member of the Labor government in Britain turned Conservative. . . . He attacks the 'myth' that socialism is a barrier against communism. He recalls the actions of the Socialist parties in Eastern Europe and France and Italy as examples of how the socialists were not only powerless against the Communists but allied with the Communists. Mr. Thomas believes the only difference between socialism and communism is in degree; adoption of either results in loss of civil liberties and in reduced standards of living."— *Current History.*

THOREAU, HENRY D. *Civil Disobedience.* 1849. Many editions. 29 pp.

Thoreau (1817-1862) was an extreme nonconformist and individualist—so extreme that the doctrine of this essay (inspired by a night spent in jail for Thoreau's refusal to pay his poll-tax) comes close to anarchism. "I heartily accept the motto," he begins, " 'That government is best which governs least'; and I should like to see it acted up to more rapidly and systematically. Carried out, it finally amounts to this, which also I believe—'That government is best which governs not at all.' "

He claims the right of personal secession. "The authority of government," he declares, "can have no pure right over my person and property but what I concede to it." If everyone claimed the right of withdrawal and noncooperation, and disobedience of whatever laws did not entirely accord with his own ideas of justice or wisdom, government would become impossible. (On the other hand, I do not mean to imply by this objection that the individual is *never* under *any* circumstances justified in refusing obedience to a government or a particular law: such refusal may sometimes be the only method of reducing injustice or preventing despotism.)

Thoreau's case is powerfully argued in a taut and elevated prose. Although some of the conclusions at which he arrives are too sweeping, he gives us many pearls of truth along the way.

TOCQUEVILLE, ALEXIS DE. *Democracy in America.* 1835. Many editions. (Knopf. 1945.) 2 vols. 452 pp. 518 pp.

This is by far the best book ever written about America, and the most penetrating book ever written about democracy. It won instant acclaim, not only in the writer's native France, where Royer-Collard declared: "Nothing equal to it has appeared since Montesquieu," but in England, where John Stuart Mill hailed it as "among the most remarkable productions of our time." Its central theme is that democracy has become inevitable; that it is, with certain qualifications, desirable; but that it has great potentialities for evil as well as good, depending upon how well it is understood and guided. In the view of de Tocqueville, the greatest danger that threatens democracy is its tendency toward the centralization and concentration of power: "If ever the free institutions of America are destroyed, that event may be attributed to the omnipotence of the majority."

There is revived interest in Tocqueville today because of what seems like the uncanny clairvoyance of his prophecies. For example (this by a Frenchman in 1835): "There are at the present time two great nations in the world, which started from different points, but seem to tend towards the same end. I allude to the Russians and the Americans. . . . The principal instrument of [America] is liberty; of [Russia] servitude. Their starting point is different and their courses are not the same; yet each of them seems marked by the will of Heaven to sway the destinies of half the globe."

But the special reason for including *Democracy in America* in this bibliography is that, as John Bigelow wrote in his Introduction to the 1904 (Appleton) edition, it is "an intellectual arsenal in which the friends of freedom will long come to seek weapons." F. A. Hayek has written of de Tocqueville and Lord Acton: "These two men seem to me to have more successfully developed what was best in the political philosophy of the Scottish philosophers, Burke, and the English Whigs than any other writers I know."

TOCQUEVILLE, ALEXIS DE *The Old Régime and the French Revolution.* London: Murray. 1856. 511 pp. (Doubleday Anchor Books. 1955. 300 pp.)

This book appeared some twenty years after *Democracy in America.* It is marked by the same luminous logic and eloquence. "The peculiar object of the work I now submit to the public is to explain why this great [French] Revolution [of 1789], which was in preparation at the same time over almost the whole continent of Europe, broke out in

France sooner than elsewhere; why it sprang spontaneously from the society it was about to destroy; and lastly, how the old French monarchy came to fall so completely and so abruptly. . . .

"Many will perhaps accuse me of showing in this book a very unseasonable love of freedom—a thing for which it is said that no one any longer cares in France. . . .

"[Yet] despots themselves do not deny the excellence of Freedom, but they wish to keep it all to themselves, and maintain that all other men are utterly unworthy of it. Thus it is not on the opinion which may be entertained of freedom that this difference subsists, but on the greater or the less esteem we may have for mankind; and it may be said with strict accuracy, that the taste a man may show for absolute government bears an exact ratio to the contempt he may profess for his countrymen."—From the Preface.

TOCQUEVILLE, ALEXIS DE. *Recollections.* Columbia University Press. 1949. 331 pp.

"No Nineteenth Century student of history and politics . . . better understood the direction in which European society was evolving than the Count de Tocqueville. He knew that he was living in an age of continuous revolution and that this process, if accompanied by further concentration of power, could lead nowhere but into a tyranny unrestrained by either custom or religion. . . . The *Recollections* begin with the February Revolution of 1848, and are continued until the end of Tocqueville's ministry. . . . The book, however, is less valuable for its historical content than for the political and philosophic lessons abstracted by Tocqueville from his experience and observation. . . . His great passion was for the dignity of the human person and for the liberty necessary to its preservation. What he dreaded about democracy was the destruction of this dignity, not so much by violence as by the insidious regimen of mediocrity."—J. M. Lalley, in *Human Events.*

TOLEDANO, RALPH DE. *Spies, Dupes and Diplomats.* Duell, Sloan & Pearce. 1952. 244 pp.

"The spies are those, American and non-American, who have served the Soviet Union so assiduously during the past decade and more. The dupes are a number of highly placed citizens of the United States who, through misguided liberalism, bad judgment, or just plain muddle-headedness, also have served to further Russian aims. The diplomats, for the most part, are in the Departments of State, Defense, and Justice, and, if we can believe what we read, they also showed a surprising lack of insight and vigor where Soviet intrigue was concerned. It is the author's thesis that, taken together, these three categories of individuals have aided immeasurably the Russian design for world conquest. More particularly, he charges them with having made possible the Communist conquest of China, the present weakened state of Japan, and the tragic division of Korea."—*Christian Science Monitor.*

TOLEDANO, RALPH DE, AND LASKY, VICTOR. *Seeds of Treason.* Published for *Newsweek* by Funk & Wagnalls. 1950. 270 pp.

The story of the Hiss-Chambers case and the Hiss trials, by two reporters—Ralph de Toledano of *Newsweek* and Victor Lasky of the *New York World-Telegram*—who covered the case for their respective journals. "A fine professional job. . . . A delightfully readable presentation of all the evidence required for the forming of a fair judgment on a most puzzling case. . . . To many, its outstanding excellence consists in the clear light it throws on the process by which an heir of the American tradition is turned into a traitor to his country."—*Catholic World.*

TREVELYAN, G. M. *Life of John Bright.* Houghton Mifflin. 1913.

A portrait of the life and times of the great exponent of free trade, by an outstanding British historian.

TUCKER, JOSIAH. *A Brief Essay, etc.* 1750. *Four Tracts.* 1774. (*A Selection from His Economic and Political Writings.* Ed. by R. L. Schuyler. Columbia University Press. 1931. 576 pp.)

The PI refers to Tucker as "a racy forerunner of the Manchester School, especially on questions of colonial trade." He is regarded by F. A. Hayek as one of the founders of true individualism. In his *Elements of Commerce* (1756) he wrote: "The main point is neither to extinguish nor to enfeeble self-love, but to give it such a direction that it may promote the public interest by promoting its own."

UTLEY, FREDA. *Lost Illusion.* Philadelphia: Fireside Press. 1948. 288 pp.

The author has rewritten her book, *The Dream We Lost,* and now calls it *Lost Illusion.* It is "her account of herself as an English communist who was converted romantically, she now believes, to the Russian version of communism, lived for years in Russia, was progressively disillusioned by the change from original communism to ruthless industrialism, and got away to the United States."—*New York Herald Tribune Weekly Book Review.* "A book like Miss Utley's is a powerful educational instrument for democracy because of its honesty, its humility, its information, and above all for the unescapable moral issues it places before the intellectuals of the West."—Sidney Hook, in *The New York Times.*

UTLEY, FREDA. *Last Chance in China*. Bobbs-Merrill. 1947. 408 pp.

This book proved to be prophetic. Reviewing it on its appearance in 1947, *The New Yorker* wrote: "A treatise on the situation in China, based on a trip the author, for many years a strenuous convert to anti-Communism, took through the East shortly after the war. Miss Utley views everything with alarm; she believes that the United States has badly mismanaged its Chinese affairs and, by hamstringing Chiang Kai-shek, has practically invited the Chinese Communists to overrun the East."

UTLEY, FREDA. *The China Story*. Regnery. 1951. 274 pp.

"Immediately after the war the market was flooded with books favorable to the Chinese Communists. Miss Utley has presented the other side of the case more thoroughly and more ably than any other American publicist. Her story throws a good deal of light (if some-times controversial light) on one of the most burning and tragic issues of American foreign policy."—W. H. Chamberlin, in the *Christian Century*.

VALTIN, JAN. *Out of the Night*. Alliance Book. 1941. 841 pp.

"There is no better picture of the life of a secret agent floating about the Communist underworld of the twenties, and no more horrible and convincing account of conditions in Nazi prisons and concentration camps. But beyond all the things which make it more readable than any 'thriller' are the profound political morals of the decline into sordid intrigue, corruption, and mechanical obedience of the international Communist movement."—A. P. W., in the *Manchester Guardian*.

VAN SICKLE, JOHN V., AND ROGGE, BENJAMIN A. *Introduction to Economics*. Van Nostrand. 1954. 746 pp.

This stands out as one of the few introductory college economic textbooks today that are frankly and positively liberal in the tradi-tional meaning of the term. It is notable for the simplicity and skill of its exposition. While its own conclusions are conservative, it explains clearly and objectively, for example, what is meant by "Keynesian economics." The authors place special stress on the importance of functionally correct wages to the performance of a private enterprise system. There is also a discussion of communism, socialism, and planning as alternatives to capitalism.

VENNARD, EDWIN, AND WINSBOROUGH, ROBB M. *The American Economic System*. Evanston, Ill.: Row, Peterson & Co. 1953. 96 pp.

The authors attempt to give a simple explanation of the American economic system. Their book contains over a hundred illustrations in one to four colors, and illuminating charts and tables. Their theme is that the American people are better housed, better clothed, and better fed than any other major group of people in the world because of their free, or comparatively free, market economy.

VERRIJN STUART, COENRAAD A. *De Wetenschap der Economie en de Grondslagen van Het Sociaaleconomisch Leven.* Haarlem, Holland: Erven F. Bohn. 1947. 319 pp.

A notable book by an eminent liberal Dutch economist.

VIERECK, PETER. *The Shame and Glory of the Intellectuals.* Beacon Press. 1953. 320 pp.

An eloquent and stimulating, although often confused, book. Its author preaches a "new conservatism" but wants to "take conservatism away from the conservatives." His central argument is that it is our duty to fight the evil of totalitarianism in all its forms, and that the shame of the intellectuals lies in their failure to fight the terrorism of Stalin with the same vigor that they fought that of Hitler.

VLUGT, EBED VAN DER. *Asia Aflame.* Devin-Adair. 1953. 294 pp.

An historical survey, by a native of Holland, and an influential editor and lawyer, of the growth of Red Russia's influence in the various countries and regions of Asia during the last three decades. "If in addition to the convincing text of this book, there were need of authoritative recommendation, it might be mentioned that the author's views are fully in accord with those of General Albert C. Wedemeyer, who writes the Foreword."—Joseph McSorley, in the *Catholic World.*

VOIGT, F. A. *Unto Caesar.* Putnam. 1938. 303 pp.

An analysis of political conditions in Europe—particularly the fundamentals of fascism and communism and Great Britain's role in keeping the peace. The author was a member of the staff of the *Manchester Guardian.* "A brilliant, circumstantial and thought-provoking book."—*The* [London] *Economist.*

VOLTAIRE. *Works.* Many editions.

Voltaire (1694-1778), particularly after his three-year visit to England from 1726 to 1729, became one of the great influences of the eighteenth century for toleration and personal liberty. But if any one-volume anthology devoted to the libertarian side of his thought has been selected and compiled from his voluminous works, I do not know of it. Such a selection should include much from his *Lettres Philosophiques sur les Anglais* (1733). (See also LORD MORLEY's *Voltaire.*)

WALSH, EDMUND A. *Total Empire*. Milwaukee: Bruce Publishers. 1951. 293 pp.

"Father Walsh, regent of the School of Foreign Service of Georgetown University, is a lifelong student of geopolitics. . . . As director of the papal relief mission to Soviet Russia, Father Walsh witnessed the Bolshevik Revolution. These first-hand observations plus his own encyclopedic knowledge enable him to examine the grave question: Why has Russia's attempt thus far succeeded where Germany's failed?"—*The New York Times*.

WARREN, CHARLES. *Making of the Constitution*. Little, Brown. 1928. 832 pp.

"For the first time in a single volume all the contemporary material relating to the formation of the Constitution has been brought together and the history of the Constitutional Convention is presented, day by day. Mr. Warren has assembled the letters of the public men of the day, the delegates and others, and has printed also the editorials and articles from the contemporary newspapers, presenting thus not only the thoughts of the men who were at work upon the Constitution or were otherwise influential in the country, but the conditions and the public opinion of that time. . . . *Making of the Constitution* measures up to every demand of authoritative history, alike in its scholarly research, its liberal humanitarianism and its smoothly flowing style."—*The New York Times*.

WASSON, R. GORDON. *The Hall Carbine Affair*. New York: Pandick Press. 1941. 1948. 190 pp.

The author, a vice president of J. P. Morgan & Co., seizes on an oft-told episode in the life of the elder Morgan, founder of the banking house, in which he is alleged to have sold to the government during the Civil War some condemned arms at a profit that would have been exorbitant for first-class weapons. Mr. Wasson delves into the contemporary records and reveals with very careful documentation exactly what took place. Then he turns to the spurious version of this episode, identifies its inventor as Gustavus Myers, tracks down its successive embellishments at the hands of later anti-capitalistic "economic historians," and shows how the myth got itself firmly embedded into the American credo. The disclosure is important for the light it throws on how cynical hostility to present big business leads to the invention and acceptance of historic slanders. Allan Nevins calls the Wasson book "a capital piece of work."

WATTS, V. ORVAL. *Away From Freedom: The Revolt of the College Economists.* Los Angeles: Foundation for Social Research. 1952. 105 pp.

A vigorous answer to Keynesism, from an uncompromising advocate of free enterprise. Dr. Watts takes off from the criticisms of Keynesism previously made by such writers as L. Albert Hahn, Ludwig von Mises, and the late Benjamin M. Anderson. His analysis of the technical aspects of Keynesism leaves something to be desired, but his discussion of its moral and political weaknesses is admirable. He points out in detail how it teaches disregard for property rights, disparages self-reliance, foresight, thrift and enterprise, puts its faith in bureaucracy and coercive authority, and is fundamentally hostile to free trade, free markets and individual liberty.

WATTS, V. ORVAL. *Union Monopoly: Its Cause and Cure.* Los Angeles: Foundation for Social Research. 1954. 88 pp.

Dr. Watts argues that present labor union monopolies are the product of a special government license granted to unions to use violence, coercion and compulsion, and that this state of affairs is further aggravated by denial to employers of what ought to be their legal right of choice. Dr. Watts also argues that, in spite of all their specially granted privileges and immunities, unions have not raised the over-all share of employees in the product of industry. The book is well organized and contains an excellent analysis of the defects of the Wagner Labor Relations Act of 1935, and of the subsequent Taft-Hartley Act.

WATTS, V. ORVAL. *The United Nations: Planned Tyranny.* Devin-Adair. 1955. 160 pp.

The author argues that the United Nations as presently constituted is "not liberal but reactionary," and that it is "a blueprint for tyranny and perpetual war instead of an instrument of peace."

WEAVER, HENRY GRADY. *Mainspring.* 1947. Irvington, N. Y.: The Foundation for Economic Education. 1953. 279 pp.

Contends that only free men can make effective use of their imaginations and creative abilities and that the purpose of government is to protect personal liberty. An excellent introduction to the history of human freedom and the resulting moral, social, and material benefits. "Down through the ages," writes Mr. Weaver, "countless millions, struggling unsuccessfully to keep bare life in wretched bodies, have died young in misery and squalor. . . . Then suddenly, on one spot on this planet, people eat so abundantly that the pangs of hunger are forgotten." The reason for this miracle, the author contends, is not any extraordinary inherent ability in the American people, but their system of economic freedom.

WEBER, MAX. *General Economic History.* Greenberg. 1927. 401 pp.

A history of the evolution of the capitalistic spirit from a sociological point of view. The book was prepared by German editors from notes left by Max Weber and the notebooks of his students.

WEISSBERG, ALEXANDER. *The Accused.* Simon & Schuster. 1951. 518 pp.

"This is not just one more book in the rapidly growing literature on the *Chystka,* the Great Purge, of 1936-1938. It is a landmark, a monument, and an inexhaustible source of penetrating insights into the souls of the men who confess and of those who make them confess; of a few political heroes and a number of political provocateurs; of real and fictitious spies; and of thousands of simple human beings, disoriented, frightened, and often going from prison cell to execution. . . . From this source a future Dostoevsky will draw the elements and inspiration for a new *House of the Dead.*"—D. J. Dallin, in *The New York Times.*

WEST, REBECCA. *The Meaning of Treason.* Viking. 1947. 307 pp.

A profound study of the motives that have led scientists and other "intellectuals" of the Western world to betray their own countries in the service of the communist conspiracy. "Wonderfully illuminating reports on William Joyce, John Amery, and other British traitors." —*The Atlantic.* "A tour de force . . . told in memorable prose."— *Commonweal.*

In the second edition published in 1952 Miss West added new chapters containing studies of two more traitors—Dr. Alan Nunn May and Dr. Klaus Emil Fuchs.

WHITE, ANDREW DICKSON. *Fiat Money Inflation in France.* 1896. (Irvington, N. Y.: Foundation for Economic Education. 1952.) (Caldwell, Idaho: Caxton Printers.) 69 pp.

Andrew Dickson White was an eminent historian, the first president of Cornell, and American ambassador to Russia and Germany. This is a brilliant history of inflation in France in the revolutionary period from 1789 to 1797. It shows by scrupulous citation of documented data how irredeemable paper money leads to soaring prices, price fixing, scarcity, the black market, the spy system, the invasion of privacy, immorality and tyranny. A little masterpiece.

WHITE, W. L. *Report on the Russians.* Harcourt, Brace. 1945. 309 pp.

The story of a six-weeks' trip to Russia during the summer of 1944. Because it was one of the first books to break the conspiracy of silence about the shortcomings of our then "ally," its appearance met a storm of denunciation and protest. "Mr. White makes little attempt to analyze the social processes at work in Russia or to generalize about her recent history. He simply tells what he saw, heard, and felt. But, as a journalist, he was in a position to enjoy certain unique advantages. He traveled about in a way that no regular correspondent in the Soviet Union had been permitted to do in years. . . . His book has thus a unique value and ought not to be confused with the ordinary correspondent's book about Russia. Mr. White not only saw much more than most visitors, he is a better observer than most, and he tells you how things look and people behave, and how everything strikes an American, in a way that few other writers have ever done."—Edmund Wilson, in *The New Yorker*.

WICKSELL, KNUT. *Lectures on Political Economy*. London: Routledge. 1934. 2 vols. 299 pp. 238 pp.

Knut Wicksell (1851-1926) was a Swedish economist most celebrated for his theory concerning the relations between money and natural rates of interest and movements in the general level of prices. This was of more than purely theoretical interest, because it pointed to the errors that governments make in bringing on inflation by trying to maintain artificially low interest rates. But his total contribution to economics was of much wider importance than this. Lionel Robbins writes: "There is no work in the whole range of modern economic literature which presents a clearer view of the main significance and interrelations of the central propositions of economic analysis than these lectures."

WICKSTEED, PHILIP H. *The Common Sense of Political Economy*. 1910. (London: Routledge. 1933, etc.) 2 vols. 871 pp.

This brilliant book is as remarkable for the ease and lucidity of its style as for the penetration and power of its reasoning. Its real importance has only been recognized in recent years. In his Preface in 1910, Wicksteed wrote: "The Introduction will make it clear that the author makes no claim to originality or priority with respect to anything that it contains." This modest disavowal was taken too literally, and for years Wicksteed was regarded mainly as a popularizer of Jevons. But in his Introduction to the 1933 edition, Lionel Robbins pointed out that the book is "the most exhaustive non-mathematical exposition of the technical and philosophical complications [implications?] of the so-called *marginal* theory of pure economics, which has appeared in any language. . . . The book was the culmination of Wicksteed's life work. . . . Into it he poured all the subtlety and persuasiveness, all the literary charm, of which he was capable. It is a masterpiece of systematic exposition. . . . Wicksteed's place in the history of economic thought is beside the place occupied by Jevons and the Austrians."

WILCOX, THOMAS. *The Anti-Bolshevik Bibliography*. Distributed by Thomas Wilcox, 712 W. Second St., Los Angeles 12. 1955. 89 pp.
A bibliography of anti-Marxist literature.

WILLOUGHBY, CHARLES ANDREW. *Shanghai Conspiracy*. Dutton. 1952. 315 pp.
The report of General MacArthur's intelligence chief on the Soviet military intelligence operations in Shanghai, as revealed through the confessions of Richard Sorge. Contains a chapter on "Agnes Smedley and the War Department."

WILLOUGHBY, WESTEL W. *The Ethical Basis of Political Authority*. Macmillan. 1930. 460 pp.
The author has been professor of political science at the Johns Hopkins University, and his work is distinguished for scholarship and clarity. His aim in this book is to examine political authority as viewed by the moralist. He believes that political coercion "is justified to the extent that it provides a more efficient and less oppressive form of control than would exist without it."

WILSON, THOMAS. *Modern Capitalism and Economic Progress*. Macmillan. 1950. 274 pp.
"The position occupied by British liberals is defended by Mr. Wilson, and from it he directs a scathing fire against the Labor Government of his country. Like American critics of socialism, he fears the socialistic threat to human liberty, but he thinks of liberty as a fairly tough plant which can stand considerable doses of government guidance. . . . He shows that capitalism has been progressive, that it can continue so, and that the profit motive has been a safeguard to liberty."—*The New York Times*.

WILTSE, CHARLES M. *John C. Calhoun: Nationalist (1782-1828)*. Bobbs-Merrill. 1944. 477 pp. *John C. Calhoun: Nullifier (1829-1839)*. Bobbs-Merrill. 1951. 511 pp.
Of the first volume, R. N. Current wrote in the *American Historical Review:* "This study of Calhoun's earlier career, much the ablest and most thorough yet published, must take its place at once as the standard account." Felix Morley calls the two books together "a great biography." "It was time," he writes, "for a sympathetic biographer to rescue Calhoun from the avalanche of tendentious smearing under which his name has long been buried. In Mr. Wiltse's own words: 'He seemed to me the most original and in many respects the

keenest political thinker this country has produced, but few people had ever heard of him except as a defender of slavery. . . . Being of good Yankee stock, and brought up accordingly, I was a little surprised myself to discover that he didn't wear horns.' " (See the entry under Calhoun's *A Disquisition on Government*.)

WINDER, GEORGE. *The Free Convertibility of Sterling*. London: Batchworth Press. 1955. 62 pp.

A lucid, thorough, and uncompromising protest against continuation of exchange control. It is not merely a polemic, but a sort of elementary textbook on foreign exchange. The author emphasizes that exchange control involves not only price-fixing in currencies, but arbitrary confiscation of the overseas earnings of a country's own citizens. He also points out that the postwar overvaluation of sterling relative to the dollar brought about the so-called "dollar shortage" and discouraged British exports.

WITHERS, HARTLEY. *Poverty and Waste*. London: Smith, Elder. 1914. 180 pp.

"This book might have been called 'The Case for the Poor.' The author throughout is pleading for those in relative poverty. It is a frank discussion of some of the admitted faults of the Capitalistic system, and an examination of the more honest and enlightened criticisms that are made against the present order. He shows that 'There is plenty of excuse for the bitterness on the part of the workers,' and in his pleading on their behalf he sometimes seems to overstate their case and to understate the point of view of the employer and the wealthy consumer. As, however, he is mainly appealing to the wealthy and attacking extravagance, this is not necessarily a drawback. One would not get the impression from this book that Mr. Hartley Withers was an Individualist, and yet it is really one of the best arguments against Socialism that we have."—PI.

WITHERS, HARTLEY. *The Case for Capitalism*. Dutton. 1920. 255 pp.

"As a writer of popular works on economics and finance, Mr. Hartley Withers stands alone. In this book he makes many undoubted complexities appear simple and almost obvious. That the Capitalist system is 'more truly democratic and in favor of freedom than either of the rival systems' has nowhere been more clearly argued. No mere pleading for the preservation of all aspects of Capitalist society as it exists is to be found here. There is much keen criticism of certain features of the Capitalist regime. Although published in 1920 it suffers less than the majority of books which appeared about that time from the false optimism that colored most thinking and writing in those days."—PI.

WOLFE, BERTRAM D. *Three Who Made a Revolution*. Dial Press. 1948. 661 pp.

Studies of Lenin, Trotsky, and Stalin. "This is one of those rare books which are obviously destined from the moment of publication to become a source and authority for the guidance of all later writers on the subject. It is to be hoped that *Three Who Made a Revolution* will also be discovered and widely studied by a general public which earnestly wants to understand why the Soviets behave the way they do."—Hal Lehrman, in *The Saturday Review of Literature*.

WOLMAN, LEO. *Industry-Wide Bargaining*. Irvington, N. Y.: Foundation for Economic Education. 1948. 63 pp.

One of the country's outstanding authorities on labor points out the consequences of industry-wide unions. He concludes: "The problem of labor monopoly cannot be dealt with effectively unless, and until, the immunity to the anti-trust laws which organized labor has enjoyed since 1914 is withdrawn. . . . Its perpetuation . . . will in time cause the break-down of our entire anti-monopoly policy. This is the first step toward a regulated or planned economy, as it has proved to be in other countries."

WOODHOUSE, A. S. P. (ed.). *Puritanism and Liberty*. London: Dent. 1938. 506 pp.

Contains well-selected documentation of the Puritan Revolution in England.

WOODLOCK, THOMAS F. *Thinking It Over*. Declan X. McMullen Co. 1947. 292 pp.

A compilation of more than a hundred of the author's articles which originally appeared in *The Wall Street Journal*. Woodlock was a wise and farsighted defender of the free enterprise system. The subjects covered here include: "Society: Isms and Idols," "Democracy: Definition and Debate," and "Economics: Order and Disorder."

WRIGHT, DAVID McCORD. *Capitalism*. McGraw-Hill. 1951. 246 pp.

One of the most vigorous and intelligent defenses of capitalism ever made by an American economist. It views its subject from a political and social as well as a purely economic standpoint.

WRIGHT, DAVID McCORD. *Economics of Disturbance*. Macmillan. 1946. 115 pp.

A main thesis of this book is suggested by two sentences in it: "The socially tolerable rate of expansion likely to be demanded in a democratic society will probably be much faster than the 'equilibrium' rate which would ensure a permanent full employment adjustment" (p. 85). "Much of the insecurity and the instability we now decry is the result of the scientific achievement and the social democracy which we admire" (p. 98).

WRIGHT, DAVID McCORD. *Democracy and Progress*. Macmillan. 1948. 220 pp.

"Professor Wright has written the best defense of private enterprise we have seen. . . . It is an argument, brilliant in many respects, for a flexible capitalism capable of adjustment to changing conditions." —A. B. Wolfe, in *The American Economic Review*.

WRIGHT, DAVID McCORD (ed.). *The Impact of the Union*. Harcourt, Brace. 1951. 405 pp.

This is a round-table discussion, by eight prominent economists, of the economic and political consequences of labor unions. The participants are John Maurice Clark, Gottfried Haberler, Frank H. Knight, Kenneth E. Boulding, Edward H. Chamberlin, Milton Friedman, David McCord Wright, and Paul A. Samuelson. Although it is impossible to summarize here their diverse conclusions, the papers and comments are often highly critical of labor union policies, and the discussion as a whole is in striking contrast with the political dogma that the influence of labor unions has been entirely beneficent, and that the chief aim of law should be to encourage the growth of their numbers and powers.

WRISTON, HENRY M. *Challenge to Freedom*. Harper. 1943. 240 pp.

The thesis of this book, according to its author, "is simple and may be stated explicitly: the principal duty of democratic government is the maintenance and expansion of freedom." He declares in his conclusion: "The proposals of this book are all radical; none of them looks toward any reactionary policy whatever. We have been living in a world where, by a kind of double talk, the vocabulary of liberalism has been stolen by the real reactionaries. Only in a world where values have become topsy-turvy would it be possible for Hitler to describe tyranny as a 'new order,' or for bureaucracy to masquerade in the habiliments of liberalism, or for the planned economy to make a pretense of 'economic democracy.' Government by bureaucracy, control of business by administrative regulation, manipulation of the economy for political reasons—these are stark reaction. Not all the cascades of beautiful words about 'new social goals,' 'bold social engineering,' 'security from the cradle to the grave' can wash away that ineradicable fact." One of the best works in the recent literature of individualism.

ZAMIATIN, EUGENE. *We.* Dutton. 1924. 286 pp.

A sometimes obscure but haunting and powerful novel of life in a totalitarian society. It is a remarkable anticipation in some respects of Huxley's *Brave New World* (q.v.), or Orwell's *Nineteen Eighty-Four* (q.v.)—and of the realities of Soviet Russia. The last is not so surprising, as Zamiatin was a Russian writer living in Soviet Russia. His book, however, was published only in translation, outside of Russia. At the climax of the novel the authorities order a brain operation on everyone to remove the Imagination as a danger to the State. Totalitarian communist governments today perform the moral equivalent of this operation: it has come to be known as brainwashing.